Contents

Smart Learning

teaching and learning with smartphones and tablets in post-compulsory education

edited by Andrew Middleton

MELSIG

for the Media-Enhanced Learning Special Interest Group
and
Sheffield Hallam University

Smart Learning – teaching and learning with smartphones and tablets in post-compulsory education

edited by Andrew Middleton, for the Media-Enhanced Learning Special Interest Group

First published by the Media-Enhanced Learning Special Interest Group and Sheffield Hallam University, 2015

Quality Enhancement and Student Success, Level 1, Oneleven, Sheffield Hallam University, Howard Street, Sheffield, UK S1 1WB

MELSIG is online at http://melsig.shu.ac.uk and @melsiguk

Book citation: Middleton, A., ed. (2015). Smart learning: Teaching and learning with smartphones and tablets in post compulsory education. Media-Enhanced Learning Special Interest Group and Sheffield Hallam University.

e-book for Kindle (KDF) ISBN: 978 -978-1-84387-382-2
e-book e-Pub format ISBN: 978 -1-84387-381-5
Print On Demand ISBN: 978-1-84387-383-9

#smartlearning

About Smart Learning

Andrew Middleton

Smart Learning: teaching and learning with smartphones and tablets in post-compulsory education is as much about innovation in education as it is about a world in which personal technologies are changing teaching and learning.

Smart Learning continues to develop thinking, which has steadily emerged through the Media Enhanced Learning Special Interest Group (MELSIG), about a changing learning landscape rich in digital and social media. MELSIG, established in 2008, is an innovative social network; amorphous, with members coming and going, continually reflecting on and refreshing our thinking about emerging practice enhanced and transformed by new ways of teaching and learning with digital media and smart technology.

The book attempts to capture some moments from a rapidly changing world of innovative education. This is important because it is in the nature of innovators to continually progress their thinking and this can leave other people behind and cause the innovators to be stranded. Innovators can easily be dismissed as being exceptional or maverick. The thinking and practice described in *Smart Learning* should *not* be exceptional and there are signs of broad interest and acceptance or the idea. This book, through its case studies and scenarios, pins down and demonstrates the value of innovative practice with digital and social media, especially when mediated by personal smart devices. These ideas make a good, timely contribution to forming a sense of how smart devices are rapidly changing the post compulsory education learning environment.

The book includes chapters that help to situate innovative academic practice within the theory of progressive teaching and learning in post-compulsory education. It also includes thought pieces and scenarios, which are intended to challenge existing assumptions about teaching and learning and inspire new ideas.

About scenarios

It is worth looking at the use of the scenarios that appear between the chapters. Scenarios are mini-narratives and provide innovators, often working in collaboration, with a way to clarify fuzzy thinking enough to present and test ideas. Carroll (2000) says a scenario is, "a concrete description of activity that the user engages in when performing a specific task, description sufficiently detailed so that design implications can be inferred and reasoned about." This allows them to be considered in a realistic way yet abstracted from, or unobscured by, contextual detail. This helps to remove the essential idea from unnecessary background noise. Scenario generation has become a useful dimension of MELSIG workshops, allowing participants to co-imagine possibilities for the near future. See the appendix: About Scenarios for further explanation about the importance of scenarios to possibility thinking.

The scholarship of 'book making'

Smart Learning is a scholarly work and it is important to establish its credibility.

You will be aware that *Smart Learning*, like the previous MELSIG publication *Digital Voices* (Middleton, 2013), is presented in a different way to other books about educational practice and innovation. You might be holding a hard copy, but it is more likely you are reading this on screen.

e-Books often take the essential form of the traditional book and follow a traditional process to publication. This is something we, working co-operatively as an open writing collective, have tried to challenge, whilst producing a highly scholarly and useful collection of chapters infused with experience, ideas and critical thinking.

The invitation to contribute was targeted first and foremost at academic innovators active in the MELSIG network. Authors were invited to contribute high quality evidence-informed writing, especially in submitting the thought pieces.

Speculation, however, is an important part of innovative thinking, helping to conceptualise and critique emerging practice; yet this involves pioneering exploration of territories in which there can be no sense of certainty, only possibilities. In *Smart Learning* innovative thinking is best estimated by its clarity: this has been tested by the running of a thorough peer review process involving all of the contributors as a collective of peer reviewers. Each contribution has been read and commented on by at least three peers. The trust and openness amongst us, collaborating in an open writing environment (using a Google Drive shared folder), has I think been a wonderful experience and one which has created a supportive and authentic learning space for all.

Our writing process and community, therefore, epitomises the idea of smart learning: enhancing practice through social uses of new spaces.

Overview of the chapters

The relationship of the personal smart device to a personalised experience of learning encapsulates the essential, emerging idea of smart learning conceptually.

Made up of thought pieces, research, case studies and scenarios, *Smart Learning*, is prescient and helps us to think further about ideas such as self-organised learning spaces (Wheeler, 2009) through its descriptions of rich contexts for smart learning.

Section 1: Thought Pieces

In *Thinking about smart learning* Andrew Middleton introduces the idea of smart learning and the scope of the book. He explains how the idea of 'smart learning' encapsulates a perfect storm of ideas that help to redefine educational space. The ubiquitous use of personal devices by students and teachers heralds an era of personalisation which is evident in the maturing of 'mobile learning' and the pervasiveness of social media. Our engagement in using and producing rich digital media and our growing experiences of BYOD and openness, and our changing digital capability, all signal a marked change in the way we perceive ourselves as teachers and students. This introductory chapter establishes the case for the book's focus on smart learning.

Social media for learning – a framework to inspire innovation introduces a framework to support curriculum design and staff development. Andrew Middleton and Sue Beckingham describe the framework and its purpose to orientate academics and learning design collaborators in considering the strengths of incorporating social media within the curriculum and, in doing so, supporting students to learn. They introduce social media and what it means to higher education before looking closely at the seven elements that make up the framework and how they are derived from established educational principles.

Catherine Hack, in *Applying learning analytics to smart learning – ethics and policy*, argues that as the concept of Bring Your Own Device (BYOD) gains traction across the higher education sector there is a growing need to evidence the impact of deploying mobile devices; this can be difficult when many of the intended benefits can be intangible. As learning analytics become both more sophisticated and user friendly, the possibility for teachers to track and interrogate the complete student online learning experience – 'click-by-click' or 'tap-by-tap' is now a reality. Research and scholarship in this changing learning landscape can involve the analysis of private and public student data from institutional and open resources. Whilst this can be deeply informative and have positive impacts for developing more effective and personalised learning experiences, it raises important ethical issues of trust, privacy and autonomy. This thought piece considers these principles in the context of current institutional policies and calls for more transparency to support practitioners in negotiating this legal and ethical minefield.

The concept of BYOD remains the focus for our consideration in Santanu Vasant's chapter *Bring Your Own Device – policy and practice in higher education*. Vasant's thought piece presents some background information on BYOD, how the movement came into existence, and its significance to higher education. He highlights some of the advantages and disadvantages of BYOD and the issues around the implementation of BYOD within an educational institution. He explores some current policies and practice around BYOD and how they can be addressed in staff development and the work of other central service units in higher education to foster greater engagement amongst all staff. The piece offers some insight into how best to support this emerging area in terms of technology and pedagogy and concludes with a future vision for BYOD.

Engagement and inclusivity is the focus of Denise Turner's thought piece, *Psychosocial aspects of engagement with social media and digital technology – personal thoughts from the frontier*. She explores the psychosocial aspects of engagement: what stops people engaging; why; how do we help people to engage; how does our language and behaviour contribute to or mitigate this? It considers the relationship of engagement and inclusivity, and how social media and smart technologies may support a necessary broader view of inclusivity that begins by including people who may not wish to be included but have to be! This thinking has led to the development of a smart app for social work assessment and interviewing.

Helen Webster asks *(How) should smart technologies for learning be taught?* This captures one of the central themes of the book and ideas about smart learning with personal devices. Part of the attraction of smart technologies in education is that they are designed first and foremost to be easy to use, presenting no barriers to adoption by learners. However, the use of personal smart technologies by students and staff in higher education signals the need to reconsider digital literacy and its importance to learning, teaching and employability. It may be that the digital literacies required for smart learning are perhaps more diverse and complex than those we have considered to date.

Following on from this, and pre-empting several case studies in *Smart Learning* that consider the experience of academic CPD, Simon Thomson sets out the 4E Framework. The visionary activities evident in *Smart Learning* highlight how important it is to critically reflect on early practice and to construct useful representations of the pioneering excursions being taken by innovators and early adopters. In *Building a conversational framework for e-learning to support the future implementation of learning technologies* Thomson sets out the framework he has devised to encourage staff to think about ways in which technology can enable, enhance and enrich learning experiences and empower learners. He questions our current technology deployment models and asks whether technology really is the solution, especially when we may not have identified the question. The piece draws upon his experience of using the 4E Framework and demonstrates its impact in supporting institutional decisions around the use of mobile devices.

Ros Walker responds to the question that often arises amongst people who can see a trend but don't know why it is important. *What shall we do with our iPads?* looks at the development of a framework for introducing mobile devices into schools. The chapter shows how the ideas within the framework developed. She describes how it can be used in a variety of educational settings as a 'discussion piece' to formulate an action plan. The chapter is accompanied by a digital version of the framework. Walker shows the amount of planning and thought required if mobile devices are to be used successfully in an educational context.

In *The TARDIS effect – how mobile phones could transform teaching and learning* Caroline Keep and Mark Feltham muse on previous visions of the future. In 1963 the BBC launched the science fiction television series *Dr. Who* in which 'The Doctor' explored the universe (and continues to do so through his various regenerations) in his TARDIS, a machine that's 'bigger on the inside' and that allows him to travel anywhere in time and space. Some 50 years later we too can do the same, albeit virtually, using mobile devices. This opens up an exciting constellation of possibilities for teaching and learning. In this short piece Keep and Feltham envision a 'Who-topian' paradigm shift in teaching and learning with mobile technology at its core.

Section 2: Research and case studies

Change at scale

Throughout *Smart Learning*, and in higher education itself, the challenge of estimating readiness is evident. Technically it seems we are ready, and culturally too, we are more open. But how ready are we to change our expectations and our actual practice as teachers and learners to make good use of our personal devices?

In *HE BYOD – ready or not?* Anne Nortcliffe builds upon previous studies which have shown increasing student ownership and usage of smart devices by students. At the time of this study in 2014 more than 1,300 academics at Sheffield Hallam University had connected a mobile device to the university email exchange server. Students are embracing BYOD to support their learning, in particular seeking out apps that will assist them as learners in tasks relating to personal organisation, productivity, referencing material, communication, and multi-tasking. Nortcliffe's study looked at the gap in knowledge about the academic use of smart technologies and the extent to which this aligns with student ownership and usage in their university lives. The chapter discusses the large quantitative study of students and staff, which she conducted at Sheffield Hallam University to answer this.

The theme of institutional readiness continues in Simon Thomson's chapter *Taking the tablets – should you bring your own or use those prescribed?* BYOD is now an established term for the use of student or staff personal devices for learning and teaching activities. However Leeds Beckett University wanted to examine the potential impact of a 1-to-1 tablet deployment where staff and students had the same device. The 2012 Horizon Report states that "students at universities and colleges have ever-increasing expectations of being able to learn on these devices whenever and wherever they may be" and suggested that tablet computing would have a time-to-adoption horizon' of one year or less. While higher education has not yet seen the large adoption suggested in that report, it is clear that research into the use of such devices is expanding. The focus of this project was to explore the impact, specifically with regards to learning and teaching; however, it also highlighted staff and student digital literacy needs, their expectations of using such technology and the centralised support and infrastructure required. This case study outlines our experience of that 1-to-1 deployment and examines the benefits and challenges in comparison to a BYOD approach.

How do social media-enhanced learning environments compare to traditional learning environments in the eyes of students? How ready are students to bring learning to their own devices and spaces? Mark Feltham and Caroline Keep report on a case study of 350+ first year undergraduate bioscience students who were allowed to choose how they wished to learn and be assessed in *Oh, the places you'll go − smart learning in the natural sciences*. Students could choose to work as individuals or in groups, either didactically through 'traditional' lectures and workshops at university or creatively via Facebook at times and places of their choosing. They present data on how and where students engaged with social media, their use of mobile devices and their preferred methods for demonstrating their learning. They argue for the use of mobile technologies in combination with social media as an exciting alternative approach to traditional classroom teaching.

Making it personal − a case study of personal smart device usage by higher education Art and Design students provides an overview of some of the lessons learnt from a project undertaken as part of the Higher Education Academy Changing the Learning Landscape programme during the academic year 2013-14. Elaine Garcia and Martial Bugliolo set out the project in which eight students from differing Art and Design discipline areas (high digital, mid digital and low digital) were provided with a smart tablet device (iPad mini, Google Nexus 7, Kobo Arc and Kindle Fire) for the year and were asked to provide regular feedback about the usefulness of the device for both educational and personal purposes. This case study provides an analysis of their views. It discusses issues that should be considered before purchasing smart tablet devices for students, such as the need to consider the type of device that will be purchased, the discipline area of the student and the personal nature of smart tablet devices.

Arguably one of the best known and innovative open learning experiences in UK higher education in recent years has been BYOD4L — Bring Your Own Devices for Learning. Its first iterations have been built around a mission to explore the possibilities that digital and social media afford. In *BYOD4L — learning about using our own devices using the 5C framework* Chrissi Nerantzi and Sue Beckingham share the 5C framework developed for this open event which, at the time of writing (2014), had been offered twice in collaboration with colleagues from different institutions in the UK and Australia and partners in the US and Germany. BYOD4L is an open learning opportunity for teachers and students who are interested in learning about how they can utilise their devices for informal, formal as well as lifewide learning, teaching, personal and professional development. BYOD4L was a facilitated, fully mobile, open CPD offer for academic staff and students. It was developed using freely available social media. BYOD4L itself, as an open educational resource and stand-alone course was made available under a Creative Commons licence. Its aim was to enable individuals from around the world to learn together using an inquiry-based approach and the 5C framework: Connecting, Communicating, Curating, Collaborating, Creating (Nerantzi & Beckingham, 2014). This provided a scaffold for participants to familiarise themselves with the main ideas associated with the concept of Bring Your Own Devices and how they can be applied to learning. The framework allowed participants to progressively develop confidence and competence in using their own devices for a variety of learning and teaching applications from simple to more complex using critical and creative thinking techniques.

Openness is reflected in the new ways we as academics, students and developers work together, including across institutional boundaries as described in BYOD4L. This is further evidenced in the next CPD case study which has built upon Helen Webster's *10 Days of Twitter* model.

Chris Rowell offers *Reflections on 10 Days of Twitter for Regent's University London* in a case study that describes the process of setting up, running and evaluating this short online course for staff. Each day over ten days a new post was added to the course *Wordpress* site. Each blog post described a new feature or way of using Twitter, how it could be used to enhance the course participant's own professional practice and concluded with a 'ten minute activity'. The study outlines aspects of the course that worked well, challenges it faced and suggestions to others who might like to run a similar course at their own institution.

Change in practice

Smart learning is evident any model of teaching and learning that seamlessly accommodates technology as a part of the learning environment. It may enhance what is already done or it may transform teaching and learning completely. The following case studies demonstrate how e-learning or technology enhanced learning is leaving behind the shackle of a provided, monolithic Virtual Learning Environment to extend the ways we learn and teach together by being more socially and interactively engaged.

Shelly Stevenson and Bianca Wright reflect on how they have applied BYOD to their teaching in *Back pocket learning − enabling 'digital natives' to use smart devices to ensure understanding of the threshold concepts of journalism.* This research used a case study of a first year journalism course at Coventry University to explore the concept of 'Back Pocket Journalism' and how it is taught in the selected Journalism course. The focus of the study was on the broader principles of journalism practice in the context of technological tools. The journalism students were empowered by encouragement to use their smart phones to capture news, edit and upload via smartphone apps, with news creation, reporting and coordination using the smartphone as the 'news hub' as well as the recording device. The foundation to this is using the phone as a research tool, using apps, social media and the actual telephone to gather information. This teaching approach was predicated on the theoretical foundations of digital literacy training, which demonstrated the potential of these tools to aid in the shift from a traditional pedagogical approach to an andragogical one, as proposed by Knowles (1980). The study pointed to the need for a digital literacy approach that builds on the foundational skills of the student cohort.

For over 6 years Dave Kennedy and Daphne Robson have been bringing well-established pedagogies for small groups into larger classes by using interactive learning activities and touch screen technologies. In their chapter *Bringing well-established pedagogies into interactive lectures* they address the importance of immediate feedback to students; something that was well-known when master-apprentice systems for learning were set up many years ago. But the economics of delivering education to large groups of students in classroom situations has meant that the frequency and usefulness of feedback to students has been compromised. They have overcome this problem by using a classroom activity based on Anderson *et al.'s* Active Learning theory (2007) which involves the following sequence of events:

- Teacher sends a question to the students from a touch screen device;
- Students answer it using their touch screen device;
- Teacher retrieves all answers from students electronically;
- Teacher displays students' answers to the class, selects several to discuss with the class and annotate.

In this way, students receive feedback for several different answers, and their own or similar answers will often be chosen. Students comment that they like seeing other students' answers as it helps them to avoid mistakes. They learn from seeing alternative strategies for solving problems and from the teacher-led discussion of why an answer is wrong. They have used technologies including *Classroom Presenter* with tablet PCs for 6 years, *Ubiquitous Presenter* with any browser device, and *Dyknow Vision* with touch screens. However, they note it is easier for students to use a device with a larger screen such as a tablet.

Michelle Blackburn and Joanna Stroud describe how the concept of the lecture theatre, once only understood as a teacher-centred learning environment, has been disrupted through the integration of personal smart devices. *Voices from 'the other side' – using Personal Response Systems to support student engagement* is an account of active learning by an academic and a learning technologist working collaboratively. They describe how they have given students a voice in class using smart technology in the form of *Socrative*, a Personal Response System (PRS). *Socrative* was used to enable the tutor to pose questions to large groups of students using their personal devices with the results being collated automatically and displayed in real time. The study reveals several benefits to using PRSs in class, including: gauging understanding, making learning fun, encouraging deeper discussion, promoting collaboration, delivering feedback at speed, giving everyone a voice, gathering data, and evaluating the academic's practice. The chapter concludes with some tips for successfully using PRSs.

Interactive learning should allow the learner to challenge and evaluate themselves. Care is needed to ensure such self-evaluation is safe and formative. Juliette Wilson argues that a game-based approach can be safe, formative and enjoyable. In *Un-pop quiz – a case study of motivating student engagement through smart games* she describes how she has introduced *Socrative* as a smart game, using it to stimulate engagement with preparatory reading amongst undergraduate Sociology students. The use, benefits and challenges of such smart games are considered. Research has shown how poor engagement with preparatory reading amongst Sociology students affects their learning. This study found that students liked the smart game when they used it and that it enabled less vocal students to participate. However, effective engagement was dependent upon the way the activity was framed: whilst 'game' communicates a safe learning environment to students, 'quiz' evoked such resistance that many students opted out altogether. The study indicates that smart games using apps such as *Socrative* have the potential to stimulate the engagement of undergraduate students with preparatory class material and encourage the class participation of less vocal students.

Challenging learners' expectations of university is an important theme for smart learning. In *Using social video to capture reflective voices* Diane Rushton and colleagues present an example of how the *YouTube Capture* smart device app can be used to promote reflective learning by recording the reflective voices of learners. A video reflection method was used in a Business course involving two tutors and their 60 students, many of whom were international students. The students were expected to work in pairs each week summarising and reflecting on key concepts towards providing evidence for an end of module reflective report. The *YouTube Capture* app is introduced and the rationale for using it is set out. Immediacy was a key factor in ensuring that learner and facilitator reflection was effective. While the purpose was to capture reflective voices, this case study explains why a video, rather than audio-based, approach was used.

Catherine Hack uses a *Google Spreadsheet* to support students as they collate and curate evidence. In *Collaborative curation in the classroom* she describes how she has established small collaborative groups, which involve students in searching both traditional and social online media for articles on the growth of genetically modified (GM) crops in order to answer the question: "Is the UK media biased against GM crops?" The structure of the spreadsheet facilitated the organisation and analysis of the information retrieved, with the activity supporting her students as they developed search strategies and established criteria for evaluating the credibility of sources and evidence. The activity encouraged the students to consider the stakeholders in an important bioethical issue, and identify alternative perspectives on the associated risks and benefits; a useful precursor for undertaking more formalised bioethical reasoning.

Social media, and specifically social networking, extends the learning environment and disrupts simple ideas of formal or informal physical or virtual learning in Neil Withnell's case study, *Using smart devices to enhance learning – the use of Twitter and blogging in nurse education*. He describes how he set up a Twitter account and accompanying blog site for the undergraduate nurses within their academic department. In this ongoing joint partnership, staff and students share the responsibility for curating the Twitter account on a weekly basis and then reflect on their week by writing blog posts or using video blogging. Within nine months the Twitter account had accrued over 2,500 followers and generated over 3,200 views to the blog. The initiative has developed the students' skills and professionalism as they have received excellent feedback from across the country.

Section 3: Apps for learning

In this section the role of smart apps and their significance to learning are discussed. In the first chapter *Approaching apps for learning, teaching and research* Fiona MacNeill discusses effective, time efficient strategies for discovering and integrating useful apps into the academic workflow and offers some teaching scenarios where an app can be used to solve a specific problem or to fill a new niche. Fiona says the search and selection of apps for learning, teaching and research is a common barrier for new users of smart devices. Initial forays into the respective app stores can reap confusing and unrewarding results. This can be frustrating, especially for new users, and can promote the perception that the device is limited when compared to a desktop computer. Finding time-efficient strategies for app discovery in tandem with strategies for using apps in your teaching arsenal is key to the successful use of a smart device. MacNeill outlines pragmatic strategies for integrating apps into existing workflows and considers teaching scenarios where an app can be used to solve a specific problem or to fill a new niche.

In the second chapter in this section on apps, *Being smart: using apps lifewide*, Andrew Middleton looks at a selection of apps used by educators. He identifies how, for many, the most important apps are those that are used lifewide. The chapter draws upon findings from a survey of academic smart device advocates to consider the qualities and functionalities of their chosen apps. Personalisation of technology, inclusive interactivity, seamless lifewide integration, communality, the increased authenticity of the learning environment, and the incorporation of rich digital mediation are highlighted as being important.

Finally...

This book is about learning in the age of personal, flexible and connected smart devices and aims to develop our appreciation of how different our world is now, even when compared to ten years ago. It asks, if the world has changed radically in this time of digital and social media, how well are we responding to the opportunities and challenges that smart learning afford us?

I hope that you find the many ideas in *Smart Learning* make connections with your own practice and help you to adapt it to make your own experience, and those of other academics and students, richer and more rewarding.

References

Carroll, J.M. (2000). Five reasons for scenario-based design. *Interacting with Computers*, 13, 43 – 60.

Middleton, A., ed. (2013). Digital voices: A collaborative exploration of the recorded voice in post-compulsory education. MELSIG & Sheffield Hallam University.

Wheeler, S. (2009). Learning space mashups: Combining Web 2.0 tools to create collaborative and reflective learning spaces. *Future Internet*, 1(1), 3 – 13.

SECTION 1 THOUGHT PIECES

Thinking about smart learning

Andrew Middleton

Introduction

The idea of smart learning serves to encapsulate approaches to teaching and learning that in some way benefit from the use of smart technologies. With student ownership of smart technologies being at over 95% according to a recent survey in my own institution, they have undoubtedly change the way we engage with life, work and study.

This chapter establishes the idea of smart learning as something much more than an innocuous change of landscape. It argues that the smart learning landscape not only affects us, but empowers us to enhance and transform education by connecting the technical phenomenon of the ubiquitous personal device to the phenomena of social media, rich digital media, mobile learning, BYOD, openness, and digital literacies. Separately they are fascinating; together they create a 'perfect storm'.

Smart devices are distinguishable as being portable, multi-functional, location sensitive, wirelessly connected technologies like smartphones and tablet PCs. Technically they are also distinguished by their incorporation of 'apps': usually free or inexpensive software applications that are task orientated.

Smart learning, as discussed in this book, emphasises *learning* and the difference that personal, and *personalised*, technology makes to a student's engagement with their study. Smart learning assumes that the learner is at the heart of their learning: teachers, peers, technologies and the learning environment are, in effect, support actors and props to that purpose. This point needs to be emphasised because it would be easy to misinterpret its significance: personal smart technology increases a learner's independence. Its potential, therefore, is to enable and empower the learner in a way that has not been possible before. This chapter explores this proposition.

Further, it explores how the phenomenon makes the context for engaging in study more personal and potentially self-directed by making possible new ways of being which are more open, connected and augmented by personally richer contexts.

While this proposition of smart learning invites us to assess opportunities and challenges available to post-compulsory education, it is not an entirely new phenomenon. Instead it can be understood as a convergence of many ideas in the Connected Age (Dahlstrom, Walker & Dziuban, 2013), some of which are as old as the hills and some that are still forming. Some of these ideas are set out in figures 1 and 2.

Disruption through the convergence of innovative thinking

Smart learning allows us to regroup and reconceptualise recent innovative thinking about academic innovation and ensure that important phenomena are firmly embedded within a *learning* landscape.

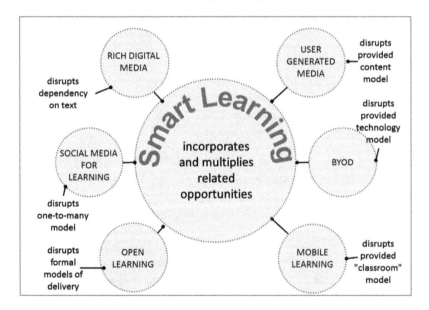

Figure 1. Smart learning: disrupting the learning landscape by converging and multiplying key ideas for progressive learning spaces

Arguably some important ideas have struggled to gain a foothold with teachers and learners because they appear to complicate, rather than enhance, what is superficially experienced as a straightforward, widely accepted relationship between the teacher and the learner. Innovative propositions for teaching and learning have to make an excellent case to warrant any attention. The excellent case, therefore, for smart learning is that it is now technically easy to expand the spaces we use for working together as teachers and learners, making our learning relationships richer, more person-centred (whatever our role), more social, more authentic, more flexible, more open and more situated in a rapidly changing digital world.

Figure 1 clarifies this expansion. We are no longer solely dependent upon the medium of text, as user or producer. Learning is more accessible and more challenging because we can make or use any media to convey, interrogate or apply knowledge. We have the flexibility of using technology in ways that suit us as individuals, wherever we are and whatever we are doing. Our assumptions about the formality of learning are disrupted and we are able to recognise the importance of different collaborators and contexts for learning and social media can help us to make meaningful, lifewide connections.

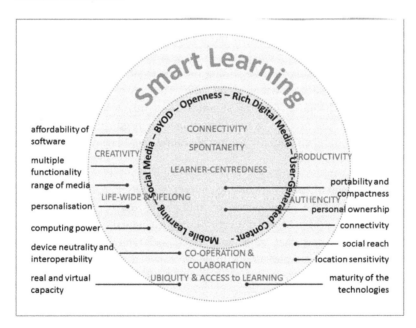

Figure 2. Defining factors and attributes of smart learning

Figure 2 shows how the idea of smart learning incorporates key ideas that combine to deliver and surpass the promise of mobile learning: BYOD, Social Media for Learning, openness, rich digital media and user-generated content. Associated with these concepts are numerous characteristics (in black) that define smart learning according to the attributes they afford (in pink).

Mobile learning

Mobile learning has provided a focus for innovation and research about technology-enhanced learning since the turn of the century. In many ways ideas about smart learning are an affirmation of that work. Kukulska-Hulme (2005), for example, set out and explored the attributes that define mobile learning. She listed these as: spontaneity; personal; informal; contextual; portable; ubiquitous; and pervasive. The same attributes explain the importance of smart learning today. What is different, however, is the maturity of the technologies, their affordability, usability, connectivity, context sensitivity, real social reach, the nature of their ubiquity and the pervasiveness of the technology. These are coupled with the compact computing power, its capacity and virtual capacity, the commonplace integration and customisable functionality of the devices, the user-base and expectations. These facets exist in the wider context of the social web (Wheeler, 2009), something that has emerged gradually and more recently. Ten years ago the pieces were beginning to come together technically, but it has been the massive growth in social networking *behaviour* that has been the significant change factor. The significance of this is how the user's relationship with technology is now determined by needs they define for themselves, creating an exigency for incorporating smart behaviour into all they do.

The phenomenon of social networking amongst today's students grew out of and surpassed the phenomenon of 'txting'; the use of mobile Short Message Service (SMS). SMS has a very limited functionality compared to today's widely used chat apps and other social media (Thomas & Bradshaw, 2013). Examples of its innovative use in higher education recognised its pervasive presence amongst students, but outside of small-scale innovations, SMS has largely been used as an administrative tool educationally (Jones, Edwards & Reid, 2009).

The term 'technology-enhanced learning', increasingly used to replace the term 'e-learning', emphasises how technology is used in the service of learning (HEFCE, 2009). Despite this, development units in higher education have not always found it easy to change their role, or its perception, from technology advocacy to learning enhancement and the 'problem' of technology acceptance and integration has tended to remain the dominant discourse in the case study literature. However, the habitual, lifewide use of social media by students, and increasingly their tutors, has inverted the outlook for the integration of technology: the end-user's expectations of education now suggest a more general readiness to bring what they do outside of the classroom with technology into it by incorporating their social networking behaviour.

The advent of the smartphone, and then its widespread ownership, began to address a major barrier to exploring at scale how mobile technologies, including phones, PDAs and portable media players, can improve teaching and learning by delivering the promised ubiquity of all-in-one multifunctional, constantly connected devices. This is why it is critical to focus on *personal*, rather than institutionally provided, technology.

The discourse around mobile learning provides insight into the possibilities of smart learning when we reflect on the ways in which it has been described:

- Mobile meaning portable handheld devices;
- Mobile meaning on the move;
- Mobile meaning being in remote, non-traditional, or authentic places;
- Mobile describing our capacity to enhance learning with technologies in non-wired environments;
- Mobile meaning our capacity to teach and learn in, across and through a range of physical and virtual spaces seamlessly;
- Mobility as something that makes the formal spaces we use more valuable, independently and socially;
- Mobility as something that makes the informal spaces we use more valuable, independently and socially.

While this focus on mobile learning has been inspirational and useful, it is timely due the proliferation of smart devices available to teachers and learners to reassess mobile learning as something that is underpinned by ubiquitous technology and is not technically exceptional (Beetham, 2011). The promise of smart learning is that it is commonplace and versatile, and accentuates a non-formal (Eraut, 2000) and holistic (Beckett & Hager, 2002) space for learning and, because of that, it can enhance the meaning of what is being learnt. Its unusual promise, as a technology-enhanced approach, is that it can promote heutagogy (Hase & Kenyon, 2000; Blaschke, 2012); a self-determined approach to learning. Furthermore, it challenges simple understandings of formal, non-formal, informal and even incidental learning (Dobozy, 2014). Due to the ubiquity of personal devices, developments in this area are less likely to be dependent on special funding; just special thinking.

Bring Your Own Device

The philosophy of Bring Your Own Device (BYOD) is that the employee (or student or tutor in the case of smart learning) uses their own technology to access their online working environment. The immediate access, flexibility and personalisation afforded by the device helps the learner to engage more effectively with their work in ways that suit them, wherever they are, whatever they need to do and at any time. There are similar benefits for the academic using their own device too. The main benefits in industry are that BYOD improves productivity and happiness (Mobile Enterprise, 2011). Education provides a different context in terms of learner engagement, though for staff the issues about productivity and security are similar.

In industry BYOD practice emerged as a reaction by employees to the constraints of technological infrastructure provided by organisations, and their associated IT policies. BYOD allows employees to circumvent these constraints by creating a more personalised and productive technology infrastructure for themselves (Caldwell, Zeltman & Griffin, 2012). It is indicative too of how a personalised and distributed approach is more flexible for the user and more strategically agile than a managed and unwieldy environment.

The design of IT infrastructure in large organisations begins with security. Productivity, therefore, is first affected by the risk of technological weakness and becomes managed by impersonal and inflexible one-size-fits-all policies. Such policies have a knock-on effect on the organisational culture, acting as a stranglehold that potentially locks down or excludes desirable behaviours that could promote creativity and innovation, collaboration and networking.

It is not realistic, nor appropriate to dismiss risks out of hand; however, organisations like universities need to think differently about how risks associated with the incoherent adoption of BYOD are managed (Traxler, 2010). It may be, for example, that organisations have to invest less in creating robust closed systems and much more in developing digital literacy to safeguard good practice. For students this investment in developing their digital literacy is significant in terms of their employability: at least 63.5% of smartphones used for business are owned by employees (Mobile Enterprise, 2011) and employers need their staff to be productive and responsible.

BYOD in education

Smart devices are disrupting our lives for better or worse and the phenomenon is something that education cannot ignore.

Higher Education Institutions (HEIs), in the main, have so far had to provide the campus-based computing used by staff and students underpinning innovative technology-enhanced pedagogy. This has given universities, like other big organisations, the control they have needed to ensure that learning technologies are reliable, safe and well-supported. This phase (approximately 1990-2017) will be viewed as a stopgap or transitional phase in years to come. Apart from being unwieldy, computer technology was until relatively recently not commonplace, and was inflexible and expensive. This began to change at the turn of the century and in the following decade, especially with the development and proliferation of lighter, more robust and powerful laptops and netbooks. Students increasingly arrived at university with a mobile phone and a laptop (e.g. University of Sheffield, 2011; Dahlstrom, Walker & Dziuban, 2013; Nortcliffe, 2015). This creates a problem for IT administrators, as Traxler (2010, p.158) says, "Universities cannot afford, procure, provide nor control these devices but they cannot ignore them either."

In 2003 RIM BlackBerry released its convergent smartphone (BlackBerry, 2014); a mobile phone renowned at the time for its integration of email and inclusion of a QWERTY keyboard, text messaging, web browsing and other wireless information services. This first attracted business users. The integration of affordable SMS tools coupled with suitable phone contracts later made them attractive to younger people too. Initially, however, they didn't have touch screens or the range of functionality subsequently found in the 'apps' of their competitors' devices. In retrospect, these features came to define what we now know as smartphones.

Apple released its *iPhone* in 2007 and then its *iPad* in 2010, both running Apple's iOS platform. Google launched its *Nexus* line of smartphones and tablets running the Android operating system in 2010. Subsequently the smartphone and tablet market has exploded, with brands including Samsung, Amazon and Microsoft adding to the to and fro of market share.

Smart technologies are now ubiquitous on campus (Nortcliffe, 2015). The challenge to educators at this point is less about whether students have the technology (though issues about inclusivity do remain), but more about whether we can influence their use of it. If students are bringing their own technology and using it to manage their lives in general, how do we move to a position where the use of devices is widely expected and accepted? According to 2013's US ECAR study (Dahlstrom, Walker & Dziuban, 2013), students in higher education are ready to use their devices more for academic purposes and look to their tutors and institutions for opportunities and encouragement to do so.

Ward (2013) on the Voxburner website discussed how their Youth Insight Report 2012/13 had found that 96% of surveyed students owned a laptop, whereas only 10% own a tablet. This is a rapidly changing situation; however, without the selection and installation of apps by the student, smart devices like tablets will not do everything that the students or their university expects them to do. This is confirmed by the students who were interviewed by Ward. They indicate how their tablet functionality supports note taking in lectures but is not capable of producing "proper" assignments. This suggests our thinking about what 'proper' means must change. In the short term, institutional support for the effective setting up and use of personal devices introduces challenges that are new to the sector.

Smartphones and tablets are powerful in terms of connectivity and the gathering and presentation or playback of content. If suitable apps have not been installed by the device owner and if expectations for academic work are not designed with the possibilities of new media in mind, smart devices can be relatively limited in what they can do in terms of the content production and hand-in requirements currently prescribed for academic work in many cases.

Expectations for formal academic work among students and their tutors, and ultimately their institutions, still have to change: for the student it seems a greater awareness is needed for how to install the free or cheap powerful apps which can provide them with the necessary functionality; for the academic, a reconsideration of what is important in assessing student work, especially in terms of useful academic protocols in the Digital Age; for universities and academics, a greater appreciation of assignment formats that exploit online social media tools and the need to develop appropriate academic and digital literacies.

Online or cloud-based social media production tools such as Google Drive, blogs, wikis, and video or audio sites need proper consideration, especially as they can be accessed equally well from a range of fixed and mobile devices and because they *are* social. Socially based study, exploiting a range of media, is feasible now in ways that it were not before. Academia needs to break away from assumed traditional practice and continually ask itself whether the removal of constraints allows us to reshape the way we teach and learn together. Institutions should review policies and guidance and pro-actively support the exploration of rich media tools.

Device neutrality, ubiquity and social connectivity, all enhanced by a non-discriminating cloud-based technical environment, change things. Academia, however, still has some way to go before it will accept student assignments delivered in these formats, or in other rich media formats.

Concerns amongst educators

The Groupe Speciale Mobile Association (GSMA, 2012) highlights some barriers to the adoption of BYOD approaches in UK education. These barriers include the reluctance of some teachers to allow students to bring their own devices into class and concerns over the digital divide. Nielsen (2011) in the context of K12 education in the US, challenges some of the arguments that more conservative educators have voiced about embracing BYOD for learning. Of these, several warrant proper consideration here.

The deepening of a digital divide is a real issue for all, though perhaps more so for those in school level education. In post-compulsory education, especially if we look at rates approaching 100% ownership smart device of smart devices (GSMA, 2012), it is less of an issue. But education, at any level, cannot risk excluding any student by introducing unreasonable conditions for engagement. It is unethical and illegal. Inclusivity, in a broader sense, is something that requires urgent and serious thought therefore, although this works in two ways: the use of BYOD for learning can both enhance and reduce inclusivity. Much more research is needed in this area in terms of assisted technology and usability design. The answer for the moment is a mixed economy in which students are encouraged and supported to use their own devices as an option to other institutional provision (e.g. Feltham & Keep, 2015).

A concern noted by Nielsen (2011) is to do with interoperability; specifically that content is determined by the 'weakest' device. Like several of the concerns highlighted by Nielsen, this seems to come from the paradigm of content driven curricula where content has been provided in non-standard formats using proprietary tools and distribution methods. Higher education is moving away from proprietary formats, though Microsoft Word and PowerPoint, for example, remain dominant. Nevertheless, a growing awareness amongst content providers of interoperability and the advent of social media and cloud-based services continues to create greater access to both content producers and users. Wheeler's (2010) notion of the Cloud Learning Environment provides a sense of how learners will manage their engagement in the future. More than this, a BYOD teaching philosophy recognises the principle of 'device neutrality' (Alokaily, 2013) and ensures that assignments can be completed on any device and this helps to shift attention away from the device to the learning outcomes.

Another real concern, and one that can be evidenced by strolling through any university learning centre, is the distractive nature of mobile devices and social networks. The phenomenon has been referred to as 'the age of distraction' (Weimer, 2014) and Kuznekoff and Titsworth (2013, p.236) say,

> ...instructors remain concerned that such connection to the social world [in class] disconnects students from learning, leading some to ban all electronic communication devices from lectures... students potentially split their attention in ways that cause them to miss important details presented during class.

The loudest and most frequent complaints, they say, come from those academics who are firmly committed to lecturing. However, the argument against the student use of mobile phones in lectures is that they don't notice information and cannot retain it as well those who are paying close attention. Smart learning supports the challenge to didactic lecturing methods and the assumption knowledge retention is a key indicator of learning. Academia has known for a long time that effective teaching methods are ones that promote learner engagement and social interactivity around a topic (Chickering & Gamson, 1987). Recent large-scale research by Freeman *et al.* (2014) highlights how the lecture format is a relatively ineffective way of teaching compared to active learning methods.

It may be that it is time to challenge the central role that the lecture has in the experience of students now that the barriers to engaging large numbers of students through a course have been whittled away by new technologies. The advent of the 'Flipped Classroom' (Bergmann & Sams, 2012) provides one useful model, amongst many, for engaging students more interactively and user-owned devices have a large role to play in such methods.

Nevertheless, whatever your stance, we *do* need to pay attention to each other in face-to-face situations whether we are learners, tutors, peers or others. *Absent presence* in which one's physical presence is over-ridden by more pressing engagement with disembodied conversations (Traxler, 2010 citing Gergen, 1996) challenges the very idea and value of a university education. Being able to concentrate and give each other the benefit of our actual presence is enriching and so important. Again, the answer to this would seem to be about developing metacognitive appreciation and critical digital literacy.

In contrast to concerns about distracted students, there is an emerging appreciation of non-formal (Eraut, 2000), lifewide learning and learning ecologies (Jackson, 2013): while students on campus may be accessing 'irrelevant' media, students off-campus are equally able to access 'relevant' media. Developing our collective understanding of how students do 'get the task done', especially in the wider context of their work and social lives, is an area that requires more attention. The connected world beyond campus provides a rich context for study, but to make more use of time off campus universities may need to put more effort into developing student's self-regulation capabilities.

Coming to understand BYOD in education

The Bring Your Own Devices for Learning (BYOD4L) course, first run collectively by academic educational developers mostly located in the UK in 2014, explored the full potential of using smart technologies and social media, both in the content of the course and in the way it was delivered (Nerantzi & Beckingham, 2015).

As in the rest of society, the pervasive 'always on' dimension of smart technology is something that changes habits, expectations and inevitably practice in education. The teaching-learning dynamic, for example, must change; partly to reflect what students expect to do, but also to exploit the removal of constraints that now allow us to connect, communicate, curate, collaborate and create in new ways (Nerantzi & Beckingham, 2015). Moving on from the idea of MOOCs (Massive Open Online Courses), BYOD4L has adopted a collaborative peer-led approach to CPD by using a fluid learning environment based around social media. While the main focus of the BYOD4L 'social space for learning' (rather than 'course') was learning enhanced by one's own devices, the experience of taking part in the initial iterations of BYOD4L demonstrated clearly how the use of smart devices and social media together create an immersive social learning environment.

BYOD4L is an early experiment in a more self-directed and peer-supported way of learning through smart and social media, though there are many similar approaches beginning to be taken. Each instance of such a programme generates new thinking and indications are that higher education will benefit enormously from imaginative consideration of such approaches.

Understanding the opportunity of BYOD in education

In understanding why BYOD is an important opportunity, and more than just an inevitability, the idea of habitation is useful perhaps; a habitat being a natural place for life and growth.

The ubiquity of technology signals independence: a lack of dependence on technology being provided for us and, indeed, a disrupted view of provision in general (Figure 1). By owning and using our own accessible, portable, highly functional and connected devices, as in industry, we are not bound by unnecessary constraints and we are free to challenge assumptions we have held about learning technology and, indeed, learning itself. Some of these are raised elsewhere in this edition, but for the moment let us reflect on some assumptions we may have about education. Learning is predominantly,

- abstracted from society and separate to other aspects of life;
- constructed around a timetable;
- better when face to face;
- something that is taught (from the front);
- facilitated through the written word, especially texts produced by academics and noted authors.

I am not going to argue either way for any of these statements. It is enough for the moment to say that in this book we discuss the veracity of these ideas about higher education, and hear about alternative approaches and thinking that challenge our assumptions. However, viewing learning as being a lifewide and a lifelong habit about continuous growth, it seems BYOD provides the learner with an opportunity to continuously reflect through life, wherever they are, on matters as they emerge, so heightening the meaning and the application of learning.

Social Media for Learning and Web 2.0

Following on from BYOD, smart learning can be understood in the context of the 'social web' (Wheeler, 2009) and social media.

The idea of Web 2.0, as outlined by O'Reilly (2005), describes a second generation digital environment where the Web is no longer just a place in which static information is placed by experts. It has become a platform for harnessing collective intelligence; where data is dynamic and abundant; where software is in perpetual beta, and where the behaviour and attitude of the people who use it is more important than technology itself. It is a living, social, creative and collaborative space designed for its inhabitants rather than its landlords (White & Le Cornu, 2011).

The advent of digital social media and an appreciation of how it can be used to enhance learning has been concurrent with, and arguably inseparable from, the emergence of ubiquitous personal smart technologies. For some this common proliferation has contributed to their disinterest in either of them; each compounding perceptions of a growing trivialisation of education perhaps or, at best, an escalation of a learning environment that is always in flux and too complex to grasp.

Social media is diverse in its form and purpose. Facebook and Twitter are perhaps most familiar to students and staff, but only occupy one end of a continuum around networking. But Google, while originally established as a search engine, has grown into a suite of social media tools including YouTube that allows anyone to use, produce, collaborate, store, retrieve and communicate in any number of ways. The amount of social media tools and providers is too numerous to discuss here, but they now pervade the lives of anyone who has an Internet connection.

What *is* important to discuss here, is how education comes to understand the relevance of social media to teaching and learning. To this end Middleton & Beckingham have proposed a Social Media for Learning Framework (2014; 2015) intended to support academic innovators when considering how social media can be used to enhance and transform their teaching.

It is discussed in more detail in the following chapter but is introduced here to help establish the scope of smart learning.

Social Media for Learning is...	Examples of what can be done
Socially inclusive ▸ supporting and validating learning through mutually beneficial, jointly enterprising and communally constructive communities of practice; ▸ fostering a sense of belonging, being and becoming; ▸ promoting collegiality.	Use Padlet to collate ideas from a virtual brainstorm
Lifewide and lifelong ▸ connecting formal, non-formal and informal learning progression; ▸ developing online presence; ▸ developing digital literacies.	Encourage students to establish a LinkedIn presence for their employability
Media neutral ▸ learning across and through rich, multiple media.	Post 'Concept Clips' (screencast or video explanations) to YouTube and invite students' comments as the basis for flipped lecture approach
Learner-centred ▸ promoting self-regulation, self-expression, self-efficacy and confidence; ▸ accommodating niche interests and activities, the 'long tail' of education.	Used a problem-based approach underpinned by a group co-production activity in Google Docs
Co-operative ▸ promotes working together productively and critically with peers (co-creation) in self-organising, robust networks that are scalable, loosely structured, self-validating, and knowledge-forming.	Assign student groups complementary tasks to build a comprehensive, credible online resource using Google Sites

Open and accessible	
▸ supporting spatial openness (without physical division); ▸ supporting temporal openness i.e. synchronously and asynchronously; ▸ supporting social openness i.e. democratically, inclusively; ▸ supporting open engagement i.e. in terms of being: geographically extended, inclusive, controlled by the learner, gratis, open market, unconstrained freedom, access to content.	Use Open Educational Resources and promote Open Educational Practice
Authentically situated	
▸ making connections across learning, social and professional networks; ▸ scholarly; ▸ establishing professional online presence and digital identity.	Invite 'experts' to speak to/with your students via Skype or in a Google Hangout

Table 1 Social Media for Learning Framework (Middleton & Beckingham, 2014)

Steve Wheeler has continually pushed forward thinking about technology's relationship with learner engagement. In his blog post *Web 3.0: the way forward?* (2010) he offers ideas for the future of education. He identifies how, not so long ago, "multimedia brought the world into the classroom" and posits that "smart technologies will take the classroom into the world." The suggestion is central to smart learning, that we are no longer bound by the physical walls and wired connections that have previously determined what we can do as teachers and learners. He compares the different stages of the Web's short history and imagines that beyond the social media that characterises Web 2.0, the future Web will be defined in terms of the degree of information and/or social connectivity we experience and the extent of the user's active and productive engagement. From this an idea of Education 3.0 emerges. However, others such as Jackie Gerstein (2013) have described this more in terms of heutagogy (Hase & Kenyon, 2000) and less as a specific outcome of technological change.

Openness

Openness provides a further important context for understanding smart learning.

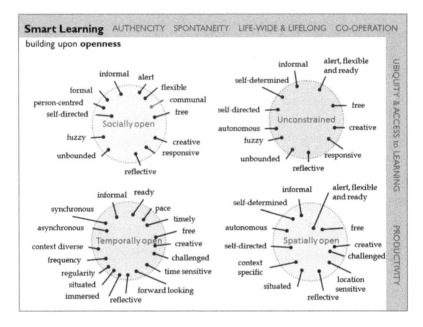

Figure 3. Smart Learning – building upon openness

A recent growing interest in openness comes from the emergence of open source software, the development of Creative Commons licences for content, and the expansion of social media sites including YouTube and Wikipedia. Knowledge sharing is the essential facet of openness, though openness assumes many different meanings even when talking specifically about Open Content in the discourse of academic innovation in the Connected Age (Attwell & Pumilia, 2007).

Attwell and Pumilia (2007) explain that open knowledge has the benefits of not only sharing knowledge, but promulgating, proliferating and sustaining it, ensuring that it has much more impact; thus exemplifying Lave and Wenger's ideas of situated learning, communities of practice and legitimate peripheral participation (1991).

Peter and Deimann (2013) raise the need for more discussion about the meaning of openness given the sector's interest in Open Educational Resources, Open Educational Practices and Massive Open Online Courses (MOOCs). The emergence of MOOCs has drawn attention to the different ways that openness is used. In general, MOOCs are understood in two different ways: in one camp the value of the MOOC is associated with ideas of an open connected community (cMOOCs); in the other (xMOOCs) the meaning of openness is much more to do with open enrolment. In the xMOOC content-centred model "learner responsibilities focus on consuming the course content and completing evaluations to assess understanding of that content" (Ahn *et al.*, 2013, p.162). Clarà and Barberà (2013, p.129) explain that, "xMOOCs are not pedagogically driven, and the consequence is that they assume pedagogies mainly based on behaviorist psychology." In the former, openness is important to the connectivist (Siemens, 2005) ideas that inform its social pedagogy, whilst in the latter the pedagogical approach ignores the social potential of having large numbers of people enrolled on the course. Openness, while important in this smart learning picture, is not simple. Even amongst transformational innovators it is clear similar sounding ideas can be poles apart.

Anderson (2013, p.2) picked up on the need for more clarity and lists the following meanings of openness in education:

- Open access beyond a particular geographic local, e.g. distance learning, online learning;
- Open ideology and academic freedom;
- Open learning content "having no restrictions on revision, re-use, sale and enhancement (as in open source software and most open educational resources (OERs)."
- Open enrolment as inclusivity, being without regard to prerequisite knowledge or other demographic data such as gender or religion;
- Freedom to start and to determine the pace of a course in our continuous enrolment undergraduate programs;
- Free and open - gratis or free of charges for participants.

The idea of education as being an open-ended, lifewide and lifelong phenomenon provides a further way of understanding openness.

Downes (2009) discusses openness in the context of knowledge-generating networks. He identifies the qualities as being the free flow of communication within and without the network and the ability of community members to easily participate in activities. This idea of knowledge-generating networks aligns closely with the thinking of some cMOOCs in which learning has a collective purpose. This marks the contrast with xMOOCs where knowledge is represented as being a comparatively static commodity.

Ideas of open scholarship have emerged in recent years too. Scholarship, composed of seven basic functions or principles, is found in the acts of: discovering, annotating, comparing, referencing or acknowledging, sampling, elucidating or illustrating, and publishing or communicating (Unsworth, 2000). In the connected digital age scholarship must inevitably change (Borgman, 2007), and Weller (2011), for example, discusses how scholarship is being positively disrupted as open data becomes more available precipitating the exponential development of knowledge.

Openness can also be thought of structurally. Smart learning may create an opportunity to move away from formal structures to some extent. For example, assessment tasks and feedback on them can become more a matter of negotiation in a more authentically situated curriculum. Some of the ways we think about engaging post-graduate students in open, negotiated curricula may start to have more bearing on the undergraduate experience. In the short term we may begin to see this as a dimension of transition, metacognitive development and CPD for example.

For each of these meanings there are further nuances. The idea of open learning content and Open Educational Resources (OERs), for example, is closely related to the idea of Reusable Learning Objects which was developed at the turn of the century (Littlejohn, 2003). This area is quite problematic in terms of smart learning because the idea of 'content' is itself difficult. It suggests that teaching and learning is something that can be packaged, shared and reused. Wiley (2009), for example, describes the "4Rs" of open content: how it can be reused, revised, remixed, and redistributed.

The idea of reusable open digital resources in higher education has always been difficult. In the UK the government funded the Teaching and Learning Technology Programme (TLTP) programme in the early 1990s and later the Fund for the Development of Teaching & Learning (FDTL) in the UK (Baume, Martin & Yorke, 2003). These and other initiatives, like the JORUM content repository in the UK, have espoused and promoted reusability, but adoption of materials has been underwhelming when compared to their aspirations. The OPAL report *Beyond OER: Shifting focus to open educational practices* (2011) identifies a lack of institutional support; tools for sharing and adapting resources; user skills and time; quality or fitness of the resources; as well as a lack of trust and time as being barriers to reuse of OERs.

The idea of Open Educational Practices (OEP) may be of more use in considering smart learning (Ehlers, 2011). It builds upon the availability of OERs but emphasises the need for developing a culture of open practice first. Ehlers offers this definition of OEP,

> *OEP are defined as practices which support the (re)use and production of OER through institutional policies, promote innovative pedagogical models, and respect and empower learners as co-producers on their lifelong learning path.*

However, the idea of OEP may suffer from being too technical and too thought through, and ultimately too focused on building and sharing specified 'good' practice rather than supporting autonomous open development of practice.

Culturally, humankind knows that it learns and develops knowledge best by learning together. Ideas such as the 'Penny University' open coffee houses of the 17th century and Miner's Workshops of the late 19th century (Peter & Diemann, 2013) exemplify our natural inclination to congregate and learn socially and compare well with "powerful new platforms like YouTube, Facebook, and Twitter [which] have demonstrated... Web 2.0 is all about harnessing collective intelligence" (O'Reilly & Battelle, 2009, p.1). In the 21st century our social networks are more open, having a global reach that allows us to find niche interest groups more easily. It may be better to think, therefore, about openness in terms scholarly networking; a more organic view of open learning that does not need to conform to specifications, only communal interest in learning. This is where the connection for smart learning and social media can be made: understanding openness as being more about peer enhancement of practice for both academics and students. Our inclination for teaching and learning, wherever it is situated, to be more open and social will be more open and social because it *can be*.

I argue that all of the thinking on openness set out above misses a key point; one that is central to the idea of smart learning: learning is owned, experienced and determined by each individual learner. This can be a heutagogical view, but more than that, it is about the learner's changing view of their world and their will and ability to fluently and continually choose how to engage with and critically review it.

Rich digital media and user-generated content

Rich digital media encapsulate a range of approaches that make good use of video, audio and screencasting. Such applications tend to fall into the two high level categories of synchronous and asynchronous media, and both accentuate the value of voice as a dimension of the teaching and learning experience. They also improve accessibility as well as personal, authentic and meaningful engagement (Middleton, 2013).

The increased use in such media coalesces around the capacity of smart devices to store, access and play rich media and to also capture, edit and publish it with ease and sufficient quality. The barriers to production and distribution of audio and video (Diamond & Middleton, 2013) have diminished considerably with the advent of user-owned smart devices, especially when considered alongside the growth in social media sites like YouTube and SoundCloud coupled with the associated behaviours and familiarity of the students and staff who increasingly use them. At the same time, improved access to a wide range of social media sites makes embedding such content easy and suggests the use of rich media in education will proliferate.

The computing power, storage capacity and multimedia capability of 'bag-sized' smart devices challenge the dependence that academics and students have had on specialist technology to work with rich media as users and producers. It follows that the dependence that education has had on the written word to the exclusion of other media is also challenged.

In computing terms this can be thought of as a transition from the first generation era of provided, tethered computing to the second generation of personal wireless devices. Table 2 provides a view of the two paradigms.

The proliferation of rich digital media in education and the user-generation of such content not only promise a reconceptualisation of educational content, and its value, it "requires new ways of recognising quality" especially when such content is made open (Attwell & Pumilia, 2007, p.S218). However, quality itself may come to be redefined "as not an absolute property inherent in an object, but something to be negotiated in the context of use" (*ibid*).

This leads us to look at the importance of digital literacies.

First generation era of provided, tethered computing	Second generation era of personal wireless devices
▶ Desktop computing; ▶ Hard drive and networked storage; ▶ Tethered network connection from campus or home; ▶ Predominant use of Office-type software and web-based information; ▶ Multi-functional, specialised and sophisticated hard-to-learn software packages; ▶ Text is the predominant media; ▶ Email communication; ▶ Virtual learning environments used to structure and present information.	▶ Portable and personally owned computing; ▶ Large capacity storage synchronised to ever-present cloud storage; ▶ Wireless connectivity from anywhere; ▶ Applications are diverse for staff and students facilitating communication, social connectivity, curation and management of digital artefacts, co-operative working including collaboration, and creativity and production using multiple media; ▶ Mono-functional, specialised, unsophisticated 'good enough' (Weller, 2011) easy-to-use software apps; ▶ Text and images are the predominant media, but the use of video and audio is growing; ▶ Email continues to dominate communication though social media channels continuously engage academics and students wherever they are; ▶ Virtual learning environments remain and social media extend their reach and the need to engage formally, informally and autonomously, and in various ways.

Table 2. Broad brush comparison of first and second generation eras of digital learning and teaching technology

Digital literacies

The ongoing need to develop the digital literacies of students and staff is key to the successful adoption of smart learning.

Jisc infoNet (2014) define digital literacies as "those capabilities which fit an individual for living, learning and working in a digital society" (2014) and include,

- Information literacy;
- Media literacy;

- Communication and collaboration skill;
- Career and identity management skills;
- ICT literacy;
- Learning skills;
- Digital scholarship.

This definition is useful. In terms of smart learning and the enhancement and transformation of teaching and learning, however, the definition does not squarely address the need to develop our understanding of *teaching* in the connected and Digital Age. The promise of smart learning, and the inevitability of this age, is that the nature of teaching and learning will rapidly change and this disruption is likely to be far reaching over the next ten years. It is neither desirable nor possible to stand still. A much more sophisticated appreciation of teaching, learning and digital literacies is needed to properly accommodate this. The emphasis on skills in this definition (as with knowledge) does not seem to fit with what is really needed in this age: an idea of literacies, or rather capabilities and fluencies that describe people who can adapt creatively and critically in the world.

Smart learning opportunities and challenges

Smart learning recognises a change in the learning and teaching landscape. The exploration of associated ideas has revealed that, with the proliferation of user-owned smart devices, it is a good time now for us as academics, students, and managers of post-compulsory education to assess our assumptions about learning environments, associated technologies and how we can work with these.

The idea of smart learning is most helpful in developing our understanding of change. By proposing the notion of smart learning it becomes possible to recognise and reflect on what is different and the opportunities and challenges that this change brings.

It is not straightforward however. This chapter concludes with a table that lists the opportunities and challenges of teaching and learning in the era of smart technology (Table 3). This list is not comprehensive by any means, but it does indicate some of the complexity of a shift from a prescribed learning environment to one that in many ways is more open; and this complexity is itself the major barrier for both teachers and students.

To extend a metaphor, not many will see the wood for the trees and until some reliable paths have been constructed, entering the forest will continue to be fraught with danger. If smart learning is valuable and even inevitable, developing digital literacies, both conceptually and practically, is critical for post compulsory education.

Stakeholder	Opportunities	Challenges
Teachers	▸ Increased independence and flexibility; ▸ Increased interdependence amongst teachers, students and others; ▸ Access to and engagement with real world evidence, situations, and people; ▸ Appreciation of teaching spanning formal and non-formal spaces, across and through a range of physical and virtual spaces seamlessly; ▸ Anywhere, anytime, anyhow; ▸ Academic identity aligned to professional experience; ▸ Less dependence on wired learning environments and infrastructure; ▸ 'apps': usually free or cheap software applications that are task oriented and simpler to support; ▸ Accentuates learning over technology; ▸ Social media opens possibilities of authentic networks and functionality; ▸ Promotes creativity and innovation, collaboration and networking and so develops course identity.	▸ Time management; ▸ Changing practice i.e. enhancement or transformation requires knowledge, effort and confidence; ▸ Support for change; ▸ Support of diverse environments and tools; ▸ Cost and management of personal or borrowed devices, software and connections; ▸ Digital literacies for academics; ▸ Managing student distraction; ▸ Defining and managing teaching that spans formal and non-formal spaces; ▸ Ambiguity of intellectual property and changing notions on comodifying knowledge; ▸ Managing, categorising or describing content and sharing and using 'content' when the meaning of content is ambiguous.

Learners	<ul><li>Increased independence and flexibility;</li><li>The experience of learning is more valued and integrated with lifewide activities and commitments;</li><li>Appreciation of and expectations for learning that is socially situated spanning formal, non-formal and informal spaces;</li><li>More emphasis given to learning about one's own capability to ensure learning</li><li>is sustainable;</li><li>Identity development and the notion of 'becoming' is valued, making learning more authentic, especially when aligned to professional experience;</li><li>Spontaneity and creativity are more valued attributes of a graduate;</li><li>Learning is more 'customisable' making for a more personalised experience;</li><li>Learning is more situated and meaningful;</li><li>Vertical course connectivity and connections through to alumni and professions are more possible;</li><li>All-in-one multifunctional devices promote 'anywhere, anytime, anyhow' learning;</li><li>Increased appreciation of learner-developed 'Personal Learning Environments (PLEs)';</li><li>Immediate access and flexibility help the learner to engage more effectively with their work in ways that suit them;</li><li>Promotes creativity and innovation, collaboration and networking and improves productivity and happiness;</li><li>Available and affordable apps;</li><li>Access to technology is not dependent on others;</li></ul>	<ul><li>Learning is posited as being lifewide and lifelong and so is open-ended and problematic by nature;</li><li>Spending significant time developing one's digital literacies, metacognitive and independent learning capability;</li><li>Imbalance of subject-based study with learning literacies;</li><li>Pervasive distraction of social media;</li><li>Time management is more complex in a lifewide environment;</li><li>Finding reliable support;</li><li>Cost of devices, software and connections;</li><li>Education in and of itself is valued less than learning with a purpose;</li><li>Personal Learning Environments (PLEs) are conceptualised by the learner;</li><li>Making judgements about the effective use of smart technologies and PLEs when learning in HE is new and challenging;</li><li>Data management from diverse apps;</li><li>Exposure of learning to the wilds of the social web introduces new ethical issues for the learner, education and knowledge.</li></ul>

Learners continued	▸ Technology-mediated learning can happen in more and different spaces on and off campus; ▸ Data and content generated through learning remains widely available to them wherever they are; ▸ User-generated content can be published and used, developed and validated by peers; ▸ The learner's network can be extensive, geographically and socially.	
Institutions	▸ Reputational development of a thriving teaching and learning community; ▸ Ongoing engagement with alumni by valuing authentic connections and lifelong learning; ▸ Partnerships with new or other students and teachers in other places; ▸ Commonplace and versatile technology is user owned; ▸ Adoption of technology is not dependent on special funding; ▸ Improves creativity, innovation, productivity and happiness of teachers and students; ▸ Strategically agility is enabled by having a more flexible approach to technology, social media and networks.	▸ All of the above; ▸ Data management and security; ▸ Lack of control and monitoring; ▸ Influence over staff and student use of smart technologies including good ethical practice, intellectual property rights, etc. ▸ Threat to quality and changing understandings of quality; ▸ Exposure of learning to the wilds of the social web introduces new ethical issues for the learner, education and knowledge; ▸ Development of digital literacies and the meaning of digital literacy in a changing world.

Table 3. Smart Learning : Opportunities and challenges of teaching and learning in the era of smart technology for teachers, learners, and their institutions

Conclusion: being smart

Smart learning describes the meeting of human *being* and a new breed of personal, ubiquitous, and multifunctional technologies.

> *Our cameras, our microphones, are becoming the eyes*
> *and ears of the Web, our motion sensors, proximity*
> *sensors its proprioception, GPS its sense of location...*
> *Sensors and monitoring programs are not acting alone,*
> *but in concert with their human partners... Our devices*
> *extend us, and we extend them.*
> (O'Reilly & Battelle, 2009, p.8)

Smart learning, then, is about learning in the age of personal, flexible and connected smart devices and our appreciation of how different our world is now; even when compared to ten years ago. The use of the term smart learning implies a question: it asks, if the world has changed radically, how well are we responding to the opportunities and challenges that smart and social media afford us?

There are at least three ways of understanding this idea. All of the following are true:

1. Smart devices provide us with *alternative* ways to do what we already do. Sometimes these alternatives are more convenient.
2. Smart devices provide us with *better* ways to do what we already do. Improvements are largely due to having more ready access to networked technologies and therefore the information and people that make teaching and learning richer.
3. Smart devices provide us with ways to do better things that are *different* to what we were able to do before. In this way we should consider how we should *transform* our practice.

There is a fourth point that challenges the assumption that the "we" in the first three points are people with roles that we recognise.

4. Smart devices provide the independent learner with access to rich and useful information and social networks. These networks can exchange and use data dynamically, disrupting pre-existing conceptualisations of knowledge and learning.

This fourth point challenges the very idea of education as being hegemonic, knowledge-centred and provided. It is about the ideas of Connectivism (Siemens, 2005) and Experiential Learning (Fenwick, 2003), valuing how we learn, work, live and grow through the connections we foster. It acknowledges that experience and learning are "so closely inter-twined that in many respects they mean the same thing" (Beard, 2015, p.1). It is also about heutagogy (Hase & Kenyon, 2000) – the self-determination of learning. It can be understood in terms of how formal education prepares its graduates as lifelong learners, but also in terms of a threat to formal education as we have known it and the need for positive, disruptive innovation. In part, this book is about the future of post-compulsory education and our role in it, but it reflects thinking and practice that is actual and emerging now.

The idea of smart learning, however, will challenge the expectations of students and their teachers and this creates a challenge for innovators and those that support innovation.

References

Ahn, J., Butler, B.S., Alam, A., & Webster, S.A. (2013). Learner participation and engagement in open online courses: Insights from the Peer 2 Peer University. MERLOT Journal of Online Learning and Teaching, 9(?), 160–171

Alokaily, R. (2013). Device neutral assignments for mobile learning in an English language classroom. *QScience Proceedings: Vol. 2013, 12th World Conference on Mobile and Contextual Learning (mLearn 2013) 10/2013; 2013.* DOI: 10.5339/qproc.2013.mlearn.29.

Anderson, T. (2013). *Promise and/or peril: MOOCs and open and distance education.* March 2013. Online at: http://www.col.org/SiteCollectionDocuments/ MOOCsPromisePeril_Anderson.pdf.

Attwell, G. & Pumilia, P. M. (2007). The new pedagogy of open content: Bringing together production, knowledge, development and learning. *Science*, 6(April), 211–219.

Baume, C., Martin, P., & Yorke, M. (2003). Managing educational development projects: Effective management for maximum impact. London: Routledge.

Beard, C. (2015). Experiential learning: Towards a multi-disciplinary perspective. In: Humberstone *et al.*, eds, *The International Handbook for Outdoor Education*, Routledge: London.

Beckett, D. & Hager, P. (2002). *Life, work and learning: Practice in postmodernity.* London: Routledge.

Beetham, H. (2011). How far have we (really) come? *16th Annual SEDA Conference "Using Technology to Enhance Learning"*, 17 - 18 November 2011, Birmingham, UK.

Bergmann, J. & Sams, A. (2012). *Flip your classroom: Reach every student in every class every day.* Washington, USA: International Society for Technology in Education.

BlackBerry website (2014). *A short history of the BlackBerry.* Online at: http://www.bbscnw.com/a-short-history-of-the-blackberry.php

Blaschke, L. (2012). Heutagogy and lifelong learning: A review of heutagogical practice and self-determined learning. *The International Review of Research in Open and Distance Learning*, 13(1), 56–71.

Borgman, C. (2007). Scholarship in the digital age: Information, infrastructure, and the Internet. Cambridge, MA: MIT Press.

Caldwell, C., Zeltman, S., & Griffin, K. (2012). BYOD (Bring Your Own Device). *Competition Forum*, 10(2), 117–121.

Chickering, A. & Gamson, Z.F. (1987). Seven principles for good practice in undergraduate education. *The American Association for Higher Education Bulletin*, March 1987.

Clarà, M., & Barberà, E. (2013). Learning online: Massive Open Online Courses (MOOCs), connectivism, and cultural psychology. *Distance Education*, 34(1), 129–136.

Dahlstrom, E., Walker, J.D., & Dziuban, C. (2013). *ECAR study of undergraduate students and information technology, 2013.* EDUCAUSE Center for Analysis and Research. Online at: http://net.educause.edu/ir/library/pdf/ERS1302/ERS1302.pdf

Diamond, S. & Middleton, A. (2013). Sound infrastructure for academic innovation. In: A. Middleton, ed. *"Digital Voices: a collaborative exploration of the recorded voice in post-compulsory education."* MELSIG & Sheffield Hallam University, 107–117.

Dobozy, E. (2014). Using the theory and practice of 'built pedagogy' to inform learning space design. In: L. Scott-Webber, J. Branch, P. Bartholomew & C. Nygaard, *Learning space design in higher education.* Farringdon: Libri Publishing.

Downes, S. (2009, February 24). *Connectivist dynamics in communities.* Blog post. Online at: http://halfanhour.blogspot.co.uk/2009/02/connectivist-dynamics-in-communities.html

Ehlers, U-D. (2011). Extending the territory: From Open Educational Resources to Open Educational Practices. *Journal of Open, Flexible and Distance Learning*, 15(2), 1–10.

Eraut, M. (2000). Non-formal learning, implicit learning and tacit knowledge. In: F. Coffield, ed., *"The Necessity of Informal Learning".* Bristol: Policy Press.

Feltham, M. & Keep, C. (2015). Oh, the places you'll go: Smart learning in the natural sciences. Chapter in this edition.

Fenwick, T. (2003). Reclaiming and re-embodying experiential learning through complexity science. *Studies in the Education of Adults*, 35(2), 123–141.

Freeman, S., Eddy, S.L., McDonagh, M., Smith, M.K., Okoroafor, N., Jordt, H., & Wenderoth, M.P. (2014). Active learning increases student performance in science, engineering, and mathematics. *Proceedings of the National Academy of Sciences of the United States of America*, 111(23), 8410–8415.

Gergen, K.J. (1996). Technology and the self: From the essential to the sublime. In: D. Grodin & T. Lindlof, eds., *"Constructing the self in a mediated age".* Beverly Hills, CA: Sage, 127–40.

Gerstein, J. (2013). *Education 3.0 and the pedagogy (andragogy, heutagogy) of mobile learning.* User Generated Education blog. Online at: http://usergeneratededucation.wordpress.com/2013/05/13/education-3-0-and-the-pedagogy-andragogy-heutagogy-of-mobile-learning/

Hase, S. & Kenyon, C. (2000). From andragogy to heutagogy. Ultibase, RMIT. Online at: http://ultibase.rmit.edu.au/Articles/dec00/hase2.htm.

Jackson, N. (2013). The concept of learning ecologies. In: N. Jackson and G.B. Cooper, eds., *Life-wide Learning, Education and Personal Development E-Book*. Online at: http://www.life-wideebook.co.uk/uploads/1/0/8/4/10842717/chapter_a5.pdf.

Jisc infoNet (2014) *Developing digital literacies*. Available at: http://www.jiscinfonet.ac.uk/infokits/digital-literacies/

Jones, G., Edwards, G., & Reid, A. (2009). How can mobile SMS communication support and enhance a first year undergraduate learning environment? *ALT-J, Research in Learning Technology*, 17(3), 201 – 218.

Kukulska-Hulme, A. (2005). Introduction. In: A. Kukulska-Hulme & J. Traxler, eds., *Mobile learning: A handbook for educators and trainers*. Open & Flexible Learning series. London and New York: Routledge.

Kuznekoff, J. H. & Titsworth, S. (2013). The impact of mobile phone usage on student learning. *Communication Education*, 62(3), 233 – 252.

Lave, J. & Wenger, E. (1991). *Situated learning: Legitimate peripheral participation*. Cambridge, UK: Cambridge University Press.

Littlejohn, A.H., ed. (2003). Reusing online resources: A sustainable approach to eLearning. London: Routledge.

Middleton, A., ed. (2013). Digital voices: A collaborative exploration of the recorded voice in post-compulsory education. MELSIG & Sheffield Hallam University.

Middleton, A. & Beckingham, S. (2015). Social media for learning framework: A framework to inspire innovation. Chapter in this edition.

Middleton, A. & Beckingham, S. (2014). *Social media for learning framework*. Media-Enhanced Learning website. Online at: http://melsig.shu.ac.uk/?page_id=669.

Mobile Enterprise (2011). Best practices for mobile device support: The enterprise guide to smart support for smart devices. Online at: http://mobileenterprise.edgl.com/white-papers.

Nerantzi, C., & Beckingham, S. (2015). BYOD4L: Learning about using our own devices using the 5C framework. Chapter in this edition.

Nielsen, L. (2011). 7 Myths about BYOD debunked. *Transforming Education Through Technology Journal*, September 2011.

Nortcliffe, A. (2015). HE BYOD: ready or not? Chapter in this edition.

O'Reilly, T., & Battelle, J. (2009). Web squared: Web 2.0 five years on. Web2 special report. Web 2.0 Summit. Online at: http://assets.en.oreilly.com/1/event/28/web2009_websquared-whitepaper.pdf

O'Reilly, T. (2005). What is Web 2.0? Design patterns and business models for the next generation of software. Online at: http://facweb.cti.depaul.edu/jnowotarski/se425/What%20Is%20Web%202%20point%200.pdf

Peter, S., & Deimann, M. (2013). On the role of openness in education: A historical reconstruction. *Open Praxis*, 5(1). doi:10.5944/openpraxis.5.1.2.

Siemens, G. (2005). *Connectivism: A learning theory for a digital age*. Online at: http://www.elearnspace.org/Articles/connectivism.htm.

Thomas, D. & Bradshaw, T. (2013). Rapid rise of chat apps slims texting cash cow for mobile groups. *The Financial Times*. Available online at:

http://www.ft.com/cms/s/0/226ef82e-aed3-11e2-bdfd-00144feabdc0.html#axzz2g6bvtwTC.

Traxler, J. (2010). Students and mobile devices. *Research in Learning Technology*, 18(2), 149–160.

University of Sheffield (2011). *Student mobile device survey*. Online at: https://www.sheffield.ac.uk/polopoly_fs/1.103665!/file/mobilesurvey2011.pdf

Unsworth, J. (2000). Scholarly primitives: What methods do Humanities researchers have in common, and how might our tools reflect this? In: *Humanities Computing: formal methods, experimental practice, Kings College, London, 13 May 2000*. Online at: http://people.brandeis.edu/~unsworth/Kings.5-00/primitives.html.

Ward, G. (2013). *University students in UK still buying laptops over tablets*. Voxburner. Online at: http://www.voxburner.com/publications/107-university-students-in-uk-still-buying-laptops-over-tablets

Weimer, M. (2014). The age of distraction: Getting students to put away their phones and focus on learning. *The Teaching Professor blog*. Online at: http://www.facultyfocus.com/articles/teaching-professor-blog/the-age-of-distraction-getting-students-to-put-away-their-phones-and-focus-on-learning

Weller, M. (2011). The digital scholar: How technology is transforming scholarly practice. London: Bloomsbury Academic.

Wheeler, S. (2009). Learning space mashups: Combining Web 2.0 tools to create collaborative and reflective learning spaces. *Future Internet*, 1(1), 3–13.

Wheeler, S. (2010). Web 3.0: the way forward? *Learning with 'e's. blog*. Online at: http://steve-wheeler.blogspot.co.uk/2010/07/web-30-way-forward.html.

White, D. & Le Cornu, A. (2011). Visitors and residents: A new typology for online engagement. *First Monday*, 16(9), 5th September 2011. Online at: http://firstmonday.org/article/view/3171/3049.

Wiley, D. (2009, 16 November 2009). *Defining "Open"*. Online at: http://opencontent.org/blog/archives/1123.

Scenario: Active learning with Dyknow Cloud

Daphne Robson

Aroha wants to introduce more active learning into her lectures. She has looked at using Personal Response Systems such as Socrative or PollEverywhere, but is put off by the difficulty of writing multi-choice and short answer questions that would challenge students appropriately when they are learning a new concept. So now she has decided to use Dyknow Cloud and for students to use their own mobile devices, preferably in pairs. She enters existing problems into Powerpoint slides and imports them into the browser-based Dyknow Cloud, which hosts active learning activities. From her own tablet she sends out problems to students who enter, draw, or write answers on their tablets, smartphones or laptops. At appropriate times, Aroha retrieves students' answers then displays them to the class. As she does so, annotates the answers, comments and leads a class discussion. In this way, students receive feedback on a selection of answers, and are thus exposed to different strategies for answering problems, tips, and common mistakes.

Key tool: Dyknow Cloud

Social media for learning
— a framework to inspire innovation

Andrew Middleton and Sue Beckingham

Introduction

The Social Media for Learning (SM4L) framework has been constructed to demonstrate how social media can be used by students and academics to promote learning. The framework supports innovation through curriculum design and has also been used in staff development activities to clarify how social media provide academics with a powerful and dynamic context in which to foster active student engagement.

This chapter introduces the seven elements in the framework, each of which present a design principle associated with a theory for effective learner engagement. Each of these principles will be introduced and then illustrated with an example for how it informs effective and imaginative curriculum design incorporating the use of social media. The SM4L framework follows the *Viewpoints* approach to mediating collaborative design activities (O'Donnell, Galley & Ross, 2012).

In sum, the framework is a structured set of principles which can be used separately or in combination to inspire the design of effective social-media enhanced pedagogy.

Background — social media

Social media are websites and applications that enable users to create and share content or to participate in social networking (Mao, 2012). The concept echoes O'Reilly's idea of Web 2.0 (2005) which describes a changed digital environment where the Web is a platform for harnessing collective intelligence; where data is dynamic and abundant; where software is in perpetual beta and attitude is more important than technology. It is a social, creative and collaborative space in which "small pieces are loosely joined." The emergence of Web 2.0 predated the common usage of the term social media but contains all the essential ideas. The conceptualisation signals a paradigm shift in the way we now communicate and engage with ideas as both users and producers. This technical restructuring of the Web has subsequently matured into a personal and social movement which has claimed the platform for interpersonal connectivity. This 'social web' now spreads beyond PCs to the connected devices we wear and carry, therefore personalising O'Reilly's articulation of 'the Web as platform', a space for harnessing collective intelligence, thriving on shared data and forever improving. Its tools are lightweight, intended to be simple and functional, and span devices to create a rich user experience.

What does this mean for education?

The Web, as we know it now, is pervasive; it is no longer a resolute, impermeable and immobile repository of information. Its strength is found in the things people do and say together - just as education's strength is in the things people say and do together. This Web has moved from its original static incarnation in the 1990s, through a dynamic phase in the 2000s, to what now is best described as a thriving phase as represented by PennyStock's *Internet in Real Time*. The advent of smart devices ensures that this thriving web, and the teaching and learning it supports, is also unbounded.

Voss and Kumar's (2012) analysis of the literature examining the use of social media, albeit in American universities, found that it addressed the themes of visibility, listening, engagement, relationships, trust, authenticity, and branding. In relation to our student-centred framework the ideas of listening, engagement, relationships and authenticity stand out as being most relevant to learning. Visibility, in terms of managing one's digital presence, is also important in relation to employability.

The Social Media for Learning Framework

The framework emerged by bringing together thinking which had begun separately for each of the authors into a collaborative focus. By comparing our perceptions of social media, why it was important to higher education learning (and sometimes why it is not), the framework emerged quickly. It cannot be definitive, but its purpose is to be useful as a mechanism to stimulate conversation.

In this section each element of the framework is introduced as it would be set out in a design workshop. A short discussion about the principle and some ideas that illustrate how it can be interpreted and applied follow each element.

Socially inclusive

▸ supporting and validating learning through mutually beneficial, jointly enterprising and communally constructive communities of practice;

▸ fostering a sense of belonging, being and becoming;

▸ promoting collegiality.

The Socially Inclusive element begins by describing inclusion in terms of Communities of Practice (Wenger, 1998), seeing social media as something that brings people together for mutual benefit and purpose. It acknowledges the importance to learning of identity and of being part of something, a sense of belonging; thus, social media values an ontological view of learning in this sense.

Latterly we have raised questions about the access to learning that social media may promote or hinder (see Denise Turner's chapter in this edition).

Example of media being used in a socially inclusive way

We use 'inclusivity' in the broadest sense and intend, by doing so, to unproblematise it; especially its narrower connotation and association with 'disability': if we learn to design inclusively we should habitually develop a positive consideration for all users.

The use of Padlet to collate ideas from a virtual brainstorm describes why this element is helpful. Padlet is a web-based tool which can be accessed from browsers on fixed or mobile devices to post succinct responses to a question, problem or scenario. All participants have the right to add notes, in various media, to what is in effect a virtual corkboard and all participants are able to see and review the postings as they are made. The idea of 'virtual brainstorm' indicates that all participants do not need be present in the same physical space. The use of a virtual tool in any case, has reduced the significance of co-location for the learning activity. The use of a 'board' metaphor dispenses with a hierarchical presentation structure, thereby removing ideas about valuing one idea against any other and this promotes equity in the collective thinking activity.

Lifewide and lifelong

▸ connecting formal, non-formal and informal learning progression;

▸ developing online presence;

▸ developing digital literacies.

This element emphasises the learner's life as being an intrinsic dimension of their formal engagement with their course and emphasises ideas found in constructivist theory about building on what already exists. It challenges, therefore, the tendency for learners and their tutors to rely on extrinsic factors for motivation. By having a lifewide appreciation of learning, the academic is able to think more broadly about the learner's environment and how each student is able to arrive at significant learning points in their own way *and* within the context of their formal course.

This element also encourages us to think about a lifelong digital presence and commitment to learning and so points us towards conceiving of digital literacies as capabilities that both empower us and safeguard our futures.

Example of media being used in the context of lifewide and lifelong learning

The professional networking tool LinkedIn provides a good illustration of this. For example: *Encourage students to establish a LinkedIn presence for their employability.* But it is also worth thinking about the concept of life blogging: the act of systematically recording everything you do, see or think as a way of developing capabilities as a reflective and critical thinker. This latter activity is extreme and ultimately obsessive sounding when intentional, but increasingly many of us leave traces of our actions, views and thoughts in myriad places. We all need to learn to manage our digital presence wisely and one way of learning to do this is to establish one's professional self methodically by using techniques like academic blogging for intelligent, reflective thinking. Reflective blogging assignments, therefore, demonstrate an important academic use of social media.

Media neutral

▸ learning across and through rich, multiple media.

The Digital Age is not bound by the constraints of previous eras in which thinking and ideas were inevitably the preserve of an elite selected to navigate their ways through long-standing academic paths ritualised by the conventions described by the written word!

While it is unnecessary perhaps to deride our academic tradition, it becomes clear how we now have the opportunity to expand and democratise the learning environments we use for higher thinking. It is now important for academia to recognise that different media promote different thinking by different people and that this is valuable. Knowledge, as a commodity, is no longer as important as it was (Siemens, 2005) and this frees higher education from obsessing on knowledge to do more of what it should be good at: supporting the creative mind so that it is able to fluently and critically play with and contribute to knowledge and the development of those that use it.

Media neutrality can be found in Kress's ideas (2003) about the inseparability of form and meaning, for example, which alert us to the importance of coming to know multiple media, whether that understanding is predominantly about format, technology, or context.

The proposition of media neutrality could have been expressed as media fluency, though that may have over-emphasised a sense of technical competence. It is more about the capability to use the right medium or media for the right job.

Example of media being used to demonstrate media neutrality

The posting of Concept Clips (screencast or video explanations) to YouTube is something that is gaining ground as appreciation of techniques such as the 'flipped classroom' and media intervention grows. The attraction of YouTube itself, especially because it is populated by an abundance of 'naive' footage, has contributed to more academics realising that making their own clips is possible and that it is something their students are likely to be able to do (see Rushton *et al*'s chapter for an example of rich media being used to change student's approaches to learning).

Learner-centred

▶ promoting self-regulation, self-expression, self-efficacy and confidence;
▶ accommodating niche interests and activities, the 'long tail' of education.

The Digital Age, as already noted, comes out of a previous era in which teaching and learning has largely been defined by its constraints. This is most notable in the dependence upon the lecture theatre, a technology seen in ancient civilisations, but which came to serve academia reasonably well from the setting up of the first universities in the late 14th century (Peter & Deimann, 2013). Learner-centredness challenges the academic to be more creative in considering use of learning space, whether that is formal, informal, physical or virtual.

Example of media being used to foster learner-centred pedagogy

Social media immediately finds a natural home in this area and the examples are immediate and abundant when thinking about its relationship to project-based learning, problem-based learning and enquiry-based learning for example. Using a problem-based approach, a group co-production task can be underpinned by structured activity in Google Docs in which students work collaboratively, drawing on their complementary strengths to analyse and resolve the assigned problem and present the results of their work coherently.

Co-operative

▸ promotes working together productively and critically with peers (co-creation) in self-organising, robust networks that are scalable, loosely structured, self-validating, and knowledge forming.

Peer co-operation is a well-established principle of good teaching in undergraduate education (Chickering & Gamson, 1987) and is evident in most effective university-level courses. Informally, it captures the rationale of learning at university: the idea of finding value in being together as opposed to being purely satisfied with using books in isolation to acquire knowledge for example. Formally it is found in collaborative methods such as group work. Laurillard's notion of a Conversational Framework (2002) reflects the co-operative interchange and progression of thinking underpinning learning at university. Fundamentally it comes back to mutuality and valuing each other.

Example of media being used to foster co-operation

The Bring Your Own Devices for Learning open learning experience (see the chapter by Chrissi Nerantzi & Sue Beckingham in this edition) explains how the tweetchat method brought participants together each evening, full of energy, engaging each other frenetically with a set of five questions over an hour. The nature of this activity, which takes place around a common hashtag in Twitter (i.e. *#BYOD4LChat*), is that five questions are posed through the hour that allow diverse participants to respond with their own answers, further questions and examples so that the body of learners, by working together, formulate a deep and rich understanding of a given topic.

Open and accessible

▸ supporting spatial openness (without physical division);

▸ supporting temporal openness i.e. synchronously and asynchronously;

▸ supporting social openness i.e. democratic, inclusive;

▸ supporting open engagement i.e. in terms of being: geographically extended, inclusive, controlled by the learner, gratis, open market, unconstrained freedom, access to content (Anderson, 2013);

▸ being open to ideas.

Openness is a very open set of ideas! As the framework highlights, it can refer to space, time, or social interaction amongst other conceptualisations, and attitudes. Openness is a useful concept to explore both in curriculum design and staff development, whatever your take on it. Any discussion usually serves to highlight how closed down we are and often this is through habit and lacking the confidence or resource to do other than what we have known; our collective tendency is often for closed thinking. As discussed in the previous chapter, *Thinking about Smart Learning*, developing an appreciation of openness requires adventurous thinking and hypothesising about what smart learning might come to mean. For today's student, however, it immediately challenges many of the assumptions we may have about learning spaces, how we relate to learning, how we use time, and how we might work together.

Example of media being used in an open way

An obvious example might be about using Open Educational Resources (OERs) or what used to be known as Reusable Learning Objects. However, while these ideas may be desirable in an ideal world, they often lead us to think about a particular understanding of 'content': something that can be packaged. Good teachers know that *conversation*, not *content*, is king. Conversation establishes the *context* for learning.

While OERs and the practice of using them, Open Educational Practice (OEP), is a rich and profitable area to explore more deeply, in this chapter a different example is offered; one that describes autonomous learning in which the students have a sense of being unbounded and responsible to each other. For example, the academic openly discusses how important it is that learning happens outside the classroom and listens for examples from the students about how, where and when they do something connected with "uni". The academic may refer to the practice of former students and how they have benefited from self-organised Facebook Groups or Google

Hangouts, or just forming informal support networks to keep each other organised. The academic's role, here, is to value social interaction and seed autonomous interaction with social media. This presents challenges for the tutor: how is openness actually enacted and supported? How should social media be managed in an open learning environment? What is the real driver for openness in a given situation? Is it to make the experience richer, more authentic or to provide the learner with more room for creatively engaging?

Authentically situated

- making connections across learning, social and professional networks;
- scholarly;
- establishing professional online presence and digital identity.

Social media helps us to make strong connections with the world around us and, whatever our discipline, the world establishes the ultimate context for our learning and scholarship. This externalised conceptualisation of learning can enhance the meaning of both being at university and in learning, and of situating and understanding the subject matter itself.

Rule (2006) suggests that authentic learning actively engages the learner in the real world problems of professionals, open-ended inquiry and metacognition, and discourse amongst a community of learners, whilst empowering the learner to direct their own learning. Herrington and Oliver (2000) propose nine critical characteristics for authentic learning that include active learner engagement in a real life context, the modelling of processes and access to roles, collaboration, reflection, learner articulation, scaffolding and meaningful assessment.

Example of media being used to harness authentic situations

Authenticity is evident in many educational podcasting applications and is found in the variety of voices, the connections that can be made to the real world, and the open-ended activity it promotes and supports. For example, invite 'experts' (people who know the external context) to speak to or with your students via Skype or in a Google Hangout. Running and recording conversations like this can generate a rich, long-lasting resource base.

Developing the framework

The framework has so far served its purpose well: to stimulate creative thinking about academic practice and the curriculum. Making it 'better' is problematic: it is important that it is open-ended and not assumed to be complete. In the same way, it has been important in this chapter to avoid listing examples in detail because, as we have said, *conversation* is king and to be overly prescriptive would be self-defeating.

The framework will develop now by the way you draw upon it or apply it. For example, you can develop your own examples with academics as a workshop activity.

Acknowledgement

We would like to thank Simon Thompson for useful suggestions which have been embodied in the writing of this chapter.

References

Anderson, T. (2013). Promise and/or Peril: MOOCs and Open and Distance Education. Online at: http://www.col.org/SiteCollectionDocuments/MOOCsPromisePeril_Anderson.pdf.

Chickering, A. W., & Gamson, Z. F., eds. (1987). Seven principles for good practice in undergraduate education. *AAHE Bulletin*, March: 3−7.

Herrington, J. & Oliver, R. (2000). An instructional design framework for authentic learning environments. *Educational Technology Research and Development*. 48, 23−48.

Kress, G. R. (2003). *Literacy in the new media age*. London: Routledge.

Laurillard, D. (2002). *Rethinking university teaching, 2nd edition*. London: Routledge Falmer.

Mao, J. (2014). Social media for learning: A mixed methods study on high school students' technology affordances and perspectives. *Computers in Human Behavior*, 33, 213−223.

O'Donnell, C., Galley, R. & Ross, V. (2012). The art of the designer: Creating an effective learning experience. *Blended Learning Conference*, 13th June 2012, University of Hertfordshire, UK.

O'Reilly, T. (2005). *What is Web 2.0? Design patterns and business models for the next generation of software*. Online at: http://facweb.cti.depaul.edu/jnowotarski/se425/What%20Is%20Web%202%20point%200.pdf.

Pennystocks (2014). *The Internet in real time*. Online at: http://pennystocks.la/internet-in-real-time

Peter, S., & Deimann, M. (2013). On the role of openness in education: A historical reconstruction. *Open Praxis*, 5(1). doi:10.5944/openpraxis.5.1.2.

Rule, A. (2006). Editorial: The components of authentic learning. *Journal of Authentic Learning*, 3 (1).

Siemens, G. (2005). *Connectivism: A learning theory for a digital age*. Online at: http://www.elearnspace.org/Articles/connectivism.htm.

Voss, K. A., & Kumar, A. (2013). The value of social media: Are universities successfully engaging their audience? *Journal of Applied Research in Higher Education,* 5(2), 156-172.

Wenger, E. (1998). *Communities of practice: Learning, meaning, and identity*. Cambridge. Cambridge University Press.

Scenario: Common room reps

One outcome of a pre-enrolment activity run by Julie in Facebook for her new Writing students is most of them have already got to know each other and got themselves organised. She has found out, through informal chats with some of the students, that there are 'ring leaders' - key students who seem to make sure everyone else in the group is up to speed with announcements. Julie is reassured that, even though students don't go into Blackboard often enough for her liking, they are looking after each other in Facebook and she knows to touch base with the course 'ring leaders' every now and then to make sure they understand critical information.

Key tool: Facebook

Applying learning analytics to smart learning
— ethics and policy

Catherine Hack

Learning analytics

"Customers who bought items in your basket also bought…" We are all familiar with the outputs (if not the underlying concepts) of business analytics, whereby retailers analyse previous buying behaviour to suggest products or services. These analytics use data-mining techniques, to extract 'previously unknown and potentially useful information from data' (Frawley, Piatetsky-Shapiro & Matheus, 1992, p.58). These techniques have been used in a wide range of fields from healthcare to detecting fraud, and are now being applied to education (Romero-Zaldivar, Pardo *et al.*, 2012). Learning analytics combine technologies from computer science: data and text mining, and data visualisation with pedagogy, social science and psychology, to gain a greater insight into how students learn online.

As learning analytics moves from the domain of computer science research into practice, and from the hands of senior management to individual teachers, these tools will allow practitioners to undertake more nuanced analysis of the impact of social learning activities.

Analysing tweetchats – an illustrative example of ethical issues in Social Learning Analytics (SLA)

As an illustrative example some learning analytics have been applied to the tweetchat facilitated by @LTHEchat, a collaborative project to discuss learning and teaching in Higher Education.

Network analysis

Figure 1 provides the network analysis of a tweetchat produced using Martin Hawksey's *TAGSExplorer* tool. The tool allows rapid identification of the 'top tweeters', and archiving the tweets for further analysis. Network analysis allows the monitoring of the community as it grows, coalescing around information providers or forming smaller sub-communities. It can also be used to identify participants who appear to be disengaged.

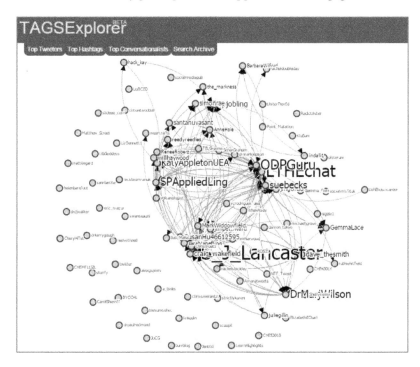

Figure 1: Network analysis of tweetchat produced using TAGSExplorer

Analysis of the discourse

Whilst visualising the network can provide some insight into the dynamics of the community, analysis of the actual discourse can be more informative of how well each participant understands or contributes to the topic. The discourse could be analysed to identify a range of a parameters, e.g. the number of questions posted by an individual, the number of posts that could be classified as off-topic, or that contain factual or conceptual errors, or provide links to other resources. This type of analysis could be very informative of learner engagement, understanding or dispositions.

Ethics of social learning analytics

What are the ethical issues arising from this analysis? Is the analysis acceptable if the tweetchat were part of a course, and the network and discourse analysis are used to provide directed feedback to a student? What if this was a retrospective analysis as part of a pedagogical research project then? Does it require informed consent? If the data has been put in the public domain does this make it acceptable to collate and analyse it for research? What if you want to integrate the SLA data with other institutional data, student grades or their educational or social history?

Policies for using student data

Current regulations and policies for using student data from learning analytics (in the UK) are covered by Common Law, the Data Protection Act (DPA) (1998) and the Human Rights Act (1998). In higher education this requires that student data is only obtained and processed in accordance with the legitimate interests of the institution. Typically students are informed that their personal data may be used for various teaching, research and administrative purposes. There is a tacit agreement that students agree to their data being used for these purposes when they register with the university. Does this only apply to the data that students share with the university or data they share via social media or on open resources? Some institutions stipulate that data may only be used for internal research, and the majority of UK universities require ethical review of all research involving data or material relating to human subjects which is not in the public domain. Evidence suggests that pedagogic research in general is not always submitted for ethical review (Regan, 2013). There are many reasons posited for this lack of compliance, including lack of clarity on:

- the distinction between research activities which require ethical review and scholarship or audit activities which do not;
- the extent to which projects which access corporate and public data are legitimised under the Data Protection Act (1998) or whether they require ethical approval and informed consent.

This situation may be exacerbated as data produced from social learning analytics is readily available, alongside the need for more evidence-based research on how students learn online.

Autonomy, trust and privacy

Kincaid and Pecorino (2005) argue that there has to be an element of paternalism in higher education due to the imbalance in knowledge and expertise between the teacher and the student. This unequal relationship requires that the student surrender some personal autonomy to the institution trusting that it will do them no harm and will endeavour to provide benefits through providing effective learning opportunities. The respect of privacy and the sharing of decisions about how personal data is managed and analysed is an important element in retaining student trust. An institution has statutory duties with regard to data protection and can be held liable for harm or loss caused where the legal duty has not been met. However data privacy is one of the most controversial aspects of online and digital interaction (Romero-Zaldivar *et al.*, 2012; Pardo & Siemens, 2014), with key players questioning whether the right to privacy exists in an environment where people are willing to share their personal information in return for free services (Mantelero, 2013). As the big online players (*Google*, *Facebook*, *Twitter* and *YouTube*) trade personal information for the right to access their services, are we complicit if we expect students to use these services in order to engage in collaborative or constructive learning activities? The recent Eurobarometer survey on 'Public perception of science and, research and innovation' (European Commission, 2014) indicated that "citizens do not consider the protection of personal data to be a high priority". However this may be indicative of either a focus on other priorities (health, employment and education), a lack of serious security breaches, or a lack of information or understanding of the scale and depth of personal information that is held by companies and institutions (Floridi, 2014). Furthermore, evidence suggests that students are unaware of the extent to which universities can track their online activities (Slade & Prinsloo, 2014).

Conclusions

As teachers make wider use of open educational resources and the diverse range of apps available on mobile devices, and are less constrained by the institutional VLE, the application of learning analytics to track student engagement will have greater importance. It is important to monitor and evaluate the engagement of students with external resources and assess the impact on student progression, retention and success, as well as less tangible indicators of student learning. This information is critical to support individual students as well as inform the wider academic community for BYOD to become more widespread in education. However the use of student data has implications for the relationship of trust and respect between institutions and students. Whilst UK Higher Education Institutions have policies in place for the ethical oversight of research activities undertaken under their auspices, there is variable application and adherence to these policies with respect to pedagogic research. As analytical tools become more widely available, and the desire to apply them to pedagogic research to gain a greater understanding of the impact of the current changes in the learning landscape, it is critical that institutions develop policies for the use of learning analytics for scholarship and research activities.

References

Data Protection Act. (1998). (c29). London: HMSO.

European Commission (2014). Public perceptions of science, research and innovation. *Eurobarometer Special Surveys*. Online at: http://ec.europa.eu/public_opinion/archives/eb_special_419_400_en.htm.

Floridi, L. (2014). Technoscience and ethics foresight. *Philosophy & Technology*. Online at: http://link.springer.com/article/10.1007/s13347-014-0180-9/fulltext.html

Frawley, W. J., Piatetsky-Shapiro, G., & Matheus, C. J. (1992). Knowledge discovery in databases: An overview. *AI Magazine*, 13(3), 57−70.

Hawksey, M. (2011). Twitter: How to archive event hashtags and create an interactive visualization of the conversation. Online at: https://mashe.hawksey.info

Human Rights Act (1998) (c 42). London HMSO.

Kincaid, S. & Pecorino, P. (2005). The profession of education: Responsibilities, ethics and pedagogic experimentation. Online at: http://www.qcc.cuny.edu/

Mantelero, A. (2013). Competitive value of data protection: The impact of data protection regulation on online behaviour. *International Data Privacy Law*, ipt016.

Pardo, A. & Siemens, G. (2014). Ethical and privacy principles for learning analytics. *British Journal of Educational Technology*, 45(3), 438−450.

Romero-Zaldivar, V., Pardo, A., Burgos, D. & Delgado Kloos, C. (2012). Monitoring student progress using virtual appliances: A case study. *Computers & Education*, 58(4), 1058−1067.

Regan, J. (2013). Risks to informed consent in pedagogic research. *Journal of Perspectives in Applied Academic Practice*, 1(1), 25–29.

Slade, S., & Prinsloo, P. (2014). Student perspectives on the use of their data: Between intrusion, surveillance and care. In: European Distance and E-Learning Network 2014, 27–28 October 2014, Oxford, UK, 291–300.

Scenario: Placement meetup and peer support

In between tutor visits Joe and Sam, Teacher Education students now on placement in different schools, support each other using Skype. They 'meet' at the end of the school day once a week. Usually they're sitting in their respective classrooms, but last week Joe said "Take me on a tour!" So Sam and Joe had a bit of fun walking around with their tablets running the Skype app. Using Skype's live video connectivity they compared the different facilities in their schools and this prompted quite a discussion about different practices. They reported this as being reassuring; each of them had commented on how isolated they had felt and uncertain they were about the quality of the experience they were having.

While on their extended placements the students collaborated at a distance using Skype or Facetime - the live video communication tool on iOS. The synchronous visual and auditory medium helped to create a feeling of support and was "More interesting than working on your own!"

Key tool: Skype, or could use Google Hangouts or FaceTime.

Based on an idea by Ros Walker, taken from MSc. Dissertation (MELSIG workshop)

Bring Your Own Device
— policy and practice in higher education

Santanu Vasant

Introduction

> 'Today your cell phone has more computing power than
> all of NASA in 1969 when it sent two astronauts to the
> moon'
> - Professor Michio Kaku, theoretical physicists and
> futurologist writing in his book Physics of the Future
> (Kaku, 2011).

This quote sums up the power of the mobile devices that many of us carry in our pockets and the potential they have for learning. This echoes the thoughts of my A-Level Physics teacher who used to say that every student in school has a 'Star Trek tricorder' in their pocket these days and all they do is text their friends!

In this chapter I explore the concept of Bring Your Own Device (BYOD), how it has been implemented in some organisations and the policy and practices needed for successful implementation.

BYOD is "the practice of allowing the employees of an organisation to use their own computers, smartphones, or other devices for work purposes" (Oxford Dictionaries Online, 2014).

Responding to changing habits

The BYOD movement has been increasing over the past few years in many sectors and notably so in higher education. It was first mentioned in a paper by Ballagas *et al.* (2005) who were German, Swiss and English university researchers, investigating how members of the public could bring their own devices to interact with large public displays. They found it was possible for smartphones with cameras, such as the Nokia 6600, to interact with large display units detailing several scenarios they envisaged. They concluded that further work on the optics on smartphones would need to be done, as accuracy was an issue.

Increased productivity is also true in other sectors, including higher education in the UK. Gidda (2014) suggests that the more students use their own device for learning, the more they will potentially use it for their learning outside of the classroom and become more familiar with their device. This may result in less computer labs being installed on campuses, although as JISC point out in an entry in their blog, the support overheads of multiple devices may negate any savings made from less fixed hardware (Curtis, 2012).

As the proliferation of mobile devices in higher education increases and the relative cost of these devices decreases, the notion of bringing your own device is seen as common as bringing your own pen, paper or calculator to university. However, the way in which staff and students use smart devices for learning is very different. Whilst the majority of students are comfortable to use their devices for learning, or at the very least see the value of such an initiative (Chen & Denoyelles, 2013; Grussendorf, 2013), the majority of staff are less comfortable to use their devices for learning and as the UCISA Technology Enhanced Learning (TEL) Survey 2014 highlights, the loaning of mobile technologies to staff remains a key challenge for TEL teams (UCISA, 2014). This also makes it difficult to put a BYOD policy in place, as discussed later.

Considering the need for policy

Before exploring the issues surrounding the successful implementation of BYOD, let us examine briefly what a potential BYOD policy would constitute for further and higher education institutions and begin to understand some of the advantages and disadvantages of implementing BYOD.

JISC Legal (2013) outline the main areas that need to be in such a policy. These include sections on system security and the role of all users of that network in maintaining that security. Further points include, the safety of all users with relation to their own device, how the institution will monitor the devices that staff and students bring in, the data protection requirements in relation to BYOD, acceptable use, what support is offered for their device and finally how breaches to the policy will be dealt with. Both JISC Legal and Intel recommend strategies that encourage users to feel ownership of the policy.

BT and Cisco found that 31% of organisations in the UK were likely to have a BYOD policy, which is lower than countries such as the US (49%) and India (46%). The research concludes there is still some policy confusion amongst UK organisations around BYOD (BT & Cisco, 2013).

Rarely does a BYOD policy in a higher education institution make reference to learning, an educational strategy or take a pedagogical rather than a technical perspective, as seen in the template from JISC Legal (2013). The policies seen in various institutions in relation to BYOD vary in scope from applying to one department to whole institution in terms of the access and the technical aspects of BYOD. Loughborough University, for example, explains BYOD and its implications to all of its staff and students (Loughborough University, 2014), while York St John University takes a different approach, using iPads to see if they could enhance an already established approach to peer review and feedback. This is an example of where a small group of academics has led innovation (Souleles & Pillar 2014, p.144).

Security

When discussing BYOD one of the first points raised by technology leaders is the risk of security breaches from unsafe devices being able to access the network to which they are connected. As Educause (2011) argues, the days of tightly controlling a university network have most likely passed and higher education institutions need to limit the amount of student sensitive data stored on devices. However, it highlights the biggest threat posed by mobile devices comes from people. Mobile devices can store and secure personal data, but only if users set up and use their devices correctly. Therefore, it is through greater education that institutions will begin to address some of these risks.

Connecting to university wireless networks

Providing access to the university wireless network is critical to the successful implementation of an institutional policy. Most universities have good wireless network coverage, but it is worth noting that activities involving a large number of devices, BYOD or otherwise, can put great demands on a network and this can impact on the success of teaching and learning activities for example (*see* the Rushton *et al.* chapter for example in which many students concurrently produce video in class).

Equal access

Another factor that is prevalent in the discourse around BYOD is that of fairness. Some students can't afford a smart device and therefore an activity involving students using their own device for learning in a lecture or seminar won't be fair on those that don't have devices. However, as JISC (2010) stated in their guide for 'engaging students with mobile learning', "80% of people will be accessing the Internet using mobile devices by 2015, organisations need to embrace mobile learning quickly". This would suggest that the vast majority of students in most UK higher education courses would have some form of smartphone, tablet or laptop and therefore University educators should consider making better use of such devices in the classroom. Microsoft makes the same point in a recent presentation (Microsoft, 2014).

The challenge of making good use of personal connected devices

Even when students have a device they bring to their place of study and have access to a wireless network researchers at one US University found that learning with their own device for many students was still something that happens outside the classroom, with little or no instruction from the academic (Chen & Denoyelles, 2013).

To understand why this is the case it is worth looking at the survey of technology enhanced learning conducted by the University and Colleges Information Systems Association in the UK every few years. In August 2014 it published its latest findings in a detailed report and found that "lack of time remains the leading barrier to TEL development, consolidating its position at the top of the list which it has held dating back to the 2005 Survey. Lack of academic staff knowledge has risen from fifth position in 2012 to second place, reversing a trend of recent years where this factor had declined in importance. Lack of money has moved down to third place, followed by Institutional and Departmental/school culture" (UCISA, 2014). This is both insightful as it is worrying. Despite significant investment in the past decade to address these issues, the report finds lack of time, skills and money as the top three barriers to developing technology enhanced learning in many institutions.

Learning spaces

In order for BYOD to be implemented successfully, after the factors of security, access and staff engagement are accounted for, physical spaces or learning spaces need to be designed in ways that are conducive to learning, with flexible seating and power sockets for devices as key elements to success.

Despite some literature around learning spaces entitled 'designing spaces for effective learning' (JISC, 2006), little has been published formally around how learning spaces impact on the learning; particularly in higher education institutions. One comprehensive publication around learning spaces is Diana G. Oblinger's Learning Spaces (2005) which proposes a model where pedagogy, technology and space are placed at the vertices of a triangle. Oblinger argues that all three are needed if successful technology enhanced learning is to take place.

Staff development

Whilst BYOD is still emerging, some UK universities are piloting initiatives via their staff development units. For some, taking a paperless route to producing workshop handouts is a first step, with staff expected to bring their own device to access PDF handouts during sessions. Others are developing guidance, looking for internal case studies or engaging with initiatives such as Bring Your Own Devices for Learning (see Nerantzi et al., 2015 chapter).

General employee engagement with BYOD (BT & Cisco, 2013) and student engagement with BYOD is beginning to be researched (Chen & Denoyelles, 2013; Grussendorf, 2013); however, the perceptions and implementation of BYOD in staff development units and other service areas is less clear. In an entry on the CASCADE blog by Dale Potter at Exeter University, he observes that, "Looking around CASCADE HQ, only 3 employees out of 30 staff members were using some their own technology on a regular basis. It would seem that whilst BYOD is becoming more common, it is only a relatively small number of employees who are doing it" (Potter, 2012).

Whilst, this is only a comment on one academic blog from a member of staff at one university, this does raise the question, "Why are academic staff in higher education not using their devices for their own learning and development?" Could this in indeed be linked to both the issues of lack of time or skills as seen by the survey of technology enhanced learning (UCISA, 2014) and an article entitled 'A supportive environment for digital literacy development' (Beetham & Jiscdigilit, 2014).

Academic digital readiness

Beetham & Jiscdigilit (2014) state that multiple factors impact on the take up of BYOD amongst staff and students, such as loss of equipment and access issues. They say that there should be a constant dialogue between both groups about issues faced. They stress that,

> Both teaching staff and students themselves tend to over-estimate students' ICT capabilities. While some students are exceptionally confident – and few are complete novices – still the norm is for students to have used only the basic functions of personal devices and services, and to have limited their exploration of educational media to those required by teachers.
> (Beetham & Jiscdigilit, 2014).

This could explain the poor take up of BYOD initiatives in universities, especially amongst staff in workshops and similar activities.

Conclusion

With these complex technical, pedagogical and cultural issues surrounding BYOD, what is the optimum situation that institutions should be aiming for in the future?

Firstly, the issues around risk and access should be addressed and as Harkin (2009) states, the BYOD policy of an organisation should involve the stakeholders, i.e. the staff and students who will use the system. Information Technology departments need to understand that users will bring in their own device and it is the role of these departments to help users manage them. In tandem with policy, practice amongst staff facing departments should change to encourage better usage of devices in workshops, so that good practice is modelled.

This will not solve the issues highlighted previously around time and skills of academics, but will foster a staff development culture that is willing to develop a framework for creative pedagogies.

Cochrane *et al.* (2014) argue that the value of bringing in new ways of learning with mobile devices far outweighs any risks involved.

Current thinking about the benefits of activities such as using apps like *Evernote*, *Flickr* and others in classroom settings and in field work (see Section 3 *Apps for Learning*) indicates how what academics and students can do now is so rich compared to even five years ago. Indeed, it could be argued that managing the risks associated with BYOD is also part of the learning journey for students and staff as they develop their digital literacies and navigate their ways through this emerging field using their own devices.

References

Beetham, H & Jiscdigilit (2014). A supportive environment for digital literacy development. Online at: https://newsletter.alt.ac.uk/2014/04/a-supportive-environment-for-digital-literacy-development/

Ballagas, R., Rohs, M., Sheridan, J.G., & Borchers, J. (2004). BYOD: Bring Your Own Device. Online at: http://www.vs.inf.ethz.ch/publ/papers/rohs-byod-2004.pdf

BT & Cisco (2013). BT and Cisco beyond your device research. Online at: http://business.bt.com/assets/pdf/it-support-and-security/BT_Cisco_Beyond_Your_Device_research.pdf

Chen, B., & Denoyelles, A. (2013). Exploring students' mobile learning practices in higher education. EDUCAUSE Review Online, October 2013. Online at: http://www.educause.edu/ero/article/exploring-students-mobile-learning-practices-higher-education.

Cochrane, T., Antonczak, L., Keegan, H. & Narayan, V. (2014) Riding the wave of BYOD: Developing a framework for creative pedagogies. Research in Learning Technology, 22 (1), 1–14.

Curtis, J. (2012). Bring Your Own Device (BYOD). Online at: http://www.jisc.ac.uk/blog/bring-your-own-device-byod-23-nov-2012

Educause (2011). 7 things you should know about mobile security. Online at: https://net.educause.edu/ir/library/pdf/EST1101.pdf

Gidda, M. (2014). Students: bring your own technology to uni. Online at: http://www.theguardian.com/education/2014/apr/11/students-bring-tech-device-uni.

Grussendorf, S. (2013). Device ownership, BYOD and social media for learning. Report. LSE. Online at: http://eprints.lse.ac.uk/51652/1/IMT_survey_2013.pdf

Harkins, M. (2009) Mobile: learn from Intel's CISO on securing employee-owned devices. Online at: http://www.govinfosecurity.com/webinars/mobile-learn-from-intels-ciso-on-securing-employee-owned-devices-w-264.

Kaku, M. (2011). Physics of the future: How science will shape human destiny and our daily lives by the year 2100. New York: Doubleday.

Karnad, A. (2014). Trends in educational technologies. The London School of Economics and Political Science, London, UK. [online] Available from: http://eprints.lse.ac.uk/55965/

JISC (2010). Engage students with mobile learning. Online at: http://www.jisc.ac.uk/guides/engage-students-with-mobile-learning

JISC Legal (2013). Bring Your Own Device policy template for further education. Online at: http://www.jisclegal.ac.uk/ManageContent/ViewDetail/ID/3073/Bring-Your-Own-Device-Policy-Template-for-Further-Education-1-May-2013.aspx.

Loughborough University (2014). BYOD@Lboro (Bring Your Own Device at Loughborough University). Online at: http://www.lboro.ac.uk/media/wwwlboroacuk/content/itservices/downloads/policy/BYOD@Lboro%20v2.pdf

Microsoft Education UK (2013). BYOD - a practical guide that will get your thinking. Online at: http://www.slideshare.net/Microsofteduk/byod-in-education-18688889

Nerantzi, C., Middleton, A. and Beckingham, S. (2015). BYOD4L: Learning about using our own devices using the 5C framework. Chapter in this edition.

Oblinger, D. and Oblinger J. L., eds.(2005). Educating the Net Generation. EDUCAUSE e-Book. Online at: http://www.educause.edu/research-and-publications/books/educating-net-generation/learning-spaces

Oxford Online Dictionaries (2014). Language Matters. "BYOD". Online at: http://www.oxforddictionaries.com/definition/english/BYOD.

Potter, D. (2012). BYOD hits the headlines. Online at: http://blogs.exeter.ac.uk/cascade/blog/2012/05/09/byod-hits-the-headlines/

Souleles, N. and Pillar, C., eds. (2014). Proceedings of the First International Conference on the use of iPads in Higher Education 2014. Online at: http://ipadsinhe.org.

UCISA (2014). UCISA report: 2014 Survey of Technology Enhanced Learning for higher education in the UK. Online at: http://www.ucisa.ac.uk/~/media/groups/dsdg/TEL%20Survey%202014_29Sep2014.ashx

Scenario: Ever develop

CPD students and professionals use Evernote to create a development portfolio in which they record evidence of how they remain in good standing. Evernote allows them to store their professional development notes in a folder they have named 'CPD'. The note making tool is accessible and synchronised to all the devices they use. Colleagues working in CPD peer groups can make shareable folders to support their peer enhancement activities.

Key tool: Evernote

Attribution: Santanu Vasant

Psychosocial aspects of engagement with social media and digital technology
— personal thoughts from the frontier

Denise Turner

I recently had a casual conversation with one of my much younger colleagues, responsible for supporting academic engagement with technology. During this brief exchange I mentioned that in my office I still had a copy of a much thumbed research book from my own student days, an entire chapter of which is devoted to 'Setting up the Card Index.' Expecting him to chuckle at my denouement, I was surprised when he simply seemed confused and then further alarmed when he said 'Hang on, what's a card index?' Standing in the sunshine of the autumn day, I found myself swiftly advancing in years, in response to his remark.

The brief discussion however, further focussed my regular musings on the rapid expansion of technology and the potential psychosocial problems of engagement with this. I have written elsewhere (Turner, 2014) of my own conversion from extreme social media sceptic to evangelist for the potential collaborative benefits of *Twitter*. My personal experience of setting up a social media 'chat' as part of a work role moved me from Winterson's (1993) fear of being 'smashed' by the machines to one where I felt part of a community of like-minded people. In my years of active *Twitter* use I have perhaps been fortunate enough not to suffer from any particularly abusive behaviour or 'trolling' and I am consequently surprised when the media seem to focus solely on this one aspect of social media engagement.

Balick (2014, p.xxix) terms such media reactions, 'knee-jerk suspicion' and takes a psychoanalytic perspective on some of these more defensive or belligerent stances towards social media. Balick's stance on platforms such as *Twitter*, echoes my own experience (Turner, 2014) of networking sites as collaborative spaces in which 'individuals communicate with others, share links to important papers, make requests and have them kindly answered, among a whole variety of other potential *interpersonal and social* experiences.' This is not to deny, of course, that people behave badly on social networking sites and the recent death of Brenda Leyland (Barnett, 2014) has focussed attention and discussion of this.

However, undeniably people also prosper on social networking sites, form communities and friendships and utilise the campaigning power of hash tags capable of social change – my own experience (Turner, 2014) is far from unique in this respect, as Bolton (2011) captures:

> *Although the technology and tools are relatively new, the concept of social networking has been around much longer than the Internet. People are naturally social creatures; that's what makes social media such a powerful concept. Social media channels allow human beings to sort themselves seamlessly into groups and factions and maintain intimate relationships at greater distances than ever before.*

Balick (2014) considers the polarisation which occurs when these positive consequences of social media are subjugated, to be a form of the 'splitting' identified in Klein's work (Klein, 1946). Rather than steering a path through the constructive or adverse consequences of social networking, thus maintaining the middle ground of Klein's 'depressive position', such platforms become either 'good' or 'bad' objects in public consciousness thus reducing the opportunity for genuinely holistic dialogue.

The conversation with my much younger colleague, described earlier, provides one potential explanation for this splitting, in that people may dread becoming overwhelmed by their lack of technological knowledge, or fear having wisdom and experience obliterated by this brave, new, digital world. I recognise this response in my own behaviour, when I returned to university as a mature PhD student (Turner, 2014). I felt I belonged only to what I had dubbed, 'the lost generation' technologically and covered my feelings of fear and inadequacy around this with irritation and defensiveness. These would also manifest in frequent outbursts to my children about the evils of being wedded to a screen, accompanied by how much better things had been in my childhood. I did not wish to be an anachronism, a dinosaur – surrounded by young people who did not know what a card index was and I felt too vulnerable to admit to this at the time.

Such vulnerability is, I suggest, another reason for defences against social media and other forms of digital technology. Bochner (1997, p.421) suggests that in academic life particularly people armour themselves against such vulnerability by maintaining distance in a manner which is both "impersonal" and "not intimate," thus successfully defending against "the invasion of helplessness, anxiety and isolation we would feel if we faced the human condition honestly." Perhaps then the previously unimagined connectivity made possible by the Internet and social media platforms brings us uncomfortably close to this human condition – to the good and the bad that people are able and have always been able to visit upon one another.

Herein, I suggest lies the key to engaging and moving forward with digital technology and in particular with social media connection. During a very recent experiment on *Twitter* devised as part of social media training for social work students I invited people studying social work at my host and other universities to contribute to a hash tag for one week only. A mature student who had only recently started using *Twitter* at his institution tweeted a request for advice in how to reference *Twitter* conversations. Within minutes he had been given guidance and instruction by a lecturer at his own university and others in the 'twittersphere' wanting to help. He replied, "I have been out of education for 16 years and we did not use Internet back then, so a lot to learn" and in this direct way was able to make himself vulnerable. Perhaps more importantly still he was also able to invite support and learning opportunities, together with giving others the permission to demonstrate their own vulnerability. The response he received from people wanting to help, give advice and share their own stories demonstrated vividly what Brown (2010) dubs the 'power of vulnerability' together with the capacity for genuine human connection which social media can exert. As I and many others have suggested such engagement carries with it risk, but so does travelling, crossing the road and even turning on the lights. We have now to engage with the power of technology in a way which holds the 'depressive position' where good and bad are contained within the same object. This calls for national/international events and conversations which truly embrace inclusivity, varying skill levels and different forms of knowledge in a holistic way which avoids 'splitting' (Balick, 2014).

References

Balick, A. (2014). The psychodynamics of social networking. London: Karnac Books.

Barnett, E. (2014). 'Trolling is never a victimless crime'. Telegraph, 9/10/14. Online at: http://www.telegraph.co.uk/women/womens-life/11144435/Madeleine-McCann-Twitter-troll-Brenda-Leyland-death-Trolling-is-never-a-victimless-crime.html

Bochner, A. (1997). It's about time: Narrative and the divided self. Qualitative Inquiry, 3 (4), 418−438.

Bolton, J. (2011). Social workers must be cautious with online social media. Community Care Online. Online at: http://www.communitycare.co.uk/2011/10/06/social-workers-must-be-cautious-with-online-social-media/

Brown, B. (2010). The power of vulnerability. TED Talk. Online at: http://www.ted.com/talks/brene_brown_on_vulnerability?

Klein, M. (1946). 'Notes on some schizoid mechanisms'. In: Klein, M. (1997). Envy and gratitude and other works, 1946-1963. London: Vintage Books.

Turner, D. (2014). Creating #teamturner: An autoethnography of connection within social work education. In: Joanne Westwood, ed., "Social media in social work education", Northwich: Critical Publishing.

Winterson, J. (1993). Written on the body. Vintage, London.

Scenario: Tell me more

Mike has set his Maths students a poster assignment each year but has been worried about the impenetrable detail they tend to include. In this assignment he wants them to focus on communicating relevant statistics. However, in his briefing this year Mike decided to drop the word 'poster' and talked about 'infographics' instead. He likes the clarity and attractiveness of the infographic format and can see how his students will respond well. "I want you to provide me with an infographic like these" he said, showing some examples from Easel.ly, Vizualize, Piktochart, Venngage and Infogr.am. "And I want you to include a QR Code linking to the spreadsheet you have used to generate the data."

Key tools: QR Code Maker, Google Sheets, Infographic tool such as Piktochart

(How) should smart technologies for learning be taught?

Helen Webster

Introduction

Smart devices, and the software apps they run, are designed to be easy and intuitive to use. Instruction manuals are largely a thing of the past for tablets, smartphones and the apps which can be downloaded onto them, and everyone has a favourite anecdote about kids who instinctively have a better grasp of their parents' iPads and mobile phones than the adults do. Do we therefore need to teach students and staff how to use smart technologies for learning in higher education? And if so, what exactly is it that we need to teach, and how would this best be achieved? These questions were my starting point when tasked with a project to encourage early career researchers to make better use of social media to disseminate their research and promote their professional profiles, thereby enhancing their impact and employability. The resulting resource, Ten Days of Twitter, grew out of the challenges I encountered exploring these issues.

The resources I developed ultimately took the form of a suite of online materials hosted on a blog, which formed the hub of a more dispersed discussion on social media. Influenced by initiatives such as 23Things programmes (PLCMC, n.d.) and MOOCs, Ten Days of Twitter (or #10DoT) aimed to support researchers (and in subsequent iterations, librarians and academics too) as they explored the functionality, but more importantly the uses and social conventions of Twitter, in the context of open scholarship. Participants accessed materials released once a day over ten (working) days, at whatever point in the day was convenient for them, and on whatever device which they habitually used. Blog posts were structured around authentic activities with the functionality being introduced around tasks associated with research as much as social media.

Digital literacy for smart technologies

The notion of 'digital natives' (Prensky, 2001), describing those who have grown up with digital technologies and who use them instinctively and confidently, is problematic and frequently untrue. It risks disenfranchising those students who for whatever reason find themselves on the wrong side of the digital divide, and disempowering staff, who may be equally capable, if not as confident, with digital technology. For this reason alone, I felt that there should be capacity for teaching both students and staff how to use smart technologies in the context of higher education. This is partly a valuable confidence-building exercise, and partly also an exploration of the cultural capital needed to be able to begin to teach yourself how to use a smart device and transfer what you have learned to any new apps you may encounter: expectations of what a device or app might be able to do, and literacy in the language of icons and other symbols which characterise the graphic user interfaces typical of smart technologies. However, for smart learning, this needs to be more than a remedial exercise in ensuring that digitally disadvantaged learners and teachers are brought up to speed. A concept of digital literacy which only focuses on the functionality and operation of smart technologies overlooks a whole array of sophisticated issues which all learners (staff and student) need to address to perceive the relevance of smart technology in learning, let alone its appropriate and effective use.

The problem of personalisation

Smart devices are personalisable and therefore personal. They are also open in terms of the types of purpose to which they can be put, and thus may be used in a variety of contexts, leisure, social, professional, and of course academic. In most cases, they belong to the student, not the institution, and may have been bought with primary aims other than study in mind; it is of course therefore the student's prerogative to decide how to use their own smart device. However, we may require that students use their own devices in particular ways in accordance with our university regulations and assessment needs. Research has suggested that students may not be as digitally literate as we, or they, assume (Bennett *et al.*, 2008, pp. 778-9; Creanor & Trinder, 2010, pp. 50-1; Littlejohn *et al.*, 2012, pp. 551). They may therefore not have fully explored or formed their own digital study preferences themselves, or they may be transferring strategies from other contexts which do not work so well in that of learning. They may also have to negotiate between study use of a device and other purposes for which it was acquired, such as leisure or social use (shaped partly by their own wishes, but also dictated by the expectations of the wider social network in which they participate) and potentially also the requirements of their employers. Likewise, staff exploring the practice of open scholarship through smart devices, whether their own or their institution's, will encounter a clash of cultures between academia and social media.

The devices therefore become a site for the creation and performance of multifaceted identities and relationships, each entailing different aims, demands, values, behaviours, cultures and social structures. When learners bring their smart devices into the context of education, they will need not only to construct appropriate new identities and behaviours in line with the aims, demands and values of academic culture (which may not at first feel very 'them'), but also negotiate the interaction and possible conflict of these new expectations, behaviours and values with those of any other contexts in which they use their smart device. Staff too, well socialised in the professional norms of academic culture, may find those of social media new and rather alien.

Any concept of digital literacy which underpins our teaching of and with smart technologies must acknowledge that learners need to be able to operate digitally within multiple contexts. This necessitates the creation of new and potentially unfamiliar identities and behaviours, each with appropriate values and norms, and will entail identifying and handling potential conflicts between their own preferences and the demands of the new context, and indeed between different contexts. It seems more appropriate, then, to speak of digital literacies in the plural, in alignment with the concept of academic literacies, in recognition of the fact that not just the university but also the workplace and social spaces are "constituted in, and [...] sites of, discourse and power," and that learning involves the need to switch between various practices according to context (Lea & Street, 1998, p. 159). More than any other digital technology, smart technologies throw this into sharp relief as they bring all this together in the same device. Moreover, teaching digital literacies in the context of smart technology must necessarily be student-centred, as the devices by and large belong to them, and in all cases are personalised to them.

Once the issue has been framed in this way, it is clear that a traditional IT training session in a computer suite, based on behaviourist teaching approaches such as demonstrating which buttons to click and options to select, simply doesn't make sense for teaching the use of smart technologies. Training learners in the functionality of an app on a uniform set of identical PCs all running the same institutionally approved software might be logistically the easiest option, but whatever the student learns in that session will not easily transfer to their own use of their smart device, which will necessarily look different. A BYOD approach would at least allow students to work with something which will look familiar, but a trainer will be faced with an unanticipatable and almost unmanageable variety of devices all customised with different operating systems, apps, Wi-Fi connection speeds and diverse personal settings, and will find it difficult to demonstrate how to use the functionality in a way which makes sense to a group. Personalised devices are also deeply personal, and a trainer-centred demonstration may feel inappropriate and even intrusive.

Moreover, the IT training model doesn't begin to take account of the digital literacies approach outlined above. Some of the provision will need to be teacher-centred, as the demands and values of the educational institution in which the smart devices are to be used are clarified. However, much of it will need to be a learner-centred dialogue, as learners are invited to reflect what new identities, practices and behaviours regarding smart technologies might be appropriate in the context of their studies, but also how these will become integrated into their studies as longer-term strategies and behaviour changes. It's one thing to show someone how to use an app, and another to help them think about how they will find time to add it to their digital study repertoire in an already busy life, or switch from a pre-existing and well established strategy to a new digital one, however much more effective it might prove to be in the long run. They will also need to consider how to integrate their study use of their device into a relationship with the other contexts in which it is used. How, for example, to keep coursework safely backed up and secure when the device may also be borrowed by their children to share content on social media or play games? Or to contribute to critical class discussion on a social media backchannel when friends may not realise they are online in a study capacity and unavailable for chat, or their workplace may have strict policies or expectations for employees' use of social media? This is a very personal process, and learners will come to very different conclusions from one another. To do this, they need to be discussing and reflecting together (which is not easily facilitated by traditional IT training spaces), and also learning in an authentic study situation (which an IT training suite is ill-equipped to mimic).

Principles for developing digital literacies

Having experimented with a variety of formats during a project to develop the digital literacy and social media use of early career researchers, including seminars, lectures, traditional IT training, I developed a set of principles which I felt should underpin any training I developed in the use of smart devices (or indeed any of the variety of devices including PCs which students might wish to run apps on).

'Training' should be situated. This means that it should be located online and on the learner's device, and in the learner's own chosen, habitual context so as to be as authentic as possible. Learning about smart learning should occur through smart technologies.

It should be tailored to the context and to the learner, exploring functionality only in the context in and extent to which it is likely to be used. This means exploring it through authentic tasks which are driven by typical learning and teaching activities, rather than an exhaustive demonstration of all the functionality out of context. It also means inviting the learner to reflect on how the technology might be integrated into their own life-study needs and also other aspects of their digital lives. Each iteration of Ten Days of Twitter, for early career researchers and subsequently librarians and academics, was customised to the kinds of things the learners might need to accomplish in the course of their work.

Such reflection necessitates participation in tasks and also discussion about the resulting reflections and sharing of experiences. Training should therefore include an element of interaction with other learners, through social media via smart technology or face to face.

In order to be integrated with the learner's own study and other habits, training should be 'bitesize' and 'just in time', fitting in with their time management strategies rather than requiring large amounts of time to be set aside especially, and introduced in the context of learning tasks they are already likely to be doing. Preferably any provision should run in real time or near-synchronous time to enable discussion with other learners.

Training should be 'open' in terms of level - with no objective benchmark for smart learning, it is very difficult to anticipate the level of potential learners as their own estimation of their abilities will vary hugely, with a very diverse range of experience to be found even on a course designated for 'absolute beginners'. A more open approach to reflection and sharing experience allows learners to explore what they need to at their own level, learning from other participants, the programme providing a scaffold for them to investigate how to use smart technologies in their own academic context.

Conclusion

Having experimented with more traditional modes of IT training, I concluded that supporting learners' exploration of smart learning was best conducted through smart technologies which themselves encouraged a more open, learner-centred approach, and which is also transferable to other apps and devices beyond Twitter. While in the Ten Days of Twitter programme there was some focus on the functionality of Twitter, the emphasis was more on how the behaviours and culture of social media could be aligned to that of scholarship, and invitations were made to reflect on how they might wish to make use of Twitter or indeed other social media platforms in their work. In some iterations of the programme there were also face to face workshops, but these were intended to reinforce the discussion and reflection rather than to demonstrate the functionality of the social media apps we were using.

References

Bennett, S., Maton, K. and Kervin, L. (2008). The 'digital natives' debate: a critical review of the evidence. British Journal of Educational Technology 39, 775–786.

Creanor, L. and Trinder, K., (2010). Managing life and study with technology. In: Rhona Sharpe, Helen Beetham and Sara de Freitas, eds. "Rethinking learning for a Digital Age: how learners are shaping their own experiences", 43–55. New York and London: Routledge.

Lea, M. and Street, B. (1998). Student literacies in higher education: an academic literacies approach. Studies in Higher Education, 23(2), 157–172.

Littlejohn, A., Beetham, H., and McGill, L. (2012). Learning at the digital frontier: A review of digital literacies in theory and practice. Journal of Computer Assisted Learning, 29(6), 547–556.

PLCMC (Public Library of Charlotte and Mecklenburgh Country) (n.d.). Learning 2.0. Online at: http://plcmcl2-things.blogspot.co.uk/

Prensky, M. (2001). Digital natives, digital immigrants. On the Horizon, 9 (5), 1—6.
Webster, H. (n.d.). Ten Days of Twittter: teaching Twitter for academics. Online at:
http://10daysoftwitter.wordpress.com

Scenario: Feedback portfolio

Mary is Course Leader and is meeting her new undergraduates on the first day of the academic year. "No better time to engage them in managing their feedback," she says to her colleagues. "Start as you mean to go on." The course team are already up to speed having been trained to promote the use of Tumblr with their students as a portfolio tool for feedback.

In the Welcome lecture Mary and the team introduce what will happen during the first semester and she explains how they will be expected to engage in independent study, manage their time, and the importance of using feedback to continuously reflect on improving their performance on each assignment. After the Welcome students use their personal devices or the PC Lab to set up a personal Tumblr account using a pseudonym. Tumblr is a micro-blogging tool: they can post text, quotes, links, photos, videos and audio recordings there.

They have been instructed to keep a weekly record of notes from activities, informal and formal feedback from their peers and tutors and a weekly self-reflection. They should include photos from group work activities to help trigger their memories. They are encouraged to 'follow' the Tumblrs of peers in their learning set and to discuss their Tumblr sites at tutorials.

Key tool: Tumblr.com

Building a conversational framework for e-learning to support the future implementation of learning technologies

Simon Thomson

Let's start this piece with a quote which aligns with my thinking and was a catalyst for some of the ideas I am about to pour out below.

> *Transformation is more about the human and organizational aspects of teaching and learning than it is about the use of technology – Laurillard (2007, p. xvi)*

This is fundamental in positioning our approach to technology in learning and teaching, yet it is often lost in the big strategic rollout of technologies and the "minimum expectations" documents which subsequently follow.

To start with we need to think a bit differently about what we currently do with technology enhanced learning activity. I am suggesting that we begin by stopping some current practices that we may have:

STOP insisting that everyone who teaches uses technology

Teaching has been around much longer than technology, and learning has successfully taken place without technology so why do we often insist that "everyone" must use technology as part of their teaching?

I can think of many excellent teaching (and learning) experiences I have had where technology was not involved.

STOP creating hoops for people to jump through

If your institution has a "minimum expectations" document, for the VLE or equivalent, then within that will likely be a series of requirements (hoops).

The intention of these documents is supposedly good - it's to make everyone use the technology (see previous paragraph). However in reality it's not a measure of quality - it's a measure of compliance.

STOP running workshops run by TEL champions.

This may seem a bit harsh because TEL champions and Learning Technologists are doing a fantastic job, but the reality is that academic colleagues expect them to be good. What is more effective is when people who have made the move from lacking digital confidence to achieving increased digital ability show what *they* have done. The best evangelists are the converted congregation, not the preacher.

Smart decisions

Therefore when planning to use smart devices in learning & teaching we should refrain from any of the three activities I identified above. Instead the focus of activity should be on the conversation, not on the device(s).

Using smart devices in an effective way means making smart decisions and that does not include insisting on their use, creating hoops or running all workshops where the experts demonstrate the potential.

So before you think about buying your smart devices, start by talking about the "why". Using the 4E Framework (*see* http://4e.digis.im) is one way in which you might wish to approach those conversations. The basis of the framework is to establish a rationale and ownership model where it is needed. The conversations should be framed around four core questions:

1. What can smart devices **enable** us to do (that we couldn't do without them)?
2. How can smart devices **enhance** what we already do (e.g. voting system in a lecture)?

3. How can smart devices **enrich** our learning experiences (such as add a global dimension to the learning)?
4. How can smart devices **empower** learners and teachers (giving them choices, such as different locations to teach & learn)?

Through these conversations we should seek to establish a clear rationale for using smart devices, but also identify clear potential positive impact. The framework is not hierarchical, there is no requirement for everyone to be empowered and the conversations are best undertaken with mixed staff and student groups.

This process can help to alleviate some of the fears associated with technology change or technology implementation. I had long recognised the physiological barriers associated with "change" specifically pertaining to technology related change. I was particularly drawn to the adapted work of Kubler-Ross and the 5 Stages of Grief model (2005).

I began to explore the 5 Stages to aspects of my own work in supporting colleagues to use technology in learning and teaching to enhance the student (and staff) experience. In using the model I mapped the 5 Stages against the typical journey I saw staff undertaking with regards to Technology Enhanced Learning (TEL).

5 Stages of Grief (with TEL comments in brackets)

1. **Denial** – This isn't happening to me. (Oh no not something else to learn).
2. **Anger** – Who's to blame for this? Why me? (Who made the decision to get this?)
3. **Bargaining** – If I can live till my daughter's wedding .... (Why can't we just stick with...........)
4. **Depression** – I am too sad to do anything. (I'm too busy to even think about it.)
5. **Acceptance** – I'm at peace with what is coming. (Actually it looks ok, might give it a go.)

I particularly like this (figure 1.) expanded version based on the Kübler-Ross model which brings in terms such as "resistance" and "self-doubt" which are particular emotions I have witnessed (and personally experienced) when approaching new technologies.

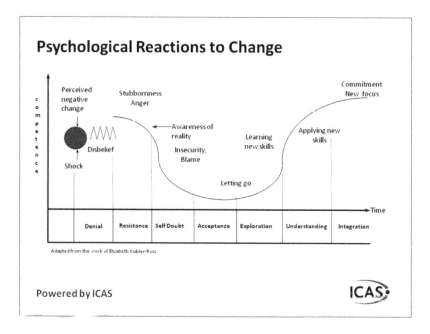

Figure 1. **Image Source:** *http://agilesutra.wordpress.com/2011/11/09/willpower-to-change-is-an-exhaustive-resource/ (with original © accredited to http://www.icas.co.za/)*

Conclusion

The value of smart device use in learning and teaching is now being explored more widely, partly through publications such as this, but also in the wider context of mobile device use. However, there are also studies (e.g. Kuznekoff & Titsworth, 2013) and reports which highlight the potential pitfalls associated with such devices if we do not have effective conversations around their purpose and value.

It is the conversations (or lack of) prior to the implementation of smart device initiatives that will see them succeed or fail, not the technology.

References

Jeffries, D. (2013). Is technology and the internet reducing pupils' attention spans? Teacher Network Teacher's blog, Monday 11 March 2013, The Guardian online. Online at: http://www.theguardian.com/teacher-network/teacher-blog/2013/mar/11/technology-internet-pupil-attention-teaching

Kuznekoff, J.H. and Titsworth, S. (2013). The impact of mobile phone usage on student learning. Communication Education, (62)3, 233-252.

Kübler-Ross, E. (2005). On grief and grieving: finding the meaning of grief through the Five Stages of Loss. London: Simon & Schuster Ltd.

Laurillard, D. (2007). Introduction. In: H. Beetham and R. Sharpe, eds., "Rethinking pedagogy for a Digital Age: designing for 21st century learning. New York: Routledge.

Scenario: The virtual flip chart

Tom has asked his Business Studies students to record group responses to a series of questions in a seminar breakout activity by using a common Twitter hashtag. Student groups, focused on different aspects of a related topic, monitor the notes being produced by each other in real time. There's a friendly competitive spirit amongst the groups who are working in different rooms. Later, findings from each group are aggregated and compared using Storify.

Key tools: Twitter, Storify

"What shall we do with our iPads?"

Ros Walker

"We're buying some iPads and we just wondered if you could come and show us what to do with them?" said the voice on the phone. This was not the first time I had heard that question. The question in my mind was 'why have you bought some iPads when you don't know what to do with them?' If we buy 'gadgets' for our home, we usually have a fair idea that they will improve some aspect of our life but this logic sometimes seems to evaporate when it comes to educational technology.

Smart devices seem to have got us particularly excited. They are brighter, more colourful, more portable, and probably more useful and versatile than any gadget we have previously owned and this combination can be intoxicating and cloud our judgement when it comes to education.

This case study explores the areas that should be considered when adopting mobile learning and how a *MasterPlan for Mobile Learning* was developed. It looks at how this can be adapted to different educational establishments and phases.

During 2011, Secondary schools were beginning to take a keen interest in the use of mobile technologies. Pilot studies have indicated that there may be "considerable pedagogic potential" (Kukulska-Hulme & Traxler, 2007, p. 181). By the first quarter of 2011, around half of new handsets sold were smartphones (OFCOM, 2011) and through personal use, many teachers were beginning to realise their potential for teaching and learning. It was also the year that the iPad2 arrived and the world began to understand the term 'app' (application) as the number of apps in the iOS app store increased from around 300,000 to half a million, equalled only by the number of downloads (Wikipedia). "These technologies offer unique possibilities to design for learning that are unlike any afforded by other e-learning technologies" explain Kukulska-Hulme and Traxler (2007, p.183). They go on to say that they are capable of supporting designs for learning which are "personalized, situated and authentic." It was natural, therefore, that schools began to explore the use of these devices in the classroom.

As with any new technology, there were successes and failures. Anecdotally, there were schools who used iPads for pupils as a recruitment incentive for 6th formers. Whilst they may have been used for learning, there was no evaluation of these projects and staff were sometimes left bewildered when pupils walked into the room with the new technology.

It was for this reason that the learning technologists at United Learning began to look for a framework to support the adoption of mobile learning. I developed a simple diagram to look at the key elements involved in a successful implementation (Figure 1).

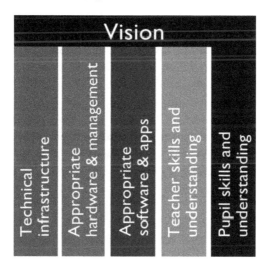

Figure 1. The Five Columns of Mobile Learning (Walker, 2013) - a first attempt at a framework for Mobile Learning, later superceded by a 'Masterplan'. Copyright creative commons Ros Walker.

This diagram was first used to highlight how an institution should have a vision for their use of technology. This would be a learning vision, which identified the skills and understanding that pupils needed and how the technology could help them to acquire them. In order for the vision to be successful, it had to be supported by the columns.

These are:

- **Technical infrastructure:** The educational establishment needs to have adequate (and ideally better than just adequate) wireless access and sufficient bandwidth. Mark Howell of Meru Networks, speaking at a conference about mobile access, said that teachers and pupils don't care about wireless – they just want it to work. It should be like a tap – turn it on and the water flows. Ideally, as we discovered later, this technical infrastructure needs to extend beyond the educational premises to the student's home.
- **Appropriate hardware and management** – At the time this diagram was published, the main decision was between an iPad, a basic Android device or a laptop (which although not a smart device, it was still mobile). There was little by way of management software.
- **Appropriate software and apps** – There was a realisation that most smart devices come with a minimal set of tools and that their potential for learning is realised through the installation of 'apps'. But how many educational establishments knew which were the best apps or how they could be used?
- **Teacher skills and understanding** - This was a time when ownership of mobile devices amongst teachers was still not high and many teachers had serious concerns about mobile devices in the classroom. Writing in 2003, Sharples (p.3) stated that, "A dilemma at the heart of networked learning is that learners can command an increasingly sophisticated set of communication and computing devices, which they are forbidden to use within formal education because they disrupt lessons and lectures." This view had started to change but was still far from the use of personal mobile devices.
- **Pupil skills and understanding** - so that they become better at independent learning, use creativity in their work and learn to communicate and collaborate effectively.

These columns appear in the order given for a particular reason. Without the infrastructure, there is no point having the devices; the right device needs to be chosen; the right software needs to be on the device and teachers and pupils need to understand how to use them.

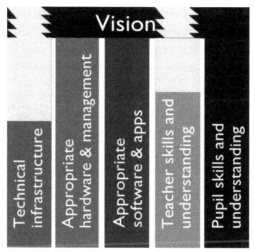

Figure 2. Failure of a mobile learning project

As an extension of the first 'model' (Figure 2) was developed to show how a project could fail. In this case, a secondary school, the Senior Management decided to allow pupils to bring in devices (BYOD). Parents and governors were consulted as part of the vision and a list was sent out a list to parents of the devices which would be appropriate. Pupils arrived in school and proudly displayed the devices (which now could be on their desks instead of in their bags). In fact, 70% had already had devices, so surely it made sense to allow their use? However, the teachers had not really been consulted. Some thought it was a good idea and some didn't, but there was inconsistent use in lessons. Also, the technical department had not been fully aware of the development or the demands that it would make on the school's network. The school already had Wi-Fi – but not sufficient coverage to manage 1100 new devices. The pupil devices kept losing the Internet; pupils played games and messaged each other when they got bored in lessons; parents began to complain. The school felt it couldn't go back on the decision now it had been made – and ended up with a big 'salvage' job, trying to create a proper vision to implement.

Whilst Figure 2 (The 5 Columns of Mobile Learning) worked well at an initial level, several schools within the United Learning group decided that they did want to pursue a full 1-1 implementation of mobile devices. Every pupil would have a device and be able to bring it to school and take it home. This would require much more sophisticated strategy and planning.

What followed was several months of consultations, visits and discussions, both inside and outside the United Learning group. We were fortunate to have access to other schools that had already implemented programmes. The final outcome of this was the 'Masterplan for Mobile Learning' (Figure 3).

A Masterplan for Mobile Learning

LEARNING VISION		Prepare	Pilot	Review	Launch	Maintain and Develop
	Technical	**Infrastructure Audit** - WiFi - Broadband - Network - Staffing - Screen Sharing	**Monitor systems** Infrastructure Develop support system Staff training Investigate MDM options	**Capacity Planning** Improve infrastructure Refine support system Commission MDM Support teacher usage	**Device Management** Implement MDM registration procedures Support roll-out via agreed systems	**Evaluate** Review provision and procedures
	Finance	**Establish Budget** Feedback from technical + provision reviews Review Leasing / Insurance options	**Purchase** Setup Volume Purchasing Plans if appropriate	**Equipment** Review provision and adjust for launch Purchase additional equipment	**Equipment** Finance agreements in place	**Maintain** Monitor monthly payments Liaise with CTO finance Process insurance claims Manage end of lease actions
	Provision	**What do we need?** - Devices - Software - Cases - Storage / charging - Screen sharing - Spares	**Pilot Implementation** Identify pilot group Develop AUP Issue devices Begin training plan	**Evaluate** Pilot group report Feedback on AUP Pilot device deployment Feedback on pilot training	**Deployment** Begin phased roll-out programme Ensure staff devices are deployed at least 8 weeks ahead of pupils	**Evaluate** Device suitability Software Repair and maintenance regimes
	Parents	**Share the Vision** Inform parents about the plans	**Engage** Involve pilot parents - Share expectations - Homework	**Inform** Meeting with parents to - Assess home WiFi & broadband provision - Feedback pilot findings	**Communicate** Parental meetings to - Discuss package details - Ownership - e-Safety - Payment options	**Monitor** - Parental perception - Parental training needs - Payment and administrative systems
	Staff	**Digital Leaders** Identify key staff - Learning pedagogy - Pilot planning	**Engage** Developing expertise Monitor impact Evaluate pilot feedback to whole staff	**Support** Staff training plan to coincide with full teacher deployment	**SAMR Model** Pedagogical shift through: - Substitution - Augmentation - Modification - Redefinition	**Evaluate** - Impact on learning - Teaching pedagogy - Training needs
	Pupils	**Pupil Engagement** Audit - Surveys - Discussion - School council?	**Engage** Encourage expertise Pupil mentors?	**Pupil Feedback** Feedback on learning experiences	**Ownership** Digital Leaders Understanding of AUP Getting started training	**Monitor** - Engagement levels - Learner independence - Impact on achievement - Pupil voice consultations

Figure 3. A Masterplan for Mobile Learning - view online at: http://melsig.shu.ac.uk/?attachment_id=895

The framework was accompanied by a full booklet. There was a realisation that the project would go through several phases, looking more like an 'Action Research cycle' as each educational establishment adapted the implementation to their needs and context. The phases were:

1. **Development of the Learning Vision** - Typically this was done by discussion within the school over a couple of days. The Learning Technologist acted as a facilitator but it was the school which looked at their development plans and identified where smart devices could make a difference. This also set a benchmark for evaluation at a later phase.

2. **Prepare** - This was the phase where several strands begin to run in parallel. The initial ideas from the 'Five Columns' were still there but with some changes and additions:

○ The technical side now had a full specification to explore including Wi-Fi, bandwidth, the school's existing network capacity, any extra staffing requirement and how smart devices could be shown on screens ('screen-sharing').

○ Finance came in as a separate item, previously not included, but now essential as larger implementations were considered and earlier lessons learned about the potential costs of improvements to the technical infrastructure and complications in purchasing software. Leasing options were adopted and parental contribution explored in some settings.

○ The hardware and software were combined into 'provision' (as it is hard to separate them in some ways) and also encompassed accessories and peripherals, such as cases, storage, charging facilities and printing.

○ Parents were included in this scenario as in the schools context, parents may be involved in the purchase and also need to be aware of how students could and should use devices in the home context.

○ Staff remained a key element of the chart with a greater role now in planning and implementing - a 'key stakeholder'.

○ Pupils also took on a greater role as it was recognised that in some of the most successful implementations, pupils had played a significant role in some of the key decisions.

3. **Pilot** - The importance of carrying out a smaller-scale 'pilot' was highlighted, providing time and space for the changes to take place.

4. **Review** - This reviews the pilot stage and allows the educational establishment to adjust and fine-tune its roll-out.

5. **Launch** - It was found that having a big launch event helped pupils and staff to see that this technology marked a change in the way that the school was going to do things. In fact, it was a chance to change far more than the technology and perhaps the most important lesson learned in the whole process was that introducing smart devices wasn't really about the device - it was about the opportunities that could now be adopted for teaching and learning.

6. **Maintain & develop** - Whilst new technology never stands still for long, there needs to be a 'breathing space' to really embed the new ideas. Many schools have used the new technology as a chance to implement 'flipped learning' or 'the creative curriculum' and allowing time for pupils and staff to grow and develop together is essential.

This framework was accompanied by a booklet with further information and 'worksheets' for consideration. This has not been included because some of the technology advice is already out of date, but the framework contains all the key elements to allow an experienced Learning Technologies facilitator to help academic staff and learners to take the key decisions towards successful use of smart devices.

As with any framework, it can be adapted to the needs of the individual organisation. Working recently with the School of Dentistry at the University of Sheffield, it was recognised that 'parents' was not a category that they required, but 'Patients' were important. There were other adjustments that needed to be made for using technology in a clinical environment.

Further Reading

The following provide further resources for developing and implementing a mobile learning strategy. Whilst geared to schools, the resources can be easily adapted for other educational settings, such as further and higher education.

- **Tablets for Schools** (http://www.tabletsforschools.org.uk/) is a charity that commissions the largest independent research programme in the world on how tablets impact learning and attainment. This research is made available as a basis for best practices for schools implementing tablet technology.
- **Educate 1 to 1** (http://www.educate1to1.org/) - A useful site with blogs by experienced managers of mobile technology, with a book containing practical advice.

References

Kukulska-Hulme, A., & Traxler, J. (2007). Designing for mobile and wireless learning. In: H. Beetham, & R. Sharpe, "Rethinking Pedagogy for a Digital Age", pp. 180-192. Abingdon: Routledge.

OFCOM. (2011). Growth of smartphones and mobile internet use. Online at: http://stakeholders.ofcom.org.uk/market-data-research/market-data/communications-market-reports/cmr11/telecoms-networks/5.20.

Sharples, M. (2003). Disruptive devices: mobile technology for conversational learning, International Journal of Continuing Engineering Education and Lifelong Learning, 12 (5/6), 504−520.

Walker, R. (2014). The five pillars of mobile learning. [Blog] (13/3/2013) Online at: http://roswalker.org/2013/03/13/the-five-pillars-of-mobile-learning/.

Wikipedia. Apple App Store. Online at: http://en.wikipedia.org/wiki/App_Store_(iOS)#mediaviewer/File:AppleAppStoreStatistics.png.

Acknowledgements

The *Masterplan for Mobile Learning* was developed whilst the author was in employment with United Learning, an educational charity managing Academies and Independent schools across the UK. It was developed in conjunction with Dan Bunker.

Scenario: Don't hold the front page - keep it rolling!

You can create 'newspapers' based on any twitter name, list or hash tag using paper.li and because any professional worth their salt these days pushes out their successes on Twitter educators are publishing weekly class papers featuring what's hot.

"By next week you will need to have found someone to follow who you hope will cover you in glory! We are going to produce a Paper.li each week. Each issue will feature stunning news items, articles, photos and videos produced by your chosen scholar guru."

This was the challenge set the class at the beginning of the year. Each week the students read the weekly newsletter looking to see how well their chosen scholars were doing in terms of column inches.

Key tool: Paper.Li

The TARDIS effect
— how mobile phones could transform teaching and learning

Caroline Keep* and Mark Feltham

Introduction

We recently surveyed over 300 first year bioscience undergraduates (Feltham & Keep, 2014) and found that more than 90% of them have in their pockets their very own T.A.R.D.I.S... and it's much bigger on the inside that we can possibly imagine. No longer does teaching and learning need to be constrained by time and space as students can travel to wherever they wish, whenever they wish by using their mobile phones to connect to the *'Internet of Things'*. Educators and students alike can view, upload, download, collate, compile and share data, ideas and resources at the tap of a touchscreen. But, we can both be so much more than simply travellers in virtual time and space! Accessing and sharing information on the move outside the classroom is just the tip of the *'Who-berg'*. We can also use these devices to interact with our environment, to collect data and control other devices as part of our teaching and learning experience and this opens up glorious new dimensions for teaching and learning.

'Who-topia' — our imagining of a transformed learning universe

Imagine the following scenario. Students sign in to their classes with their mobile phones, having scooped the session's content via their class's social media group the night before and archived it to their own mobile Personal Learning Environments (PLEs). They use their phones, in class, to interact with the materials, the teacher and fellow students in order to test their understanding, whilst sharing their views, comments and questions via a

---

* nee Kristjansson

live *Twitter* feed. The whole session is recorded in real time and uploaded to the students' phones at the end of the session. Outside the classroom their learning continues as they now use their phones to collect data for projects and use social media such as *Facebook* to ask questions and share answers. They build their own data-loggers in the university makerspace to explore ideas further and design and code their own open-source phone apps to interrogate these devices and share their data via Bluetooth to the Web. They record their progress as they go on their blogs and add in useful updates and links to their *LinkedIn* profiles at the end of the day. Unrealistic? We don't think so.

A constellation of possibilities

Automated attendance registers involving students swiping the barcode on their student cards are already in operation and barcode and QR-code scanner apps already exist, whilst free apps like *Socrative* and *Kahoot* allow students to use their mobile device like 'clickers' to interact with peers and tutors during in-class sessions (see also in this edition Blackburn & Stroud, 2015; Wilson, 2015; Kennedy & Robson, 2015). *Facebook* is already being used to deliver content, providing 24/7 support for students and allowing them the freedom to upload their work wherever they are and in whatever format they like (Barden, 2014; Staines & Lauchs, 2013; Wang *et al.*, 2012). *Evernote* is already being used as a virtual Personal Learning Environment (PLE) by some students to compile, collate, edit and create content specific to their own learning and it is now easier than ever to scoop, snip, scrape and clip information to support individual learning (*see* Nortcliffe, 2015). Live *Twitter* feeds and chats too are on the increase and provide teachers and students with a ready means of interaction (*see* Nerantzi *et al.*, Rowell, and Webster chapters) and webinars and video-blogs are becoming more common in educational settings. In addition walk-throughs are now easy to produce in real time using video capture software like *Blueberry BB Flashback*, *Action!* and *Bandicam* and we have successfully used the latter to record lectures and provide instructional materials for students.

Mobile phones are packed full of sensors that students can use to collect data on temperature, pressure, light intensity, humidity, sound levels and vibrations and there are a huge numbers of free utility apps that can be downloaded and used to turn these sensors into seismometers, range finders, wind meters, speed guns and heart monitors. Makerspaces are beginning to appear in educational settings (Sharples *et al.*, 2013;

Weinmann, 2014; Schrock, 2014; Jariwala *et al.*, 2014) providing students with a wealth of enquiry-based learning opportunities and 3D printers and physical computing devices such as *Raspberry Pi* and *Arduino* are becoming more common in our schools, colleges and universities thanks to a new wave of educational initiatives (Wakefield & Rich, 2013). Last year, for example, *Google* and *Raspberry Pi* gave 15,000 such devices to UK schools (Edwards, 2013; Brock, Bruce & Cameron, 2013) whilst *Intel* and *Arduino* have been donating *Galileo* boards to universities (Intel, 2014). *Minecraft* and *Lego* too now have educational programmes linked to Science Technology Engineering and Maths (STEM) teaching. *MinecraftEdu* has merged gaming with learning (Short, 2012; Webster, 2011) and *Lego Mindstorm* allows kids to build physical devices to learn about science (Adams *et al.*, 2010). And with these developments has come coding. It's now part of the National Curriculum in schools and children as young as 8-9 are using MIT's *Scratch* to create their own content (Wilson, Hainey & Connolly, 2012), whilst older children are using it to create their own phone apps and more advanced users 'joining the dots' by using MIT's *S4A* software to code apps that will control *Arduino*-based devices (Fields, Vasudevan & Kafai, 2014; Gupta, Tejovanth & Murthy, 2012).

Only time (and space?) will tell...

The idea that we need a paradigm shift in education is not new (Robinson, 2010) and it has long been recognised that at the heart of this shift lies a return to more creative ways of learning and teaching (Robinson, 2001; Robinson, 2006; Kelly & Leggo, 2008). Mobile technologies, we believe, provide us with an unprecedented opportunity to achieve this by allowing us to develop new, flexible pedagogies (Gordon, 2014; Ryan & Tilbury, 2013) that provide students with diverse, rich learning environments in which the creativity of the student as hacker/maker can flourish and in which learning is no longer confined in time and space. It is within our grasp therefore to move towards a more dynamic, mobile way of teaching and learning that has the potential to transform curriculum delivery (JISC, 2009; JISC, 2011), enhance student learning and see a return to creativity in the classroom and lecture hall, whether these be real or virtual.

But do we want this? And, more to the point, do our students really want this? In a previous study (Feltham & Keep, 2014) we found clear differences between students' preferred learning styles and many did indeed express a strong desire for more creative ways of learning. But, this was not the case for all students. The wholesale replacement of our current didactic teaching practices with 'TARDIS-enhanced learning' would, yes, make subjects "more alive and relevant" (Sharples *et al.*, 2013, p.33) for some, but at the same time could alienate and hence disadvantage others. So, the question is this; is our Who-topia for the 'geeks' or 'the masses'? We guess only time (and space?) will tell...

References

Adams, J., Kaczmarczyk, S., Picton, P., and Demian, P. (2010). Problem solving and creativity in engineering: Conclusions of a three year project involving reusable learning objects and robots. *engineering education*, 5(2), 4—17.

Barden, O. (2014). Facebook levels the playing field: Dyslexic students learning through digital literacies. Research in Learning Technology, 22.

Blackburn, M. and Stroud, J. (2015). Voices from 'the other side': Using Personal Response Systems to support student engagement. Chapter in this edition.

Brock, J. D., Bruce, R. F., and Cameron, M. E. (2013). Changing the world with a Raspberry Pi. *Journal of Computing Sciences in Colleges*, 29(2), 151—153.

Edwards, C. (2013). Not-so-humble raspberry pi gets big ideas. *Engineering & Technology*, 8(3), 30—33.

Feltham, M.J. and Keep, C.M. (2014) Oh, the places you'll go: Smart learning in the natural sciences. In: 'Smart Learning: teaching and learning with smartphones and tablets in post compulsory education'. MELSIG.

Fields, D. A., Vasudevan, V., and Kafai, Y. B. (2014). The programmers' collective: Connecting collaboration and computation in a high school Scratch mashup coding workshop. In: Learning and becoming in practice: ICLS 2014 Conference Proceedings.

Gupta, N., Tejovanth, N., & Murthy, P. (2012). Learning by creating: Interactive programming for Indian high schools. In: Technology Enhanced Education (ICTEE), 2012 IEEE International Conference on (pp. 1-3). IEEE.

Gordon, N. (2014). Flexible pedagogies: Technology-enhanced learning. York: Higher Education Academy.

Intel (2014). Intel Galileo University Donation Programme. Online at: http://galileodonation.intel.com/

Jariwala, A. S., Fasse, B. B., Quintero, C., Forest, C. R., Linsey, J., Ngo, P., ... and Newstetter, W. (2014). The invention studio: A university maker space and culture. Advances in Engineering Education, 4(2).

JISC (2009). Effective practice in a digital age: a guide to technology-enhanced learning. Online at: http://www.jisc.ac.uk/media/documents/programmes/ elearning/digiemerge/Emergingpracticeaccessible.pdf

JISC (2011). Transforming curriculum delivery through technology. Online at: http://www.jisc.ac.uk/publications/programmerelated/2011/curriculumdeli veryguide.aspx

Kelly, R. and Leggo, C. (2008). Creative expression, creative education: Creativity as a primary rationale for education. Destselig Enterprises Ltd.

Kennedy, D., and Robson, D. (2015). Bringing well-established pedagogies into interactive lectures. Chapter in this edition.

Nortcliffe, A. (2015). HE BYOD: ready or not? Chapter in this edition.

Robinson, K. (2001). Mind the gap: The creative conundrum. Critical Quarterly,43(1), 41-45.

Robinson, K. (2006). Do schools kill creativity. In: Presentation at TED2006 conference, Monterey, CA.

Robinson, K. (2010). Changing education paradigms. RSA Animate, The Royal Society of Arts, London, http://www. youtube. com/watch.

Ryan, A. & Tilbury, D. (2013). Flexible pedagogies: New pedagogical ideas. York: Higher Education Academy.

Schrock, A. R. (2014). "Education in disguise": Culture of a hacker and maker space. InterActions: UCLA Journal of Education and Information Studies, 10(1). Online at: http://escholarship.org/uc/item/0js1n1qg

Sharples, M., McAndrew, P., Weller, M., Ferguson, R., FitzGerald, E., Hirst, T., and Gaved, M. (2013). Innovating pedagogy 2013: Open University innovation report 2. Milton Keynes: The Open University.

Short, D. (2012). Teaching scientific concepts using a virtual world - Minecraft. *Teaching Science, 58*(3), 55-58.

Staines, Z. R., and Lauchs, M. (2013). The use of Facebook in tertiary education. Interactive Technology and Smart Education, 10(4), 285 − 296.

Wakefield, J. and Rich, L.J. (2013). Google to give school Raspberry Pi microcomputers. BBC News. Online at: http://www.bbc.co.uk/news/technology-21243825

Wang, Q., Woo, H. L., Quek, C. L., Yang, Y., and Liu, M. (2012). Using the Facebook group as a learning management system: An exploratory study. British Journal of Educational Technology, 43(3), 428 − 438.

Webster, A. (2011). Educational building blocks: How Minecraft is used in classrooms. Ars Technica (2011).

Weinmann, J. (2014). Makerspaces in the university community. Master Thesis. Stanford University.

Wilson, J. (2015). Un-pop quiz: a case study of motivating student engagement through smart games. Chapter in this edition.

Wilson, A., Hainey, T., & Connolly, T. M. (2012). Evaluation of computer games developed by primary school children to gauge understanding of programming concepts. In: *6th European Conference on Games-based Learning (ECGBL),* 4 − 5.

Scenario: Becoming professional

Professional Development Planning sits uncomfortably within the curriculum for many students who don't fully appreciate how building a professional profile takes time. Mary is course leader for Physics. In her Welcome lecture she begins by fondly remembering recent graduates using friendly anecdotes as she reviews her alumni's LinkedIn profiles. "I'll be watching your progress too. Keep building your profile," she says to her new recruits "You've got just three years to wow me."

Key tool: LinkedIn

SECTION 2
RESEARCH AND CASE STUDIES

BYOD4L
— learning to use smart devices for learning and teaching through the 5C framework

Chrissi Nerantzi and Sue Beckingham

Introduction

Opportunities to learn informally have exploded since the arrival of social media and mobile technologies. These technologies disrupt the way we learn and create new opportunities for learning (Beetham & Sharpe, 2013). Google is rapidly becoming our dynamic encyclopaedia and connecting to global sources of information and learning is normal behaviour for anyone with a question or desire to learn. This chapter discusses an open approach to learning which was designed to engage educators in HE innovatively with CPD for learning and teaching called Bring Your Own Devices for Learning (BYOD4L).

The design of BYOD4L harnessed social media, mobile learning and ideas about open learning to create a rich and interactive learning space mediated through personal smart technologies. It was conceptualised as an immersive open CPD event to be run mostly online over five days.

Previously (Nerantzi & Beckingham, 2014, in review) we have described open CPD as professional development afforded by Open Educational Practices (OEP) and Open Educational Resources (OER). Such practices and resources encompass open courses or events, online and face-to-face events and MOOCS as well as freely available and accessible materials, both digital and physical. These create opportunities for "self-directed and self-organised CPD driven by professional interests, priorities and aspirations." (Nerantzi & Beckingham, in review, p. 3)

At the time of writing three iterations of BYOD4L have informed the development of a collaborative and scalable open CPD model which presents a versatile approach to delivering CPD for institutions while the 5C framework has been used unmodified.

BYOD4L - a collaborative development

The idea of creating BYOD4L as an open event was first conceived in 2013 by Chrissi Nerantzi as a way to create opportunities for extended engagement linked to a conference, event or other development activities. Chrissi Nerantzi and Sue Beckingham developed the idea into a concept and put all the pedagogical building blocks together for BYOD4L. The Smart Learning events offered by the Media-Enhanced Learning Special Interest Group (MELSIG, see http://melsig.shu.ac.uk/) provided a useful platform to test this idea. Development through collaboration of BYOD4L was central to the approach from its outset. The authors, Chrissi Nerantzi and Sue Beckingham, based at different UK universities, developed the initial concept, the BYOD4L online presence, pedagogical design, activities and resources using a range of freely available social media technologies but also Open Educational Resources (OER) developed by Nerantzi & Uhlin (cited in Nerantzi, 2014). Further OERs were developed especially for BYOD4L which as a whole is openly licensed and also made available as a stand-alone OER course.

The main BYOD4L event site was built using Wordpress.com. Wordpress is a free tool that allows anyone with moderate IT skills to construct a web presence made up of media rich pages. New community spaces were established in Facebook as well as Google + and Twitter. In addition a closed social space using Facebook was created to provide a supported space for facilitators. Later, volunteer co-facilitators, identified through their personal networks, were invited to be involved in the lead up to first iteration of BYOD4L in January 2014. The facilitation team then consisted of 12 collaborators from nine institutions and two countries. These social media platforms and tools were chosen as these have been used successfully in the past in other open educational initiatives.

Before it was run, BYOD4L was peer reviewed by Dr Cristina Costa who recognised BYOD4L's strength and innovative character. The review was especially important for us as it provided a valuable mechanism for quality assurance: BYOD4L as an open collaborative event or course, sits outside the normal institutional quality processes that apply to other academic programmes and Cristina's experience and expertise in using social media for learning, as well as her recognition as an ALT Learning Technologist of the Year, made her a credible reviewer for this project.

In BYOD4L 'bite-size learning', which can be understood as flexible, short and just-in-time interventions (Simpkins & Maier, 2010), was recognised through the awarding of the open badge system to recognise informal learning and achievement of bite-size learning. To secure a badge participants were invited to use an online form to submit evidence of their active engagement with each of the 5Cs. Typically this was in the form of a reflective blog post. Their evidence was then peer reviewed. Facilitators were also eligible to gain credits linked to the 5Cs as a participant. Other forms of recognition were associated with BYOD4L. For example, at Manchester Metropolitan University BYOD4L was offered as a FLEX opportunity. FLEX is a practice-based CPD scheme developed by the Centre for Excellence in Learning and Teaching (CELT) with informal and formal pathways which maximises on the opportunities available within and beyond an institution. It can lead to up to 30 credits of the Postgraduate Certificate or the Masters in Academic Practice as a way to formalise informal learning, FLEX awards, which are open badges for CPD linked to learning and teaching and are a way to evidence relevant engagement. Engagement in FLEX can also help when working towards professional recognition of the HEA. BYOD4L was mapped to the UKPSF and presented opportunities to work towards professional recognition in some further participating institutions, for example at Sheffield Hallam University.

Pedagogic considerations

An engaging enquiry-based learning design was used which evolved from the design developed for the open course Flexible, Distance and Online Learning (FDOL). In FDOL a Problem-Based Learning (PBL) approach had been used and the FISh model (Focus – Investigate – Share, see Figure 1) developed by Nerantzi and Uhlin (Nerantzi, 2014).

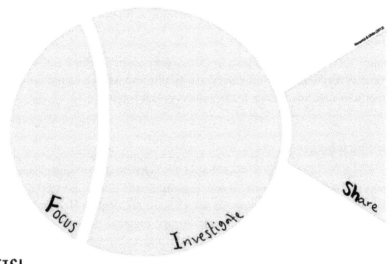

FISh

Figure 1. FISh (Focus - Investigate -Share)

Building upon this, BYOD4L used short video scenarios to trigger personal and collaborative learning. In addition a short set of varied activities were suggested for each of the five 'C' topics (described below). Each provided opportunities for personal and group learning.

Running BYOD4L

BYOD4L was offered over five days in January 2014 for the first time and was targeted at students and teachers in Higher Education, but was open to anyone else interested in learning more about using smart devices for learning or professional development. During the first week-long iteration we estimate about 100 individuals took part from 26 countries globally. As BYOD4L is registration-free, the quantitative data we hold is based on social media participation.

BYOD4L was offered again in July 2014, this time working more closely together as a cross-institutional collaboration involving five UK higher education institutions. About 100 individuals took part this time. There were similar numbers of participants in the third iteration which was offered in January 2015. The numbers are based on participation in the Google+, Facebook and Twitter. In this second iteration we encouraged participating institutions to also arrange local events to bring local communities together and extend the learning activities into face-to-face situations during the week.

January 2014, July 2014 and January 2015 were chosen to offer BYOD4L by organisers responding to facilitators' availability and when it would be best for participating institutions to maximise local engagement.

Learning together

The majority of activities were based on asynchronous engagement. However, daily tweetchats were organised to bring the BYOD4L community together synchronously for an hour. A Google + Hangout was also offered. Further opportunities to engage together were arranged in collaborators' institutions through local informal face-to-face gatherings.

The creation of a facilitation and learning community was an important part of the BYOD4L concept. The facilitators played a key role in laying the foundations for this. Participants were encouraged to actively experiment, reflect on their experience and share their thoughts, ideas and reservations openly with others. Some of these were openly shared in the form of recorded discussions and shared via blog posts and Twitter.

The 5Cs

The 5C framework was used to scaffold learning and provide a thematic focus for each of the five days, as well as creating a pedagogical rationale. This is described in more detail below. The idea for the 5Cs developed when the authors discussed how learning and development of practice in the area of smart social learning during BYOD4L could be scaffolded and supported within an open learning community (Nerantzi & Beckingham, 2014) to foster what Megele (2014, p.47) calls multilogues, "a many-to-many communication, where each message is addressed to more than one potential receiver and may be answered by more than one potential replier."

From the outset, it was intended that BYOD4L would be a bite-size open learning event offered over five days, which could also be seen as a facilitated block as used in many professional courses. Five days could potentially provide a more focused and more intensified engagement opportunity, creating suspense and excitement. It could also be seen as the starting point for the formation of an ongoing community of practitioners.

From the outset, it was intended that BYOD4L would be a bite-size open learning event offered over five days, which could also be seen as a facilitated block as used in many professional courses. Five days could potentially provide a more focused and more intensified engagement opportunity, creating suspense and excitement. It could also be seen as the starting point for the formation of an ongoing community of practitioners.

It was coincidental that the five sections of the 5C framework begin with the letter 'C'. This came from looking for a way to conceptualise a framework that would enable participants to immerse themselves in a valuable learning experience around a continuum of learning from the known to the unknown. The 5C Framework fosters critical and creative thinking and actions. It is focused around human interactions and the important role they play for learning and development more generally in a complex world. The 5Cs of Connecting, Communicating, Curating, Collaborating, Creating created such an immersive pedagogical as well as thematic structure.

Specifically the 5C framework aims to:

- enable and support opening-up and sharing of thoughts, ideas, practices with others that would lead to active participation, sharing and reciprocity (Weller, 2011);
- boost confidence and progressively develop competence in participants leading to transformative practices and behaviours (Beetham & Sharpe, 2011);
- recognise the value of smart learning by learners reflecting on their own practice and actively experimenting and exploring what can be achieved.

The 5Cs present therefore, a scaffold for learning, a stepped approach to engage with smart learning that usually starts with the more familiar and leads progressively to the more advanced or complex concepts and applications of using smart devices for learning.

While the 5Cs at first glance might look like a linear framework (Figure 2), it is important to highlight how it also can be used in a non-linear 'pick 'n' mix' way and provides further flexibility for use and application (Figure 3).

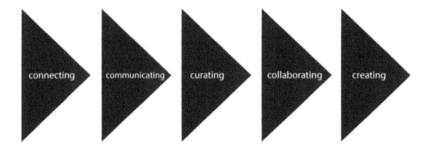

Figure 2. 5Cs linear

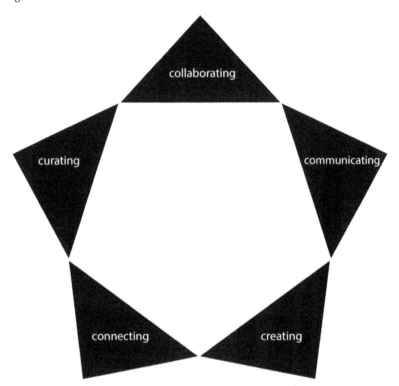

Figure 3. The 5Cs non-linear

Frameworks and taxonomies used in this way establish a manageable outline structure which help to describe the scope of the conceptual domain. It can be difficult to really understand in any great depth something that is conceptually unfamiliar without such an outline description and to analyse its validity. For the academic and learner a framework like the 5Cs might provide a reliable starting point for enquiry.

Anderson & Krathwohl (2001) **Revision of Bloom's Taxonomy**	▸ Creating ▸ Evaluating ▸ Analysing ▸ Applying ▸ Understanding ▸ Remembering
Salmon (2002; 2013) **The 5 stage model of learning and teaching online**	▸ Development ▸ Knowledge construction ▸ Information exchange ▸ Online socialisation ▸ Access and motivation
Belshaw (2011) **8Cs Digital Literacies**	▸ Cultural ▸ Cognitive ▸ Constructive ▸ Communicative ▸ Confident ▸ Creative ▸ Critical ▸ Civic
Beetham & Sharpe (2011) **Model of students' digital literacies, a developmental model**	▸ Attributes and identity (I am...) ▸ Situated practices (I do...) ▸ Functional skills (I can...) ▸ Access and awareness (I have...)
Smyth *et al.* (2011) **3E Framework**	▸ Empower ▸ Extend ▸ Enhance
Bennett (2012) **Digital Practitioner Framework**	▸ Attributes ▸ Practices ▸ Skills ▸ Access

Figure 4 A Selection of pedagogical frameworks presented in chronological order

Looking closer at the 5Cs, we retrospectively identified similarities to other pedagogical frameworks including Salmon's e-tivities (2002, 2013), Beetham's and Sharpe's (2011) digital literacy model for students, Belshaw's (2011) 8Cs of digital literacies, Anderson and Krathwohl's Revision of Bloom's Taxonomy (2001), Smyth's 3E Framework as well as Bennett's (2012) Digital Practitioner Framework (see Figure 4).

Each of these frameworks attempts to present innovative thinking about learning and teaching concepts or logics by describing a clear, high level structure. The structure enables initial conceptualisation without requiring the learner to fully appreciate what is yet to be learnt. Such frameworks establish a trust that is essential to engagement with a theoretical model. The 5Cs offers such a logic, and it is one that may have wider application.

In the following section, the rationale behind the 5Cs will be illustrated. Authentic voices of participants linked to these have been included to present insight into how individual elements of the framework worked for the learners.

The 5Cs pedagogical rationale

The 5C Framework (Nerantzi & Beckingham, 2014) has already led to successful engagement with BYOD4L through two iterations in 2014 and one in 2015. Anecdotal evidence indicates that it is changing practices while also leading to the development of a collaborative model that makes scaling-up open cross-institutional CPD possible and perhaps more manageable and sustainable (Nerantzi & Beckingham, under review).

In this section we discuss the underpinning pedagogical rationale for creating this framework to engage not only early adopters (Rogers, 1963) or digital practitioners (Bennett, 2012), but also all those who are less confident in using social media and mobile technologies, or digital technologies more generally, for learning and teaching. Practitioners might not know why and how these could be used in their professional context to enhance student learning but also for their own professional development. The 5Cs therefore present a scaffold for pedagogical engagement and development of novices and experts alike as it builds and extends confidence, competence and capacity in the context of BYOD4L. The 5Cs help to normalise the use of social and mobile media in an educational context through experiential and immersive learning and development. This helps to close the gap between everyday life and education or as Wiley & Hilton (2009) call it the daily divide where education appears to be analogue, tethered, isolated, generic, closed and people consumers in contrast to everyday life that is digital, mobile, connected, personal, creators and open.

We also hypothesise that the 5C Framework offers a useful, reusable approach to structuring further pedagogical contexts and activities which is underpinned by critical and creative thinking. The 5Cs might also provide a useful framework for developing competence, confidence and capability among practitioners in the digital age leading to the enhancement of practices more widely. It also opens up the opportunity to challenge the very culture of CPD and the way we may traditionally approach this.

Connecting

In the 5Cs the first step to learning together is connecting. This is partly about the learner gaining confidence in making connections with the event but also others; more importantly, however, it is about developing the learners' understanding of the importance of social networking, peer support and community building in forming a resilient and lasting learning network.

Wiley and Hilton (2009) note that there are multiple connections between people, information and systems today using digital technologies and acknowledge that there seems to be a connectivity gap between everyday life and education. They claim that formal education is still less connected and often operated in isolation. Siemens (2005; 2006, 29-30) introduced Connectivism as "a theory describing how learning happens in the digital age. [...] Connectivism is the integration of principles explored by chaos, network, complexity and self-organisation theories." For Siemens (2006) Connectivism enables uninterrupted knowledge creation in networks, while Downes (2005) defines it as connective knowledge. Learning based on the above is seen as a process based on connections. The connections become the enablers of social learning defined by our connectedness (Dron and Anderson, 2007). However, the notions of autonomy versus belonging linked to groups in networks is debated by some scholars. Downes (2007) for example dismisses the notion of groups in networks altogether but supports the notion of communities, while Dron and Anderson (2007) recognise that there is a place for groups in networks. Wenger *et al.* (2011, 12) on the other hand, compare connections to hooks that help individuals become part of a community. They state "being more interconnected often increases the sense of community, and a desire to learn about a shared concern often motivates people to seek connections."

This is the stage in 5Cs where technological challenges are broken down and the learners have the time to trial different approaches for connecting with others in different social spaces, on and offline; a useful reminder that learning happens everywhere. Learners take steps to connect with the event, peers, facilitators and the wider community and their little successes in this area make their experience more personal and meaningful. This starts to create a sense of belonging that can boost their motivation for engagement and participation.

The notion of interconnectedness also extends to the signposting between social spaces and the profiles people share. This can be of great value to those new to using such spaces, providing a guiding path between the spaces through the inclusion of hyperlinks within their profile, linking a blog to Twitter, Twitter to LinkedIn for example. It also serves to contextualise how different spaces can be used and the value of connecting in these different spaces.

Communicating

At this stage learners begin to use the connections they have made and reach out to others. Initially, this communication may be mostly social in nature and linked to course details or technologies used (Salmon, 2002, 2013) but conversations become progressively more focused around specific learning points and activities.

By communication we mean a two-way process and an exchange and sharing of ideas, thoughts and experiences through conversations among peers and tutors to construct meaning and learning. While Vygotsky (1978) has done extensive work in this area in the context of children's learning, Laurillard (2012, 143) notes that conversation is also valuable for adult learning as it is "powerful for stimulating the productive internal conversation that leads to learning." However, equally important is the opportunity to learn by 'listening' and developing confidence in communicating within what are, for some, new channels and spaces for dialogue.

Communication channels are determined mostly by the learners and will be characterised by their capacity to accommodate multi-directional conversations involving a plethora of voices and their perspectives, or what Megele (2014) calls multilogues. Respecting each other's voice is paramount for promoting academic debate and becoming open to new ways of thinking and new perspectives. Communication supported by social media can be asynchronous (enabling flexible engagement and deep reflection) or synchronous (just in-time communication, conversation and debate, to make personal connection with other learners, build community as well as quick decision making), using text or other media and can be among peers, tutors, and mentors, as well as in small groups and in the wider learning community or network as learning happens socially in the open.

Communication could also be seen as the first step to sharing and social curation from sharing information, resources or viewpoints that might be useful to the wider community, while others would also see conversation as a form of collaboration where the emphasis is on collaboration as a process of learning and co-construction of meaning (Dillenbourg, 1999; Stahl *et al.*, 2006) and not a shared product or output (Roschelle & Teasley, 1995; Laurillard, 2012).

Curating

At this stage, learners develop the capacity to select useful information for themselves and others in a way that can be openly shared. Curation can be used as a means to organise information by topic, but during the process of doing so the curator will review and filter out what is considered to be inferior. Care is taken to honour authorship of the items curated by citing correctly. The opportunity to add your own perspective and opinions can be seen as adding additional value, and this also opens up the opportunity for open discussion. It is another way for active participation. In a way a curator moves beyond collecting artefacts, resources or ideas (which could be seen as a more inward facing, individual or group activity), towards curating, which is a dynamic, collaborative and open activity based on mutual sharing and reciprocity.

We see the act of sharing itself as a form of curating, while Rother *et al.* (2014) note that for them sharing is actually the most important part of curating. The 5 Resources Framework for Critical Digital Literacy developed by Hinrichsen and Coombs (2010, online), for example, incorporates the dimension of "Using". Under this, finding is defined as,

> The ability to gather appropriate information, resources
> and tools for a given purpose and to recognise and exploit
> the potential in communities, information, resources and
> tools encountered. This involves processes of asking,
> searching, filtering, curation and sharing.

While in Hague & Payton (2010, online) one of the components of their digital literacy model developed for schools is, "the ability to find and select information." It is our understanding that Belshaw's (2011) *8 Essential Elements of Digital Literacies* makes indirect reference to curation via the element Critical (Ct), as in applying critical thinking when evaluating technologies. This could be extended to being critical also when accessing resources, information and when connecting with others. The perspectives included here, make it clear that curation is a filtering process of information, connections, etc. These authors present curation less as a multi-directional process in a social context, which in our view are important features of curation that distinguishes it from other forms of collecting or filtering.

Participants take part in sharing information openly with the wider community using specific tools and contributing to collections started by others. At the same time they start to select and value curated artefacts shared by peers and thought leaders in their area of interest, which may be a topic, an approach to learning, a subject specialism or other focus that is meaningful to them.

The discerning identification and selection of relevant and useful knowledge and artefacts, therefore, is at the heart of curation. Learners develop a clearer understanding of the usefulness of curating for themselves and others and how to filter what they find. The act of filtering is a metacognitive act that develops with practice. Rheingold (2012, p.5) refers to the importance of '"critical consumption of information (aka crap detection)'." The learners develop a sophisticated strategy for making use of the relevant curated resources that are available while also being responsible for giving something back to their community by sharing what they have selected. Stodd (2014) discusses how social media are helping us to develop valuable skills in curation and publishing. The very process creates its own 4Cs as it commences with collecting, critical filtering, the art of curating in a chosen space and finally communicating. Of course curating can also be an activity that that is done solely for the benefit of the individual and indeed curated collections of information may be stored away for personal use alone.

Collaborating

Building upon the co-operative spirit of curating, the learners are ready to move towards a more collaborative learning relationship by utilising what they have learnt through conversations with others. At this stage, learners co-construct meaning and work together on problems and ideas to construct shared outputs or products (Roschelle & Teasley, 1995; Laurillard, 2012) or simply share the process of meaning making and learning (Dillenbourg, 1999; Stahl *et al.*, 2006).

While in co-operative learning the focus is on the individual (Slavin, 1980; Stahl, *et al.*, 2006; Johnson *et al.*, 2007). Collaboration, however, is a move towards the collective (Dillenbourg, 1999) and requires familiarity, competence and confidence based upon the previous stages. It also requires a good understanding of what can be achieved through collaboration, how collaboration works and which tools aid collaboration in open and social learning contexts and this stage provides these opportunities supported by social and mobile media. Social skills and networking are prerequisites for this to happen, as is the willingness to open-up and share with others (Weller, 2011; Stodd, 2014). The value of collaborative learning especially to construct higher order knowledge has been widely recognised, for example see Goodyear and Zenios (2007).

Computer-supported collaborative learning (CSCL) was born in the 90s (Batson, 1988) out of a small number of projects, including the Computer Supported Intentional Learning Environment (CSILE) project by Scardamalia & Bereiter (1991) which aimed to bring learners together and help them learn collaboratively supported by peers and tutors in ways that were not possible before (Dwyer & Suthers, 2005; Stahl *et al.*, 2006). Today we have a plethora of social media at our fingertips that make this idea happen more easily and quickly as the technology has become much more user and learner friendly in ways that no longer require advanced technical expertise ensuring we can all become collaborators. Stodd (2014, 5) stresses the importance of social learning to survive and thrive with change. For him learning in the social age is social. He reminds us that, "It's no longer about providing materials for people to learn and be tested on like parrots, more about creating spaces and a matrix of resources for people to engage with to create meaning. It's about scaffolded social learning environments where we facilitate, nurture and support."

Learners reflect on their practice and explore the specific digital tools and platforms that are useful for collaboration. They are encouraged to identify opportunities for small-scale collaboration so that they can practise working and learning collaboratively and are able to reflect on and learn from this experience.

Creating

In this fifth stage, learners are confident and able to be more playful, experimental and creative. They have come to recognise the value of play for learning and are prepared to explore and play with ideas to make learning happen. Learners are encouraged to use some of the suggested digital and social media tools and explore other ones they have discovered and express themselves creatively. They learn through playful making on their own or with others. Gauntlett (2011) claims that social media are turning us all into digital creators and describes how this can be a powerful tool to engage us in meaningful learning activities. Seely Brown (2013) takes it further and notes that it is more than just making and proposes the notion of playful tinkering as an act of opening-up and being open and engaging in constant reframing of contexts to thrive in change. For him Home Sapiens (Knowledge), Homo Faber (Maker) and Home Luden (Play) are three dimensions in one that are vital for the 21st century learning.

This is the stage where learners use their curiosity to become much more adventurous and play with pedagogical ideas. They synthesise old and new ideas; both their own and these of others. They are prepared to take risks and learn from failure. Craft (2000), discusses possibility thinking: this "what if" is the question learners ask themselves and others, but the same approach to thinking also encourages them to see problems as opportunities for exploration and discovery (Jackson, 1996). This becomes the force, not just for thinking and reflection, but also for play and experimentation. The community's engagement in such activities boosts the confidence of individual learners who feel safe and supported, despite the openness. Many of the learners who engage actively with creating will perhaps have moved closer to towards the digital residents spectrum (White & Le Cornu, 2011) as they feel comfortable about sharing their unpolished creations with others as work-in-progress and are prepared to engage in meaningful conversation around their work with their peers as well as activities of (co-)creation.

Reflecting on the 5Cs and next steps

The 5Cs Framework has been developed to provide a scaffold for learning and development for a wide range of participants. The linear and non-linear application of the 5Cs provided further flexibility for engagement and scaffolded learning that can be tailored to different learning contexts to develop confidence, competence and capability. The 5Cs provides a new way to engage in academic open and collaborative CPD. Further research is required to explore the learners' experiences linked to the 5Cs in the context of BYOD4L and in other pedagogical contexts, such as online, face-to-face, blended and open learning situations as it is emerging that the 5Cs can be a useful pedagogical framework that fosters critical and creative thinking and actions in the context of CPD as well as learning more widely.

BYOD4L as a topic, the open CPD model that is evolving through this as well as the 5Cs model all continue to intrigue us. Each of these facets signals a new way of thinking, action and practice; a view of learning echoed throughout this book.

Acknowledgements

We would like to thank the MELSIG community and Andrew Middleton particularly, for embracing the idea to offer BYOD4L under the SIG umbrella. It has helped revitalise interest and engagement which we were hoping to achieve. We would also like to take this opportunity to thank all BYOD4L collaborators and participants who joined us in January and July 2014 and/ or January 2015 and for their passion and commitment. We have learnt a lot and know that none of this would have been possible without them. A special thank you goes to Ellie Livermore our project artist.

References

Anderson, L. W. and Krathwohl D. R., eds. (2001). A taxonomy for learning, teaching, and assessing: A revision of Bloom's taxonomy of educational objectives. New York: Longman.

Batson, T.W. (1988). The ENFI project: A networked classroom approach to writing instruction. In: Academic Computing. Vol. 2 Iss. 5. pp. 32-33, 55−56.

Beetham, H. and Sharpe, R. (2013). Rethinking pedagogy for a digital age: Designing for 21st Century learning, 2nd edition, Oxon: Routledge.

Beetham, H. and Sharpe, R. (2011). Digital literacies workshop. Paper presented at the JISC Learning Literacies Workshop, Birmingham. Online at: http://jiscdesignstudio. pbworks.com/w/page/40474566/JISC Digital Literacy Workshop materials

Belshaw, D. (2011). "What is digital literacy?" A pragmatic investigation, doctoral thesis, Durham: University of Durham. Online at: http://etheses.dur.ac.uk/ 3446/1/Ed.D._thesis_(FINAL_TO_UPLOAD).pdf?DDD29+

Bennett, L. (2012). Learning from the early adopters: Web2.0 tools, pedagogic patters and the development of the digital practitioner. Doctoral thesis, University of Huddersfield.

Craft, A. (2000). Creativity across the primary curriculum, Oxon: Routledge

Dillenbourg P. (1999) What do you mean by collaborative learning? In: P. Dillenbourg (ed.) Collaborative-learning: Cognitive and computational approaches, 1 – 19. Oxford: Elsevier Online at: http://halshs.archives-ouvertes.fr/docs/00/19/02/40/PDF/Dillenbourg-Pierre-1999.pdf

Downes, S. (2007). Groups vs networks, November 24. Online at: http://www.downes.ca/post/42521

Downes, S. (2005). An Introduction to Connective knowledge, 22 Dec 2005. Online at: http://www.downes.ca/post/33034

Dron, J. and T. Anderson (2007). Collectives, networks and groups in social software for e-Learning. Proceedings of World Conference on E-Learning in Corporate, Government, Healthcare, and Higher Education Quebec. Retrieved Feb. 16: 2008.

Dwyer, N. and Suthers, D. (2005). A study of the foundations of artifact-mediated collaboration. In: T. Koschmann, D. Suthers & T. W. Chan, eds., "Computer supported collaborative learning 2005: The Next 10 Years!", Mahwah, NJ: Lawrence Erlbaum Associates. 135-144. Online at: http://lilt.ics.hawaii.edu/papers/2005/Dwyer-Suthers-CSCL-2005.pdf

Gauntlett, D. (2011). Making is connecting: The social meaning of creativity, from DIY and knitting to YouTube and Web2.0. Cambridge: Polity Press.

Goodyear, P. and Zenios, M. (2007). Discussion, collaborative knowledge work and epistemic fluency. British Journal of Educational Studies, 55 (4), 351 – 368.

Hague, C. and Payton, S. (2010). Digital literacy across the curriculum. Futurelab. Online at: http://www.futurelab.org.uk/sites/default/files/Digital_Literacy_handbook_0.pdf

Hinrichsen, J. and Coombs, A. (2011). The 5 resources model of critical digital literacy. JISC, Greenwich: University of Greenwich. Online at: https://sites.google.com/site/dlframework/home

Jackson, N. (1996). Imagining a different world. In: Jackson, N., Oliver, M., Shaw, M. and Wisdom, J. (1996) "Developing Creativity in Higher Education", 1 – 9.

Johnson, W., Johnson, R. and Smith, K. (2007). The State of cooperative learning in postsecondary and professional settings. In: Educational Psychology Review, 19(15), 15 – 29.

Laurillard, D. (2012). Teaching as a design science: Building pedagogical patterns for learning and technology. Oxon: Routledge.

Megele, C. (2014). Theorizing Twitter chat. In: Journal of Perspectives in Applied Academic Practice, 2 (2), 46 – 51. Online at: http://jpaap.napier.ac.uk/index.php/JPAAP/article/view/106

Nerantzi, C. (2014). A personal journey of discoveries through a DIY open course development for professional development of teachers in higher education. Invited paper in: Journal of Pedagogic Development, University of Bedfordshire, 42 – 58. Online at: http://www.beds.ac.uk/jpd

Nerantzi, C. & Beckingham, S. (under review). Scaling-up open CPD for teachers in higher education using a snowballing approach.

Nerantzi, C. & Beckingham, S. (2014). BYOD4L: Our magical open box to enhance individuals' learning ecologies. In: Jackson, N. & Willis, J., eds., "Life-wide Learning and Education in Universities and Colleges". e-Book, online at: http://www.learninglives.co.uk/e-book.html

Rheingold, H. (2012). Net smart: How to thrive online. Cambridge: MIT Press.

Rogers, E. M. (1983). Diffusion of innovation (3rd ed.), London: Free Press.

Roschelle, J. and Teasley, S. (1995). The construction of shared knowledge in collaborative problem solving. In: O'Malley, C., eds., "Computer-supported collaborative learning", Berlin, Germany: Springer Verlag, 69 – 197.

Rother, K., Goodier, S., Nyahodza, L. and Czerniewicz, L. (2014). Curation for participation: An 8-step guide to curating open scholarly content. OpenUCT Initiative, Cape Town: OpenUCT Initiative, available at https://open.uct.ac.za/bitstream/handle/11427/8431/openuct_guide_curation_for_participation_WORKING_VERSION_151014.pdf?sequence=1

Salmon, G. (2013). E-tivities: The key to active online learning. 2nd edition, Oxon: Routledge.

Salmon, G. (2002). E-tivities: The key to active online learning. Oxon: Routledge.

Scardamalia, M. and Bereiter, C. (1991). Higher levels of agency in knowledge building communities: A challenge for the design of new knowledge media. Journal of the Learning Sciences, 1, 37 – 68.

Seely-Brown, J. (2013). Learning in and for the 21st century. Public Lecture and Answer Session. In: C.J. Koh Professorial Lecture Series No.4, Singapore: Office of Education Research,NIE/NTU.

Siemens, G. (2006). Knowing knowledge. Online at: www.knowingknowledge.com

Siemens, G. (2005). Connectivism: A learning theory for the digital age. International Journal of Instructional Technology and Distance Learning, 2 (10).

Simkins, S. and Maier, M. (2010). Just-in-time teaching. Stylus Publishing, LLC.

Slavin, R. E. (1980). Cooperative Learning. In: Review of Educational Research, Summer 1980, 50 (2), 315 – 342.

Smyth, K., Bruce, S., Fotheringham, S. and Mainka, C. (2011). Benchmark for the use of technology modules. Edinburgh: Edinburgh Napier University. Online at: http://staff.napier.ac.uk/services/vice-principal-academic/academic/TEL/TechBenchmark/Documents/3E%20Framework.pdf

Stahl, G., Koschmann, T. and Suthers, D. (2006). Computer-supported collaborative learning: An historical perspective. In: Sawyer, R. K., ed., Cambridge handbook of the learning sciences, Cambridge: UK: Cambridge University Press, 409 – 426. Online at: http://gerrystahl.net/cscl/CSCL_English.htm

Stodd, J. (2014). We all need to know about the Social Age. In Stodd, J., ed., Exploring the social age & the new culture of learning, Life-wide Magazine, Issue 11, September, 4 – 7.

Vygotsky, L. S. (1978). Mind in society: The development of higher psychological processes. Cambridge, MA: Harvard University Press.

Weller, M. (2011). The digital scholar: How technology is transforming scholarly practice. London: Bloomsbury.

Wenger, E., Trayer, B. and de Laat, M. (2011). Promoting and assessing value creation in communities and networks: A conceptual framework. Rapport 18, Ruud de Moor Centrum, Open Universiteit. Online at: http://www.social-learning-strategies.com/documents/Wenger_Trayner_DeLaat_Value_creation.pdf

White, D. and Le Cornu, A. (2011). Visitors and residents: A new typology for online engagement. First Monday, 16(9).

Wiley, D. and Hilton, J. (2009). Openness, dynamic specialization, and the disaggregated future of higher education. International Review of Research in Open and Distance Learning, 10(5), 1-16. Online at: http://www.irrodl.org/index.php/irrodl/article/view/768

Scenario: Starting points and social brainstorming

Learning is often a process of refining what you already know and adding definition to this with the support of others. Charlie uses this principle to engage his Engineering students in week one and then keep them engaged throughout the module. In the first class he establishes a class mind map using Mind 42 and shares the access to it using student email addresses.

He has already added the weekly topics and the main nodes and invites everyone to shout out what they know or expect to cover using key words. They add sub-nodes and begin to add some notes and links to these. The students are expected to revisit the mind map each week, add links and pictures. They review and update it using the last five minutes of class time each week to check that key points are included and accurate.

The map is there to promote discussion and personal research, help each student reflect on their understanding of the module topics, contribute to the way knowledge is represented and develop this with their own ideas and examples.

Key tools: Mind42, Mindmeister

Based on: Blaschke, L. (2014). Using social media to engage and develop the online learner in self-determined learning. Research In Learning Technology, 22.

Reflections on 10 Days of Twitter
for Regent's University London

Chris Rowell

Introduction

In this case study I will describe how I set up and ran a short online course called *10 Days of Twitter for Regent's University London* for staff. It was originally developed by Helen Webster to support STEM at Cambridge University. Helen made the course content available under a Creative Commons licence.

Over the last couple of years I have run a number of workshops showing staff how to set up and manage a Twitter account. I could see from the workshop attendance there was a demand to know more about Twitter and how it could be used. Whilst the immediate feedback from these sessions was good it became apparent to me that when I met these staff later they were still unsure of how to use Twitter in their own professional practice. I wanted to run the course so that staff could move beyond setting up their initial profile and making their first Tweet to real situations where they were interacting with their colleagues and their wider professional networks.

The Regent's University iteration of the course started on the 13th May 2014 and each day over the following ten days (including weekends) a blog post was published which gave an outline of the day's topic and set a short task that participants were expected to complete. The schedule started with the basics of setting up a Twitter profile, what to Tweet about, 'following people', and using hashtags before moving on to look at more complex Twitter tools such as Tweetdeck and Hootsuite.

I was initially attracted to this course because of my experience as a facilitator on the 'Bring Your Own Devices 4 Learning' course (*see* Nerantzi & Beckingham chapter) which showed me the potential of delivering an online staff CPD event that could be delivered over a short period of time focusing on a specific aspect of social media within a higher education environment.

Facilitating 10 Days of Twitter

Following Helen's guidance (http://10daysoftwitter.wordpress.com/running-10dot/) for *10 Days of Twitter*, my main task as facilitator was to put up the daily post on the blog and oversee the Twitter interactions that followed over the next 24 hours. In terms of the blog I stuck fairly closely to Helen's original posts. I changed some of the examples given in the posts to make them more relevant to the subjects taught at Regent's University. So that I made recommendations for useful people to follow in subjects like Business, Psychology, Film Studies, Fashion and Design and Languages.

I also had several comments posted on the blog and questions emailed to me which I responded to over the ten days.

I had set up a separate Twitter account (@RUL10DoT) to support the course and I used this twitter account to interact with the participants. By the end of the course I had written 401 Tweets and had 78 people following the account. Monitoring the Twitter timeline was a rewarding, but also time consuming, experience. Over the course of the ten days I averaged 40 Tweets a day on the @RUL10Dot account whilst I also maintained my own personal Twitter account (@chr5rowell).

Running the Twitter course was not my main activity over this period of time. I had to continue with my 'day job' which includes the numerous activities of being the Deputy Learning Technology Manager and it was difficult finding the time to manage all these activities.

Overall the experience of being a facilitator on the course was a good one. I really enjoyed seeing the learning and collaboration taking place. Each day I could see the number of tweets increasing and gradually interactions started to take place between the participants.

Observations about the learners

Over the course of the ten days there were over 50 participants at Regent's University who engaged with the course. The nature of their engagement varied a lot. At one end of the engagement spectrum there were 'lurkers', learning by watching and observing the blog and tweets; at the other end of the spectrum were participants who became highly active, tweeting regularly in response to the daily tasks.

The #RUL10DoT course was available to all academic and professional staff in the University. Judging by the informal feedback I received from the participants a few had never used Twitter prior to the course but several had a Twitter account in the past but were unsure of what to do with it and often could not see how it could be relevant to their own professional development. They were attracted to the course because if offered them the prospect of developing Twitter in their own professional context.

'Lurking' is a somewhat disparaging term for what I see as useful, legitimate activity. Often it is the way many people learn online (Dennen, 2008) and although it is difficult to evidence their observations many of the participants on the course told me in person they did not feel confident enough to send their own Tweets but were watching the activity on the RUL10DoT course and learning how Twitter works. Once they had signed up with Twitter they spent time just looking and watching what others were tweeting about. Through this observation they learned about Twitter conventions and some eventually gained enough confidence to start Tweeting themselves.

In fact, the 'lurkers' are essential if a successful community of practice is to emerge out of this learning activity (Arnold 2010). The experienced core (the facilitator - myself) led and guided the group and these were followed by a second group who engaged and participated every day. The third group in Wenger's words (Wenger, 1991) are the 'peripheral group', the passive participants (the 'lurkers'), who learn from the others and then may (or may not) move into one of the other groups as they learn to retweet, tweet and engage with other on the course.

Furthermore, consider the following quote from Lev Vygotsky on the Zone of Proximal Development which he defines as "the distance between the actual developmental level as determined by independent problem solving and the level of potential development as determined through problem solving under adult guidance, or in collaboration with more capable peers"

(Vygotsky, 1978, p.86). I think this is what is happening with the Twitter interactions on the course. The #RUL10DoT course created co-operative learning exercises where less experienced or competent participants develop with help from more skilful peers – within the 'zone of proximal development.'

What worked

The #RUL10DoT course was launched at Regent's Staff Conference on the 13th with a Twitter workshop on *Getting Started with Twitter* in the morning which I jointly ran with the Deputy Library Manager, Andy Horton. We had ten attendees at the workshop and four of them had never used Twitter, so by the end of the session they had all set up their accounts. The other six had accounts, but had not used them with any real purpose or did not know what to Tweet about. During the workshop we gave a brief overview of Twitter, covering many points in 20 minutes and then gave them a pack of cards adapted from Sue Beckingham's slideshow on *Getting Started with Twitter* (Beckingham, 2013 online). At that point we asked them to send a tweet using the course hashtag #RUL10DoT. It was really useful having a face to face event to 'kick off' the course as this immediately generated several tweets using the hashtag. It also became apparent that most of the staff who came to the workshop then went on to participate in the course.

When I started teaching the course I did not know how many staff members would engage with it. We can get some idea of the participation by looking at the online analytical tools supplied by Wordpress, the blogging platform, and Twitter. The course blog statistics illustrate how engagement increased. On Day One there were over 30 visitors and 47 views to the blog. By Day Two this had leapt to over 50 visitors and 188 views of the site. Not all of these would have been Regent's staff members, although I was more than a little surprised to see so many people 'checking out' the blog posts.

I found Twitter stats were equally surprising. By the end of the second day there were over 50 people using the #RUL10DoT hashtag. By the end of the course the @RUL10DoT account had 78 followers – most of them staff at Regent's University, but there were others mainly from other UK universities.

A couple of days after the course I set a course evaluation questionnaire (using Survey Monkey) and posted the link on the course blog. The results of the questionnaire were very positive showing that those who completed the course felt that it catered for their specific needs and would be useful in developing their own professional networks. It is likely that only those staff who had a positive experience of the course and stayed engaged until the end will have been aware of the evaluation. Therefore the results need to be treated with caution.

Results of the evaluation

The online evaluation survey was completed by 11 of the #RUL10DoT participants. The participants answered ten questions about their experience of the course and its value to them. The survey concluded with a question about the format of the course and interest in pursuing similar courses about social media.

1.	In which of the following categories is your main job role at Regent's University London? Academic staff 18.18% (n.2) Professional Services 81.82% (n.9)
2.	What was your general opinion of the #RUL10DoT course? Excellent 63.64% (n.7) Good 36.36% (n.4) Average 0.00% (n.0) Indifferent 0.00% (n.0) Poor 0.00% (n.0)
3.	How well did the course cater for your specific needs? Very satisfied 63.64% (n.7) Satisfied 27.27% (n.3) Partially satisfied 9.09% (n.1) Not satisfied 0.00% (n.0)
4.	Will you be able to apply what you have learnt to develop your online network? Yes 100.00% (n.11) No 0.00% (n.0)
5.	Did the course keep you engaged for the whole 10 days? Yes 54.55% (n.6) No 45.45% (n.5)

(continued)

6.	How satisfied were you with the instruction and course material on the *#RUL10DoT* website? Very satisfied 54.55% (n.6) Satisfied 36.36% (n.4) Partially satisfied 9.09% (n.1) Not satisfied 0.00% (n.0)
7.	How satisfied were you with the activities on the course? Very satisfied 45.45% (n.5) Satisfied 45.45% (n.5) Partially satisfied 9.09% (n.1) Not satisfied 0.00% (n.0)
8.	How would you rate the 'selfie' competition? Enjoyed it 70.00% (n.7) Disliked it 0.00% (n. 0) Did not do it 30.00% (n.3)
9.	Which of the following topics would you be most interested in learning about via an additional online course in the future? 5 Days of LinkedIn at Regent's University London 90.91% (n.10) 10 Days of Blogging at Regent's University London 54.55% (n.6) 7 Days of education apps at Regent's University London 45.45% (n.5) 8 Days of Media at Regent's University London 7.27% (n.3) 7 Days of Blackboard at Regent's University London 18.18% (n.2) 9 Days of Mobiles 4 Learning at Regent's University London 36.36% (n.4) 6 Days of Social Media in Education at Regent's Uni 36.36% (n.4) I do not want to do any further online courses 9.09% (n.1)
10	Do you have any further comments about the *#RUL10DoT* course? "Great work, Chris." "Fantastic idea it was! Very well delivered!" "Very good." "Have now downloaded the app on my phone, really simple to use thanks to Chris."

Table 1. Results of the #RUL10DoT course survey

The personal value of running this open course

Personally, I think there are three things of value I have gained from organising this course on Twitter. Firstly, it has given me the confidence to know that I can plan, organise and teach this type of online course. I have never been involved in a purely online course before as most of my previous experience has been working on the integration of blended learning.

Secondly, it has shown that there is a demand from the staff here at Regent's for this type of training. It is the first time our Learning Technology Team has tried this type of training with our staff. Previously, most training has been delivered in workshops or on a one to one level of engagement. Judging by the numbers engaging in the course (53 using the hashtag and 78 following the Twitter account) and our feedback so far staff really like the format of short online courses based on a specific subject.

Thirdly, it's been a useful networking experience. I have met many new people in the University through the course. Some of these staff would not have come to a face to face session because of their work loads and time constraints. Even in a University, it is very difficult for busy professionals to find time in their working day for training and CPD events. It has meant that I have developed a new type of working relationship with them and maybe this can be developed further into the future.

Challenges of running the course

One of the biggest challenges of running the course was keeping the momentum and maintaining the motivation of the learners. I could clearly see from the numbers viewing the course blog that there was a tailing off in participation from a peak of 188 views to 10 views by Day 5 of the course – admittedly this was a Sunday but I had anticipated this and had already planned a 'Selfie Competition' to boost motivation once more.

The competition was simple. Participants on the course just had to Tweet a 'Selfie' of themselves using the hashtag #RULselfie to enter. I approached the Learning and Development section of HR in the University and they gave me £100 credit to buy some prizes from the University book shop. I had a great response to the competition and numbers on the blog were boosted again by Monday. I just think adding a fun element to the course is really important!

I also tried adding more visual content to increase motivation. I embedded some existing YouTube videos into the blog and started tweeting more photos and links to videos, although in retrospect I think I could have developed this further. If I had had more time it would have been interesting to interview some of the staff doing the course about their views, questions or issues. These could have then been embedded into the blog posts and would have made excellent videos for further discussion and engagement.

Organising a purely online course was a new experience for me and I found the lack of instant feedback from the learners challenging even though Twitter is a fairly instant communication tool. At times I really wasn't sure whether to send messages or connect with people on the course. I could have been more proactive with some participants who started strongly and then faded out.

Lessons Learnt and Tips for others

There are a few lessons learnt and tips I would recommend to others thinking about running the 10DoT course:

1. **Make time** – Running the Twitter course takes up a fair amount of time which is difficult to quantify. Throughout the day I was always checking the Twitter timeline and responding appropriately. This allowed me to get on with my 'day job' but did add to my overall workload by the end of the day. If possible keep your other activity to a minimum over the 10 days. Also I ran the course over the weekend. This was a mistake. Activity dropped off considerably over the weekend and it also meant I had to administer what was going on. If I ran the course again I would just stick to working days.
2. **Motivation** – Think about the motivation factors for the learners. Even over a relatively short period, learners dropped out of the course. I used the 'selfie' competition to re-engage participants which worked to some degree but if I had had more time I think I could have done more, especially using and embedding videos into the blog. Perhaps interviewing some of the participants about their Twitter experiences would have made the blog posts more motivating and interesting.
3. **Value of face to face meetings** – When I run the course again I will organise more supporting workshops. Having the initial one on the first day really worked but next time I think I could have organised two or three more face to face sessions. I'm sure most of the participants wouldn't have turned up but it would have been a useful addition to those who wanted it.

4. **Develop a team** – Don't just run the course on your own. I asked a variety to people in the University to be co-facilitators which really just meant them helping to respond and encourage people to Tweet over the ten days. So I had a fellow Learning Technologist, a Marketing Lecturer and the Head of Careers and Business Relations as fellow facilitators. This worked really well. Andy Horton (Deputy Librarian) was great at moving the Twitter chats along and he even wrote a guest blog post on who to follow on Twitter aimed specifically at Regent's staff.

All in all it's been a great experience and I'm planning to run the course again next academic year.

References

#10Dot Ten Days of Twitter. Online at: http://10daysoftwitter.wordpress.com/

#RUL10DoT Ten Days of Twitter for Regent's University London. Online at: http://regents10dot.wordpress.com/

Arnold, N., & Paulus, T.(2010). Using a social networking site for experiential learning: Appropriating, lurking, modeling and community building. The Internet and Higher Education, Volume 13, Issue 4, December 2010, Pages 188–196 [Special Issue on Web 2.0]

Beckingham, S. (2013). Getting started with Twitter. Online at: http://www.slideshare.net/suebeckingham/getting-started-with-twitter-23557615.

Paz Dennen, V. (2008) Pedagogical lurking: Student engagement in non-posting discussion behavior http://www.sciencedirect.com/science/article/pii/S074756320700115X last accessed 17th December 2014

Horton, A. (2014). *The Search for Interesting People on Twitter*. Blog post. Online at: http://totallyrewired.wordpress.com/2014/05/12/the-search-for-interesting-people-rul10dot/

Lave, J., & Wenger, E. (1991). Situated learning: Legitimate peripheral learning. University of Cambridge Press.

Vygotsky, L.S. (1978). Mind in Society: The Development of Higher Psychological Processes. Cambridge, Massachusetts: Harvard University Press.

Scenario: The story of learning in groups

Friends, learning sets and Personal Learning Networks - lend me your ideas.

Anne is part of an established social network study group (a PLN). They take it in turns to curate their study postings and then share them back every two weeks to reflect what they've learnt together. This week it has been Anne's turn to select significant social media posts and add a narrative. Using Storify she creates a free text narrative and intersperses the free text with links to websites, blog posts, their Pinterest folders, embedded videos, photos and articles. She credits the sources of this media using hyperlinks. It's taken her all evening but now she's ready to save the Storify and share it back with her PLN.

Key tools: Storify and other social media tools

Based on slides by: Corinne Weisgerber on Slideshare

http://www.slideshare.net/corinnew/teaching-with-storify-diigo and hootsuite?ref=http://www.slideshare.net/featured/category/education

Back pocket learning
— enabling 'digital natives' to use smart devices to ensure understanding of the threshold concepts of journalism

Shelly Stevenson and Dr Bianca Wright

Introduction

Journalism is changing – the way we gather news and the way we publish it. According to Westmoreland this change is because of the introduction of the touch screen. As a result publishing is easier and broadcasting is no longer the privilege of only the wealthy. (Westmoreland, 2013) However, this paradigm shift in the profession needs to be mirrored in education, addressed in how we teach journalism, since it is often still taught in a traditional way.

This leads to problems in understanding, partially because in broadcast-heavy courses the emphasis is on learning the equipment needed to produce radio and television content rather than on the process and skill of news reporting. The time spent focusing on navigating the kit reduces the time spent learning the key concepts behind journalism. As a consequence it can sometimes become difficult for learners to understand completely what is essential to the story. They can produce technically competent radio or television packages without fully understanding what news is.

According to Nickerson 'Understanding is an active process. It requires the connecting of facts, the relating of newly acquired information to what is already known, the weaving of bits of knowledge into an integral and cohesive whole' (cited in Entwistle, 2009, p. 45). Because the threshold concepts become buried in the midst of skills learning there is an obfuscation of the theory necessary to understand how journalism works. Real learning in this case involves 'not only having knowledge but also doing something with it' (*ibid*). If the output produced sounds good but do not tell the audience the story then we have not produced anything worthwhile.

These threshold concepts which are, according to the Reuters Handbook of Journalism (2014), understanding the audience and telling the story. However, these have, in the past few years at Coventry University, been somewhat overlooked in our focus on product rather than comprehension of the fundamentals of news. Because of this it appears that some students have only a basic knowledge of journalism and the fear is that some 'even got through a degree programme …at this level' by mimicry rather than understanding (Cousin, 2006). Teaching these concepts without at the same time requiring learning complicated new kit would enable the first years to focus on understanding the journalism threshold concepts; of ethics, storytelling, news values and audience.

Rationale

With this in mind, we tested the 'Back Pocket' theory for the students in the first year intake 2012-2013 using induction to teach the core skill – how to tell a story. Back pocket journalism, a term coined by one of the researchers, draws on the concept of mobile journalism (MoJo), which emphasises the use of the now almost ubiquitous mobile technologies, specifically the smart phone, to report and produce journalistic artefacts (Mills, Egglestone, Rashid and Väätäjä, 2012). The thinking behind this is that most of our first year intake students grew up with digital technologies and could be considered 'Digital Natives'. A digital native by definition is someone who has grown up with the current technology and so has ability to use it well. (Prensky, 2001). The pilot project also took cognisance of the potential of m-learning to "have transformed pedagogy and facilitated student engagement in a variety of course contexts" (Cochrane and Bateman 2009). The support for this was an andragogical approach to facilitate learners to be 'as self-directed as possible, allowing them to be creative with assignments and projects' (Blondy, 2007), while still cementing core concepts related to the practice of journalism.

Andragogy as proposed by Knowles (1980) is an educational theory focused on adult learners with a specific emphasis on the "learner's ability, need, and desire to take responsibility for learning" (Hiemstra & Sisco, 1990). Within the higher education context, the adoption of andragogy as a teaching and learning method is mixed. Yoshimoto, Inenaga and Yamada (2007) noted that the use of andragogy at higher levels of education was more developed in Germany than in the United Kingdom or Japan. The choice to move towards an andragogical approach was motivated by the need to address issues of conceptual understanding of journalistic issues and production in an engaging and student-centred manner. Incorporating technological tools that the students use on a daily basis further relocated the required learning to a student centre rather than a classroom focus, allowing students to take responsibility for their own learning.

As this was a pilot project, it was important to gauge student readiness for the implementation of such an approach. A 2011 study by the University of Sheffield (2011) found that 99.6% of students at the university had mobile phones, with 56% owning a smartphone. While the experience of the researchers had pointed to the common use of mobile phones and tablet computers by students, it was necessary to test this assumption through some informal research. During the 'raise your hands' survey at the beginning of the academic year 2012/2013 all 37 students had a smartphone or a tablet at induction.

Once it was established that the students had access to the required devices, they were sent out to gather stories using their phones and tablets to create the 'Freshers Guide' published on iCov.co.uk, the journalism course outward facing website. The students were allowed to choose the format of their story -, audio, video, slide show, or text - it didn't matter as long as the story was clear. The aim was to direct the students attention to the main or threshold journalism concepts while creating content using what they already have in their back pocket.

They were instructed to think about their audience – someone like themselves – and find what would be appropriate to tell other first year students about the surrounding area. The students were then told that they needed to create these articles/packages/films using what was in their 'back pocket', collaborating with each other using their phones and apps.

The apps that they used were the ones most familiar to them. This had the double benefit of helping them to grasp the story without the fear of the unknown technology, and the teaching team learned new ways to gather the news when the students shared their app knowledge. This was in keeping with Knowles' idea that "curricular perspectives change from postponed to immediacy of application and from subject-centeredness to performance-centeredness (1980).

Freeing them from the 'kit' consequence enabled them to change the way they viewed what they were creating and why, and focus on the narrative. As a good journalist can tell you, storytelling is primarily about developing a 'nose for news', a shift in the way one thinks – developing the news mind. Rather than passively gathering information, a news mind looks at each thing and says 'Who? What? When? Where? Why? How? Why not?' 'Why should I tell anyone about this?' 'Does this matter?' 'Who is the audience that I produce for?' 'Would they care?' 'Should they care?'

These are the threshold concepts of journalism, what is news and who is the audience– the rest falls into place after that.

As a result of this task, the stories produced were technologically as good as what could have been produced with the University equipment available and in some cases, were a better fit for news because of the immediacy and flexibility. As these students were also the first students at Coventry University to be given a Macbook Pro with editing software, they also were the first cohort to be able to edit and manage their products without relying on established computer labs. In all, they became information gathering, mobile publishing and broadcasting pods – each of them.

This had several implications:

First – those who were 'truly' comfortable with using the technology Digital Natives were able to jump in and develop news gathering quickly, they were able to 'get' the theory behind the news and understand news values and audience theory. Unfortunately the concept of the Digital Native did not apply to all of the students, even though all had a smart device. Although some were in fact, masters of digital living, others were only just able to use a few apps and obvious technology. It was discovered that the theory that *all* young people were Digital Natives was flawed. (Bennett, Maton & Kervin, 2008) A small percentage had access to the technology but not the interest or ability to use it well. The initial group work disguised this as the others carried the 'digital sub-natives'. This small percentage had the very issue we attempted to avoid by using the mobile devices – the difficulty of learning how to use the technology while trying to tell the story. However, the majority were in fact Digital Natives and responded strongly to this approach and flourished.

This experience of differing levels of digital competence made it clear that digital literacy still is an important component of learning, even at higher education level and even among those thought to be Digital Natives. From a teaching perspective it points to the need to draw on Beetham and Sharpe's digital literacy framework (2010), which describes "how students seem to develop higher order digital capabilities on a foundation of access and functional skills." The opportunity, then, lies in assessing initial skill levels at induction and finding ways to scaffold learning, building on those foundational skills in order to aid students in reaching higher levels of digital literacy and truly embracing their supposed position as Digital Natives.

This differentiation between students within the broader Digital Native group was confirmed the following year with the 2013/14 intake. Serendipitously that cohort were not taught Back Pocket learning in the first term and instead had the equipment focused heavy teaching method of previous years. By the second term it became apparent that the students were sadly lacking in the ability to tell stories although they had followed the previous year's scheme of work – without the back pocket session during induction.

Feedback from on the previous year's team found that some students gave the appearance of initially understanding, but had no real grounding in narrative.

One of the course lecturers, Natalie Chisholm, noted that "Getting them out finding the story and talking to people was crucial in the beginning. This gave them confidence and helped them to understand the importance of the story. That was missing from the second set (year B) – they didn't gain the confidence needed to gather the stories. I feel this demonstrated Back Pocket Journalism as a valuable practice."

Her experience was echoed in that of Teaching Assistant, Simon Pipe, who said, "There was a marked difference in student satisfaction. The second group (Group B) did not feel they had been taught. They weren't able to grasp the threshold concepts because the Back Pocket method was missing in the first three weeks – everything was dominated by the kit. I've seen this professionally as well – when learning new kit, the journalism suffered because of the practical demand of the manual control. They just weren't thinking about the journalism – what the story was."

Year B had the Back Pocket Journalism and Learning session at the beginning of the second term with remedial storytelling workshops. They then had weekly 'newsdays' workshops with one-on-one feedback. Even with this support some students did not grasp fully the threshold concepts and there were a larger number of fails at the end of the year, which seems to point to the need to "frontload" the experience at the beginning of the student journey in order to ensure understanding from the outset.

A comparison of the teaching methods of the two intakes, Year A 2012/13 and Year B 2013/14, revealed telling differences in approach and outcome: Year A were taught using an andragogical approach with the Back Pocket learning beginning with induction week, while year B used a pedagogical model based on the traditional teaching method of lectures and workshops with separate later skills teaching sessions with no Back Pocket journalism/learning in induction week. At the end of the first term Year A were more confident in the area of radio and were able to produce two hour shows in groups on alternate days for two weeks. This was due to their ability to gather news more easily. They spent more time in the narrative and less time grappling with the equipment. Year B struggled with radio and had difficulty producing a half hour of content over four days. In some cases year B students gave up entirely in the news week until we readdressed this in the second term.

Future development

The case study highlighted the differences in technological proficiency between students within the same cohort and emphasised the importance of digital literacy training to ensure that all students develop to the required level of digital competence. In order to address this issue, next year there will be an online hub for student support, using peer learning as well as lecturer support, rather than just the outward-facing hub for content. The proficient 'Digital Natives' will produce 'how to' videos for this hub introducing key apps for the various mobile platforms. This will ensure students can access help on demand. This hub will have a forum for questions on digital editing and examples of Back Pocket Journalism created by the lecturers and facilitators easily accessible on the mobile devices. This content will be allowed to evolve rather than be tightly scripted, and will foster a sharing of experiences and help support the self-directed nature of andragogy (Blondy, 2007).

Conclusion

This pilot project experience and the comparison with traditional teaching approaches seems to demonstrate how Back Pocket Journalism as a teaching and learning approach allows key concepts of storytelling and journalism basics to be taught using technology that is familiar. This freed students to be creative and solidified their understanding and deep learning on their own terms, without the complications of learning new equipment, for the most part. However, it is necessary to ensure that all the students are competent users of their own back pocket technology and demonstrate the required level of comfort and familiarity with the tools used. Adopting a digital literacy approach paired with peer learning and mentoring may address these issues.

References

Bennett, S., Maton, K., & Kervin, L. (2008). Digital Natives debate: A critical view of the evidence. *British Journal of Educational Technology* (Blackwell) 39(5), 775-786.

Blondy, L. C. (2007) Evaluation and application of andragogical assumptions to the adult online learning environment." *Journal of Interactive Online Learning* 6(2) Summer, 116-130.

Cochrane, T. * Bateman, R. (2010). Smartphones give you wings: Pedagogical affordances of mobile Web 2.0. *Australasian Journal of Educational Technology,* 26(1), 1-14.

Cousin, G. (2009). *An introduction to threshold concepts.* Vol. 17. New York: Planet.

Entwistle, N. (2009). *Teaching for understanding at university.* London: Palgrave Macmillan.

Hiemstra, R., & Sisco, B. (1990*). Individualizing instruction.* San Francisco: Jossey-Bass.

Knowles, M. S. (1980). *The modern practice of adult education: From pedagogy to andragogy.* Englewood Cliffs: Prentice Hall/Cambridge.

Mills, J., Egglestone, P., Rashid, O., &Väätäjä, H. (2012) "MoJo in action: The use of mobiles in conflict, community, and cross-platform journalism." *Continuum,* 26(5).

Prensky, M. (2001). Digital natives, digital immigrants: Part 1. *On the Horizon* (MCP UP Ltd) 9(5), September/October, 1-6.

Sharpe, R. & Beetham, H. (2010). Understanding students' uses of technology for learning: Towards creative appropriation. In: R. Sharpe, H. Beetham & S. de Freitas (Eds.) *Rethinking learning for the digital age: How learners shape their experiences,* 85 – 99. RoutledgeFalmer, London and New York.

Thompson Reuters. Reuters.com. November 2014. [Online] Available at: http://handbook.reuters.com/extensions/docs/pdf/ handbookofjournalism.pdf.

University of Sheffield (2014). Student Mobile Device Survey. [Online] Available from: https://www.sheffield.ac.uk/polopoly_fs/1.103665!/file/mobilesurvey2011.pdf, (2011).

Westmoreland, O. (2013). Mobile News, a review and model of journalism in an age of mobile media. *Digital Journalism* (Routledge) 1(1), 6-26.

Yoshimoto, K., Inenaga, Y., & Yamada, H. (2007). Pedagogy and andragogy in higher education: A comparison between Germany, the UK and Japan. *European Journal of Education,* 42 (1),.

Scenario: Getting to know you - Padlet selfie gallery

Geoff and Liz were back in the office. Today it was Geoff who was looking frazzled! "I just can't remember their names. How can we expect the students to feel at home if we can't even refer to them by name? I feel so embarrassed - but I reckon I've met 150 new faces this year..."

"You're right Geoff. It is really important. And it's important that the students know each other too. Some of them look so lonely. Try this. I've run it with my classes this year and I think it's working. Create a Padlet site for each of your classes and get every student to post their name and a selfie pic or video. I also got them to add one interesting fact like the thing they are most proud of. Once we got started we all posted."

Key tools: web browser, Padlet.com, cameras on student devices

HE BYOD
— ready or not?

Anne Nortcliffe

Introduction

This chapter presents the results and analysis of a quantitative study of students and staff at Sheffield Hallam University on how they are using their own smart devices to support student learning and enhance the student experience at Sheffield Hallam University. It also looks at which smart apps staff and students use.

Background

Mobile technology has the potential to meet learners' educational needs for accessible, inexpensive, anytime and anywhere interaction (Dodds & Fletcher, 2004; Ballagas *et al.*, 2006). It was perceived it would lead to new learning technology paradigms and deeper learning environments. Already mobile technology has had an impact on student e-learning evolving from mobile learning (m-learning) and then to ubiquitous learning (u-learning) (Liu and Hwang, 2010). Shin *et al.* (2011) identified how the quality and usability of mobile technology will lead to the widespread adoption of u-learning.

Bringing Your Own Device (BYOD) for work or study is now a common reality. Smart devices are having an impact on commercial practice (Chen *et al.*, 2010; Durbin, 2011; Lin & Brown, 2007) and are changing how people work: the people they engage with, what they do, where they work and when they work are all changing because of smart technologies. BYOD is also common on campus for the majority of the student population (Hamza & Noordin, 2012) and integral to the way students support their studies (Nortcliffe *et al.*, 2013; Nortcliffe & Middleton, 2012; Woodcock *et al.*, 2012a; Woodcock *et al.*, 2012b). Salmon (2013) suggests smart technology is not a threat and should be thought of as an opportunity for academics to use and exploit in connecting with learners and, as such, is capable of transforming their learning environment. Our learners are more attuned to what is possible even if they are not currently using them for learning.

Some students are embracing smart technology for learning (Woodcock, 2011) and their rationale for adopting this technology is consistent with previous research in supporting u-learning (Traxler, 2009; Sharples *et al.*, 2009). Their rationale for adoption ease of operation (Kang *et al.*, 2011), to enable autonomous learning (Camargo *et al.*, 2011), to benefit from their user-centred capabilities, and to enable the creation of personal learning spaces (Goodyear, 2000). Goodyear (2000) also notes that personal smart technologies finally achieve the promise of accessibility, ease of use, efficiency, supportiveness, and user-friendly attraction.

In the students' eyes BYOD technologies are supporting the shift towards u-learning, (Woodcock *et al.*, 2012b). The question remains though: how well are staff and students embracing this opportunity?

At Sheffield Hallam University the IT network monitoring systems indicates that:

- 58% (2,562 of 4,421) of staff employed at Sheffield Hallam University synchronise their smart devices with the staff MS Outlook Exchange server (in the period 31/7/11 to 26/6/13). 2,101 (48%) of staff have academic roles. 68% of devices synchronised by staff were iOS devices. Only a very small proportion of these were owned by the institution.
- On average 934 out of 39139 users (34,718 students and 4,421 staff) connected to the university's Wi-Fi network each day during the 2013 second semester.

At a time when many institutions are developing digital literacy strategies (e.g. the "Digitally Ready Project" at the University of Reading discussed by Brooks, 2014), the mobility of staff and their use of technology have been identified as key themes in the University's emerging Digital Strategy for supporting student learning (Hayes, 2013). The University's Vice Chancellor has indicated that personal and institutional smart technology is and will be a critical part of the University's future strategy for developing SHU students learning, literacy and innovation (Jones, 2013). Therefore it is timely and useful to consider to the extent and nature of academic staff use of smart technologies to support learning and to enhance their practice.

Research methods

The research aimed to determine the extent of confidence amongst staff and students in using their personal smart devices and to learn how they are using them to support their 'university life'; this included student learning, teaching, support and experience of being at university in general. It considered their dependency on their devices and whether the devices were used in formal teaching and learning environments (the "classroom"). It also looked at the enabling and inhibiting factors affecting the use of personal and institutional smart devices at university.

A quantitative survey approach was adopted. Two surveys were created and distributed using Google Forms; one targeted at academic staff and the other at students. The design of both surveys was similar, but the questions were tuned so that they were appropriate for each group, i.e. staff questions refer to their work related activities teaching, assessment, CPD and research, whereas students focus on their employability development and learning activities.

The questions used a combination of open, Likert and closed questions. Some of the questions were dynamic to improve the quality of returned data, improve the respondent's survey experience and to make it more likely they would complete the questionnaire (Schmidt, 1997). This was achieved by presenting questions to a respondent dependent upon their earlier responses.

Survey design and distribution

Adhering to good survey practice (Hague, 1993), the initial section of the surveys gathered relevant demographic and classification data for each respondent. For the students this included finding out about their current level of study, their course of study and information about their smart device ownership including whether it was on contract or not, and an estimation of their confidence in using the device. For academics the introductory questions identify staff departmental/services membership, University role and their length service at the University.

After the introductory questions both surveys enquired about the main usage of their personal device. If the user responded that they only used their device for personal activities, the questionnaire continued by asking if the user had considered using the device to support their academic practice. The survey for those who responded that they used their device to support their 'university life' in some form or other continued by asking how it was used for academic purposes.

The student survey was distributed using the virtual learning environment's email communication system through each course organisation site in order to reach every student in the faculty of Arts, Computing, Engineering and Science (ACES). This faculty was chosen as it represents a broad set of staff and students including those in Fine Art, Maths and Engineering and the researcher had ready access to each of the faculty's course organisation Blackboard sites. There are approximately 5,000 students in the faculty.

Staff participants were targeted through a personal email. The mailshot distribution list was made up of all known staff members identified by University IT with a personal or institutional smart device configured to access the University's staff email system (MS Outlook Exchange). University IT services supported the research and shared our interest in understanding the extent of BYOD usage within the institution for determining how support and infrastructure can be developed. The rationale for a targeted approach, as opposed to an indiscriminate distribution, was to ensure the survey was completed by staff who could be defined as already having an interest in the study due to their declared use of BYOD for work related purposes. 1,410 staff (unfortunately it is not possible to distinguish which staff are academics and which have other University roles) were emailed.

Open question response analysis

Two qualitative research analysis methods were used to evaluate the open responses.

First, a taxonomy analysis was used to codify the open responses to questions about the five most popular apps identified by each respondent, and how they are using these apps at university (discussed in Woodcock *et al.*, 2012). Following this, a grounded theory method (Glaser, 1964) was used to codify the survey's open responses.

Common themes from the open responses of staff and students were identified relating to the challenges and enabling factors of using smart devices and apps in the respondent's university life.

Results and Discussion

240 staff from all faculties and central services and 173 students responded to their respective surveys. Though the student survey was targeted at the faculty of ACES, it appears some students passed the survey to peers in another faculty. 98% staff and 94% student respondents declared they personally owned their smart device.

The data showed how staff and students owning a personal smart device are typically using it to support multiple dimensions of their university life. However, the student data suggests that they have integrated the use of their technology into their 'university life' more than academics. It also suggests they have become more dependent upon their device(s) (Table 1).

Use of smart devices (select one of the following)	Students %	Staff %
Mostly I do not use my device(s) in relation to my studies/work. My device is for my personal, social or work life rather than my university life.	15%	8%
I use my device(s) mostly for organising my life as a whole, including my personal, social and university life.	28%	21%
In my university life I often depend upon my device(s) to help with a few select activities like checking my email, browsing the Web, making notes, arranging to meet peers, etc.	32%	36%
As with other aspects of my life, I use my device(s) freely throughout my university life. I believe its multi-functionality really helps me with many aspects of my university life. It often replaces paper in many aspects of what I do, for example.	24%	35%

Table 1: Staff and student response to multi-choice question "Proportion of smart device usage amongst staff and student users in their university, social and personal life"

The findings in Table 1 mirror the staff and student reflections in their confidence to using their devices. 12 staff in a further open question requested training for how to use their personal device more effectively to support their university life.

Table 2 depicts the taxonomy category analysis and codification of staff and students Woodcock *et al.* (2012) in response to the question "What are the five most useful tools or apps you use at university on your smart device? (Where possible include the name and primary function of each tool)."

Category	Staff (% of 170)	Student (% of 238)	Examples of common smart apps used by respondents
Office productivity and assignment preparation	51%	64%	Word processing, spreadsheets, presentations, notes, Google Drive, Trello, GoodNotes, Annotate, Evernote, Padlet, Peddlepad, Haiku desks, Snotes, Skitch, Gimp, Onenotes, Penulitmate, Google Keep
Reading information	10%	5%	PDF readers, newspapers, iBooks
Searching for, browsing information and reference	41%	46%	Web browser, dictionary, thesaurus, You Tube, TED, Kahn Academy
Audio, image and video media capture	22%	17%	Camera, sketching, graphing, voice recorders, video camera, Celtx, SnapChat
Managing learning, work or research	77%	82%	Blackboard, library, iStudiez, Diigo, group work, timetabling, personal organisation, iTunesU, EBSCOhost, CamCard, Scoop.it, Wunderlist, Easy Attendance, Calender, CountDown, Splanner, Behance. ToDo, Istudiezero, Fantastical, iCal
Social media connectivity	23%	31%	Facebook, twitter, students union app, Alien Blue, Tumblr, Blogger, HootSuite, Collaborate

Communications	86%	49%	Email, Text, Phone, FaceTime
Data manipulation	4%	3%	Calculators, convertors, formulas, Numbers, Surveys
Subject specific tools	20%	15%	Sim Monitor, Coach's Eye, SIGN/NICE, NHS apps, Periodic tables, languages, databases, programming tools, stock market, Subject quizzes, Socratives, Sensor Data, Brian Lab, Wolfram maths
Other	30%	28%	Job sites, memory training, puzzles, CV tools, backup and data storage, remote login, Alarm, Clock, Google Maps, Travel Apps, Weather, Pomodoro, BitNest, Barcode and QR code scanner, Sensor Data

Table 2: Woodcock et al. (2012) taxonomy category analysis of staff and students five favourite apps for University life.

Staff primarily report using calendar and email apps to keep on top of work, categorised here as smart device Communications. However, the data shows that students primarily report using their device to access the institutional virtual learning environment (Blackboard) and writing apps, categorised as Managing learning, work or research. The high percentage of students using writing apps indicates that they are using their smart devices for producing course related work; consistent with previous research (Nortcliffe & Middleton, 2012). This is a contrast to Nguyen and Chaparro (2012) who claimed students are primarily used iPads for personal entertainment and socialising in comparison to people in non-student role who mainly used their iPad for reading information.

The above results may well reflect a generational dimension. 60% of all students at SHU are under 21 years of age, while the average age of staff is 43 (2014). 18-25 year olds at the time of this study have been referred to as the "net generation": those who have grown up using social media and the Internet (Tapscott, 2008). Tapscott's study of 11,000 11-30 years olds identified that the Net Generation have developed new skills and approaches to digest and process information, communicate, work together and socially interact. However, Bennett *et al.* (2008, p. 6) note that,

> *"Younger people often have lower skill and knowledge*
> *levels than what might be expected based on the digital*
> *native hypothesis."*

A more recent study (Hargittai, 2010) has shown that students who have had ready access to technology (i.e. through more privileged socio-economic backgrounds) have a higher understanding and know-how of Internet technology than those from typically less privileged backgrounds. The Net Generation are confident in using technology, but their actual digital literacy skills are insufficient to navigate complex net-based technological environments and students need to develop their digital literacy (Palfrey & Gasser, 2013).

Conclusion

The results indicate that students are more confident with using and applying BYOD to support their university life than university staff. However, this confidence is more about the level of technology exposure students have had rather than being a comment of their digital literacy (Bennett *et al.*, 2008). There, therefore, an opportunity for symbiotic learning between staff and students about developing digital capability in using smart devices to support 'university life'. There is an opportunity for staff and students to work and learn together about using their personal smart technologies effectively for academic purposes and professional practice.

At an institutional level there is a need to make smart device technology readily available on short or long term loans to students from low disadvantaged backgrounds where they have had no access to personal smart technology. Those with responsibility for the professional development of staff need to understand how to support colleagues in using personal devices without invading the personal spaces represented by their devices. Nevertheless universities need to signal that the fixed technologies may be on the wane and that increasingly our smart devices will become more important to us in our university lives.

References

Ballagas, R., Borchers, J., Rohs, M., & Sheridan, J. G. (2006). The smart phone: a ubiquitous input device. *Pervasive Computing, IEEE*, 5(1), 70-77.

Bennett, S., Maton, K., & Kervin, L. (2008). The 'digital natives' debate: A critical review of the evidence. *British journal of educational technology*, 39(5), 775-786.

Brooks, G. (2014). Changing the Learning Landscape Case Study: Preparing Higher Education for the Digital Age, BETT 2014 Conference – 22 January 2014, London, UK.

Camargo, M., Bary, R., Boly, V. Rees, M. & Smith, R. (2011). "Exploring the implications and impact of smartphones on learning dynamics: The role of self-directed learning," 17th International Conference on Concurrent Enterprising (ICE), 1-7, 20-22 June 2011.

Chen, J., Park, Y., and Putzer, G. J., (2010). 'An examination of the components that increase acceptance of smartphones among healthcare professionals'. *Journal of Health Informatics,* 5(2), 2010, e16.

Costello, S. (2012). How many apps are in the iPhone App Store? About.com. Online at http://ipod.about.com/od/iphonesoftwareterms/qt/apps-in-app-store.htm

Dodds, P., & Fletcher, J. D. (2004). *Opportunities for new "smart" learning environments enabled by next generation Web capabilities* (No. IDA-D-2952). Institute for Defense Analysis Alexandria, VA.

Durbin, S. (2011). Tackling converged threats: building a security-positive environment. *Network Security*, 6, pp.5-8 Online at: http://www.sciencedirect.com/science/article/pii/S1353485811700617

Glaser, B. G. (1964). Constant comparative method of qualitative analysis. The. *Soc. Probs.*, 12, 436.

Goodyear, P.M. (2000). Environments for lifelong learning: ergonomics, architecture and educational design. In: J.M. Spector, and T.M. Anderson (eds.), Integrated and holistic perspectives on learning, instruction and technology: understanding complexity. Kluwer Academic Publishers,Dordrecht, 1-18, 2000.

Hague, P., (1993). Questionnaire design. London, Kogan Page.

Hamza, A., & Noordin, A. F. (2013). BYOD usage by postgraduate students of International Islamic University Malaysia: an analysis. International Journal of Engineering Science Invention, 2(4), 14 – 20.

Hargittai, E. (2010). Digital na (t) ives? Variation in internet skills and uses among members of the "Net Generation". *Sociological Inquiry*, 80(1), 92-113.

Hayes, A. (2013). Assistant Director-Info Systems & Technology. RE: SHU Digital Strategy. Email to A. Nortcliffe, 23rd July 2013. Personal Communication.

Jones, P. (2013). Introduction to plenary session: the University Strategy. Sheffield Hallam University, 16th July 2013.

Kang, Y. M., Cho, C., & Lee, S. (2011). Analysis of factors affecting the adoption of smartphones. *Technology Management Conference (ITMC), 2011 IEEE International*, 919-925.

Lin, P., & Brown, K. F. (2007). Smartphones provide new capabilities for mobile professionals. CPA Journal, 77(5), 66-71.

Liu, G. Z., & Hwang, G. J. (2010). A key step to understanding paradigm shifts in e-learning: towards context-aware ubiquitous learning. *British Journal of Educational Technology*, 41(2), E1-E9.

Nortcliffe, A. & Middleton, A. (2012). The innovative use of personal smart devices by students to support their learning. In: Wankel, L. and Blessinger, P. (eds) "Increasing Student Engagement and Retention using Mobile Applications:

Smartphones, Skype and Texting Technologies", (Cutting Edge Technologies in Higher Education series. Emerald, Bingley, UK, 175-210.

Nortcliffe, A. Clark, S. & Parkes, J. (2013). Digital education engagement for post PC students, *The Academic Practice and Technology (APT) Conference 2013:* Next Generation Learning Places and Work Spaces, University of Greenwich, 2nd July 2013.

Nguyen, B. T., & Chaparro, B. S. (2012). Apple iPad usage trends by students and non-students. In: *Proceedings of the Human Factors and Ergonomics Society Annual Meeting,* 56(1), 1511-1515, Sage Publications.

Palfrey, J. G., & Gasser, U. (2013). Born digital: Understanding the first generation of digital natives. Basic Books.

Salmon, G. (2013). E-tivities: The key to active online learning. Routledge.

Schmidt, W. C. (1997). World-Wide Web survey research: Benefits, potential problems, and solutions. *Behavior Research Methods, Instruments, & Computers,* 29(2), 274-279.

Sharples, M., Arnedillo-Sánchez, I., Milrad, M. & Vavoula, G. (2009). Mobile learning: small devices, big issues. In: Balacheff, N., Ludvigsen, S., Jong, T., Lazonder, A. & Barnes, S. (eds) Technology-Enhanced Learning, Part IV, Springer Netherlands, 233-249.

Sheffield Hallam University (2014). Facts and figures. Strategic Planning and Intelligence, Sheffield Hallam University, August 2014.

Shin, D. H., Shin, Y. J., Choo, H., & Beom, K. (2011). Smartphones as smart pedagogical tools: Implications for smartphones as u-learning devices. *Computers in Human Behavior,* 27(6), 2207-2214.

Tapscott, D. (2008). Grown up digital: How the Net Generation is changing your world. New York: McGraw-Hill.

Tibken, S. (2012). Google ties Apple with 700,000 Android Apps, last accessed 3rd January 2012 at: http://news.cnet.com/8301-1035_3-57542502-94/google-ties-apple-with-700000-android-apps/, September 2012.

Traxler, J. (2009). Learning in a Mobile Age, International *Journal of Mobile and Blended Learning,* 1(1), 1-12, January-March 2009.

Woodcock, B. (2011). An investigation into the benefits and limitations of mobile learning applications used for computing studies in higher education, Undergraduate computing programme project report as part of BSc Computer Networks, Department of Computing, Sheffield Hallam University, UK.

Woodock, B., Middleton, A. & Nortcliffe, A. (2012a). Considering the smartphone learner: developing innovation to investigate the opportunities for students and their interest, *Student Engagement and Experience Journal,* last accessed 12th April 2012 at http://research.shu.ac.uk/SEEJ/index.php/seej/article/view/38/Woodcock, February 2012.

Woodcock, B., Armstrong, M. Nortcliffe, A. & Middleton, A. (2012b). "Smart device potential for student learning"4th *International Conference on Computer Supported Education,* Porto, Portugal, 16th-18th April 2012.

Scenario: Audio briefing and FAQs

The students' tasks had traditionally been set out in a document. It seemed to explain everything they needed to know, but every year Jim was faced with a sea of puzzled faces when the written assignment brief was published in Blackboard. It was inevitable that he would spend 15 minutes reiterating the brief. He worried that students who had not attended the class were being disadvantaged. This year, on the spur of the moment, Jim decided to switch on the voice recorder app on his phone before he began to reiterate the brief in class. He reflected that it was probably just reassuring for the students - they seemed to understand perfectly well. Just talking through the assignment helped though. Later he published the recording he had made to the assignment folder for those who had not been there. And as he was approached by individuals later with further questions he made Audio FAQs - recordings of answers he found himself giving time after time to individuals in class.

Key tool: Voice Record app

Based on: scenarios from the MELSIG Digital Voices book

Taking the tablets
— should you bring your own or use those prescribed?

Simon Thomson

Background

During the academic year 2012/13 Leeds Beckett University (previously Leeds Metropolitan University) sought to examine the potential of a 1-to-1 tablet deployment experience with a specific focus on learning and teaching. The project was a collaborative activity between the Students Union and the Centre for Learning & Teaching. It was internally funded by the University and the evaluation activity was supported through consultancy as part of the Changing the Learning Landscape partnership managed by the Leadership Foundation. One course was selected and over the period of a single semester staff and students on that course were supported in the use of tablet devices.

At Leeds Beckett we opted to use the Google Nexus 7 (2012) tablet devices. This selection was based on our current experiences internally of using iOS, Android and Windows devices and assessing their cost per unit against functionality. The final decision was mainly based on cost (the fact we could have a larger scale experience as the cost per unit was significantly less than iOS, other Android or Windows devices), but also due to the fact that our University is a Google Apps for Education institution so we were able to set the devices up with current staff and student logins. This Phase 1 pilot ran for one semester and the success of that pilot led to the funding of the Phase 2 pilot which this case study covers. This second phase pilot ran in Semester 2 2013/14 (January 2014 - July 2014).

Course Selection

The selection of courses for the Phase 2 pilot was undertaken through an application process. We had seen from the previous pilot that when a course volunteers to be involved we are likely to see improved motivation from individuals and increased impact and output from the overall user experience. All courses in the University were invited to make a request to be involved in the project based on some selection criteria:

- the application was co-ordinated through the Course Leader;
- a maximum of 75 tablet devices per Faculty was available. Any course with more than 75 students could still apply to be part of the project as long as it could run a cohort experience of 75 students or less e.g. at a single level of study within the course;
- all staff working with the cohort have agreed to participate;
- the course team was prepared to undertake development activities.

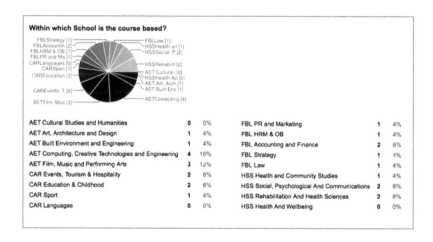

Within which School is the course based?

AET Cultural Studies and Humanities	0	0%	FBL PR and Marketing	1	4%
AET Art, Architecture and Design	1	4%	FBL HRM & OB	1	4%
AET Built Environment and Engineering	1	4%	FBL Accounting and Finance	2	8%
AET Computing, Creative Technologies and Engineering	4	16%	FBL Strategy	1	4%
AET Film, Music and Performing Arts	3	12%	FBL Law	1	4%
CAR Events, Tourism & Hospitality	2	8%	HSS Health and Community Studies	1	4%
CAR Education & Childhood	2	8%	HSS Social, Psychological And Communications	2	8%
CAR Sport	1	4%	HSS Rehabilitation And Health Sciences	2	8%
CAR Languages	0	0%	HSS Health And Wellbeing	0	0%

In total we received 25 requests, representing every Faculty and all but 3 Schools, but more importantly for the study we had requests from every level of study in the University. It was identified as part of the project aims and objectives that we would seek to capture data from the project that was from a range of levels and study modes.

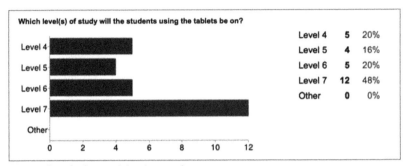

Levels of study for participating students

The process of selection was facilitated by the Centre for Learning and Teaching with discussions with the Students Union and Faculty Associate Deans for student experience (who would be overseeing the local support for the pilot).

The final selected courses represented all levels and included full and part-time study modes.

Faculty and level	Staff	Students
Faculty of Arts Environment & Technology		
BSc Computer Forensics (L5) BA Performance (L5) BA Design Product (l5)	7 4 6	68 16 44
Faculty of Health & Social Sciences		
BSc Physiotherapy (L4) & MSc Physiotherapy (L7)	15	51
Carnegie Faculty		
BA Early Childhood Education (l4) BSc Hospitality Leadership & Management (L5 & L6)	5 9	19 29
Faculty of Business & Law		

	1	14
MSc Accounting (L7) PGDip Legal Practice (L7)	9	45
Total faculty distribution (342)	56	286
Additional devices were distributed to academic librarians (4), IT systems colleagues (2), learning technologists (9) and Centre for Learning and Teaching staff (3).		
Total distribution: 360		

Table 1.

Project Management

The project was overseen by the University's Centre for Learning & Teaching (CLT), and in particular the Head of E-Learning. The strategic driver for this was due to the fact that the centre had been instrumental in securing the internal funding and co-ordinating the bid between the students union, faculties and other key services such as library and IT. CLT would also be responsible for the deployment of the devices, development activities and data collection through surveys and focus groups.

Within each Faculty the Associate Dean with responsibility for Student Experience would support course teams and, where necessary, provide additional local resources. Each course also has their own identified Academic Librarian who would also be issued with a device to support the provision of resources for mobile use. Although based in the Library, they would liaise directly with course teams to identify and purchase necessary resources for the course delivery. The project also had support from the IT services team, specifically in identifying areas of poor wireless connection and where necessary the rapid deployment of Wi-Fi architecture to support the project.

Evaluation activity was co-ordinated by the Students' Union (responsible for the gathering of student experience data) and the Centre for Learning & Teaching (responsible for staff experience data gathering and final report). The project also received funded consultancy from the Changing the

Learning Landscape fund which was used to run third party focus groups for staff and students.

Deployment, development and support

All tablet devices were registered and deployed through the Centre for Learning & Teaching (CLT). Prior to the students receiving their devices the staff undertook an induction activity where the devices were handed out and set up for use i.e. integrated with Google logins and email/calendar access etc. This gave staff at least two weeks access to the hardware before the students. During Semester 2 Welcome Week the students on the selected courses undertook an additional induction activity around the tablet project. The rationale for the project and planned activity was introduced to the students and the devices handed out. It was not a requirement for the students to take part in the research but only one of the student participants declined.

In terms of device ownership, we had seen from the first pilot that if the staff and students feel that the device is theirs they will invest more time into its use. Staff are able to keep their devices once the project comes to an end and whilst they are still employees of the University (there is also provision for them to purchase the device under a staff purchase system if they leave the University).

Students were also given the option to purchase the device after the project had finished for £50 (a significant saving on the retail price of £199).

CLT provided two additional development sessions for each course/cohort team throughout the semester as well as developing online resources to support the staff and students. CLT undertook the role of also being the first point of contact for any technical issues as well as learning and teaching support in order for us to be able to capture the full range of problems that might arise.

Key observations

There were two survey points for both staff and students in the study at Week 4 and at Week 8, with a focus group in Week 12. Survey One had 196 student responses (69% response rate) and 40 staff responses (71% response rate). Survey Two had 133 student responses (47% response rate) and 19 staff responses (34%). There was a significant reduction in the responses to the second survey and anecdotal evidence suggests that this is due to the increased demands on staff and students at that time of the semester. However the data gathered is still representative of all cohorts and courses.

Observation 1: Personal vs Professional Use

Survey data indicated that students were much more likely to use their devices for personal use as well as learning and teaching use. Staff were less likely to use the device in a personal capacity, despite being allowed and encouraged to do so.

In the figure below it is clear that students have a fairly even spread of use in both personal and study use, whereas the staff tend to focus on using the device only for work. In fact 23% of the staff indicated that they used the device entirely for work use. Based on further conversations with staff on this it appears to be related to two main points:

- That staff have historically tended to keep work and personal activity separate (i.e. separate staff PC to home PC etc.) and this was partly habitual;
- Staff still saw the device as being owned by the University and so potentially reluctant to place personal accounts (e.g. Facebook) on the device.

Please indicate approximately how much time on the device is personal v study.

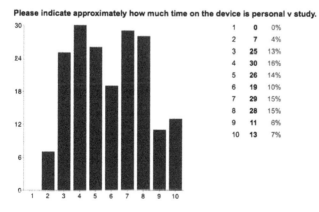

1	0	0%
2	7	4%
3	25	13%
4	30	16%
5	26	14%
6	19	10%
7	29	15%
8	28	15%
9	11	6%
10	13	7%

STUDENT: On this scale 1 would be equivalent to 100% personal use and 10 would signify 100% use in their study.

Please indicate approximately how much time on the device is personal v work.

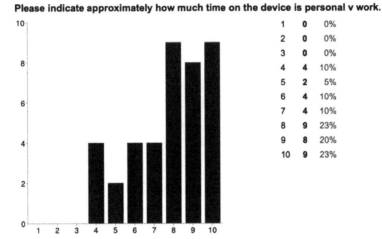

1	0	0%
2	0	0%
3	0	0%
4	4	10%
5	2	5%
6	4	10%
7	4	10%
8	9	23%
9	8	20%
10	9	23%

STAFF: On this scale 1 would be equivalent to 100% personal use and 10 would signify 100% use for their work.

Student discussions clearly indicated that they just saw it as a "device" with certain capabilities and were happy to put what they needed on the device as they would do with their own smart devices.

Observation 2: Usage Frequency

Staff and students used their devices on average 2-3 days a week, with a significant number of staff (48%) and students (45%) indicating that they used the device daily at the point of Survey One.

On average how often do you use the device since receiving it?

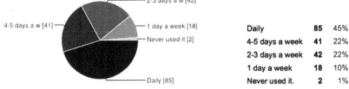

Daily	85	45%
4-5 days a week	41	22%
2-3 days a week	42	22%
1 day a week	18	10%
Never used it.	2	1%

Student Device Use - Survey One

On average how often do you use the device since receiving it?

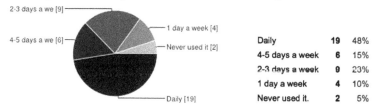

Daily	19	48%
4-5 days a week	6	15%
2-3 days a week	9	23%
1 day a week	4	10%
Never used it.	2	5%

Staff Device Use - Survey One

On average how often are you still using the device it?

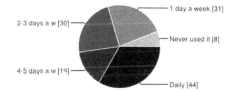

Daily	44	33%
4-5 days a week	19	14%
2-3 days a week	30	23%
1 day a week	31	23%
Never used it.	8	6%

Student Device Use - Survey Two

On average how often have you used the device since receiving it?

Daily	6	32%
4-5 days a week	4	21%
2-3 days a week	5	26%
1 day a week	3	16%
Never used it.	1	5%

Staff Device Use - Survey Two

As was anticipated, based on our earlier experience of the Phase One pilot, there was a drop is usage once the "novelty" of having the device had worn off. However it is significant to note that for both staff and students over 70% were using their devices at least 2-3 days a week.

These usage statistics indicated that the devices had integrated well into regular day to day activity and that users found value in having the devices.

Observation 3: Learning and Teaching Activities

As we were specifically interested in the use of the devices in a learning and teaching context all course teams were encouraged (but not required) to integrate the device use into learning and teaching activities. These experiences ranged from accessing the lecture slides for note taking during the lecture, to identifying specific applications for use in fieldwork activities.

In Survey One 77% of students indicated that they were using the devices in learning and teaching activities despite only 43% of staff indicating that they were using the devices as part of a taught session.

Have you used the device in a taught session?

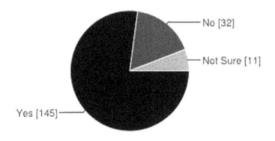

Students - Survey One

Have you used the device in a taught session?

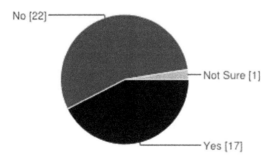

Staff - Survey One

This apparent discrepancy was further repeated in Survey Two where 67% of students indicated they were using the devices in taught sessions and only 37% of staff were using them as part of a taught session.

Have you used the device in a taught session?

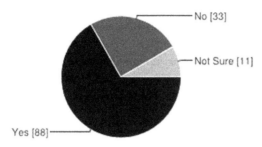

Students - Survey Two

It appears from this (and subsequent focus groups) that students are using the devices in sessions even when staff had not specifically designed activities for their use. The free form comments on the surveys indicate that the reason for this is that students are using them particularly in lectures to access slides, make notes and to refer to extended readings or access the Internet on the subject(s) being covered.

Have you used the device in a taught session?

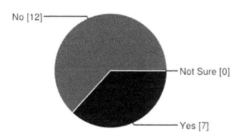

Staff - Survey Two

Notable Additional Observations: Expecting the Unexpected

The study also identified a number of additional observations that are of interest to the team and ones which we did not necessarily intend to observe.

1. We saw increased access to the student email system. Due to the fact that the devices were linked to the students' Google accounts they were more likely to access their student emails. Many students do not link their student email to personal mobile devices. As part of Pilot Two we added a question related to student email and 62% of students stated that having the device had increased their use of their student email account.

2. Increased access to the VLE (with Blackboard Mobile). A significant number of students were not aware of the Blackboard Mobile app which was a required install on their tablet devices. With the app installed students were more regularly accessing discussion areas and resources on the VLE.

3. Equality of learning experience was improved. Whilst a number of our students arrive on campus with devices, a significant number are from low socio-economic backgrounds. Having a device provided by the University means that everyone is equal in terms of device capability and functionality.

4. Staff confidence is improved with a single device deployment. Staff focus groups indicated that preparing resources, information and activities for multiple devices (BYOD) was almost impossible to achieve satisfactorily. With a single device staff had confidence in both developing activities and resources for devices, but also trouble shooting problems with students. In two identified cases students were supporting staff in the use of the devices and recommending apps for learning and teaching activities.

5. When asked for a preference with regards to BYOD or one provided by the University students did not indicate a strong preference for BYOD. 55% indicated a preference for one being provided with 43% indicating they did not mind.

Do you think students should be provided with devices like this as part of their studies?

Yes	22	55%
No	1	3%
Not Sure	17	43%

Staff, however, more strongly favoured a system where "Staff and students have the same/similar device (Staff and students same operating system and app store)".

Please indicate your preference to any potential future decisions around technology use in learning & teaching

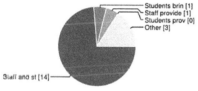

Staff and students have the same/similar device. (Staff and students same operating system and store)	74%	n. 14
Students bring their own devices. (BYOD) and staff choose their own devices (Staff and students have different devices and stores)	5%	1
Staff provided with the same devices, students bring their own devices. (Staff have the same device. Students have the different devices and app stores)	5%	1
Students provided with the same devices and staff choose their own. (Students have the same device. Staff have different devices and app stores)	0%	0
Other	16%	3

Next Steps

It is clear from the experience of this project that both staff and student experiences were significantly enhanced with the provision of tablet devices. There is also evidence to suggest that from a learning and teaching perspective having a single device deployed for all staff and students increased staff confidence and their capacity to integrate such technology into their learning and teaching practices.

Challenges identified were largely related to Wi-Fi infrastructure and more support required early on in the deployment of their devices to build confidence and capacity in staff abilities sooner. Both of these issues can be easily resolved with appropriate resource planning.

We now have to analyse our data and experience in order to make informed decisions on any future plans with regards to BYOD and 1-to-1 tablet deployment activities. What we have observed and recorded from this activity is that staff and students have an appetite for using mobile devices in learning and teaching, and that it is not just "students at universities and colleges (who) have ever-increasing expectations of being able to learn on these devices whenever and wherever they may be" (Johnson, 2012, p.6) but also our staff.

The University of East London has already provided its students with a device, perhaps recognising not just the learning and teaching benefits of a single device but also the ability to preload content and promote this as a unique selling point to students.

Whatever the future holds, whether it be BYOD or 1-to-1 deployment the growth of the mobile, smartphone and tablet market in leisure and business can no longer be ignored in educational establishments. As more and more primary and secondary schools make tablet purchases the expectations of future students in Higher Education will need to be met.

Reference

Johnson, L. (2012). Horizon Report, 2012: higher education edition. New Media Consortium/EDUCASE. Online at: http://www.nmc.org/pdf/2012-horizon-report-HE.pdf

Scenario: Over to you

Anne makes her lecture materials available in advance. She has nearly 300 Level 4 students each Friday afternoon. There's been a lot to get through this term but she has changed her approach from last year when she was struggling to cram everything into her lectures. This year she has cut out 25% of her lecture content and set up 10 minute pre-vision concept videos instead - one for each week. She has used the Explain Everything smart app to construct these based upon the content she was using in class last year. Students have been told to watch these between lectures. Now she begins each week's lecture by running a Socrative quiz about the concept videos: questions are posed by her in the Socrative app which appear on each student's device in real time in the lecture. They respond to a range of question types and Anne spends a little time clarifying and developing the answers for each question. She then continues the lecture as in previous years, though she is already thinking about expanding this 'flipped' approach.

Key tools: Socrative teacher and student apps, Explain Everything

Oh, the places you'll go
— smart learning in the natural sciences

Mark Feltham and Caroline Keep*

Introduction

Two years ago, as part of a larger collaborative project on maker education and makerspaces in HE (see e.g. Barniskis, 2014) we began formulating ideas about how we might promote and then embed flexible, smart learning into our teaching through the use of social media, mobile technologies and enquiry-based learning (JISC, 2009; 2011; Littlejohn & Pegler, 2007). Our raison d'être was to provide our students, if possible, with choices in how, where and when they learned in order to give them the best opportunities we could to develop their skills and demonstrate their learning in ways that best met their personal needs and circumstances (Gordon, 2014; Hammersley, Tallantyre & Le Cornu, 2013; Ryan & Tilbury, 2013). We describe below how we set about achieving this and some of the interesting findings that emerged when we gave students the opportunity to choose between different modes of study.

Background

In 2013-14, we taught a first year core module (Fundamentals of Scientific Research) to 363 undergraduates across six programmes (Zoology, Animal Behaviour, Forensic Anthropology, Biology, Wildlife Conservation and Geography) in the School of Natural Sciences & Psychology at Liverpool John Moores University. Its aim was to enable students to develop a range of academic, research and transferable skills related to their respective programmes. A large component of this module comprised learning about statistics, something students have in the past found an exceptionally 'dry'

* nee Kristjansson

subject that is both difficult to understand and un-engaging. In addition, the students' diversity of learning styles, together with the timetabled slot of 9 o'clock on a Monday morning, presented unique challenges regards stimulating students' curiosity and interest in ways which inspired a commitment to learning.

It was clear from engaging with students, moreover, that they varied considerably in the degree of autonomy they wanted, how they wished to learn, the pace at which they wished to work and the time they had available for study. We therefore designed the module to enable students to choose how, when and where they studied by allowing them to opt out of the 'traditional' university learning pathway of lectures and workshops supported by VLEs such as Blackboard and Moodle, and opt instead for a more 'creative' learning pathway in which lectures and workshops were replaced by creative projects and the lecture hall itself by communication via social media and mobile technologies.

We were interested in three key questions;

1. When given the choice, how many students would opt for the creative pathway?
2. How, if at all, would their performance differ from students opting to continue on a more traditional didactic learning pathway?
3. How would these students use social media and mobile technologies?

Module design

The module was divided into two halves. In Semester 1 all students alternated between both pathways, attending weekly lectures and computer workshops one week, followed by problem-based learning in closed Facebook groups the next. They could additionally opt to be assessed individually or in groups of 2-5. Computer workshops comprised traditional IT exercises in which students completed statistical tasks and used feedback sheets to show what they had learned and what they still found difficult

The social media work, however, was quite different. Every fortnight we posted a 'Taskprod' (a creative learning activity) that was designed to encourage students to solve problems as imaginatively as they wished and engage in conversation on their group pages if they hit problems.

Students then posted their work as comments to their Facebook groups in whatever format they liked (files, images, videos) using whatever devices they liked (mobile phones, tablets, laptops, PCs) and at any time they liked (day or night). The key thing was for them to demonstrate their learning how and when *they* wanted to. We then gave them feedback by liking / commenting / personal messaging / podcasting them about their posts. As we received notifications each time a student posted work or asked a question, feedback was both efficient and timely and so students could engage in these learning activities where and when it suited them in the knowledge that help was at hand should they require it.

In Semester 2 students chose one pathway to pursue exclusively. Students who opted for the 'traditional' learning pathway thereafter attended timetabled lectures and workshops and were assessed individually against a specific set of learning outcomes related to statistical analysis. Students who opted for the 'creative' learning pathway were not required to attend any timetabled classes and could additionally opt to be individually assessed or assessed in groups. Students on this pathway were taught via Facebook and were allowed to demonstrate their learning in whatever way they wished through one of six enquiry-based creative projects:

1. produce a stats guide in any style they liked;
2. produce a stats Video guide in any style they liked;
3. generate and analyse data by building and testing a Rube Goldberg Machine;
4. build and test an ornithopter,
5. carry out DIY experiments;
6. collect their own observational data.

Students on the 'creative' pathway were assessed against the same learning outcomes as their 'traditional' peers and for the latter all Q&A and feedback took place on Facebook.

How students chose to learn

Students fell into four groups based on their choice of learning pathway and their preference for working alone or with others.

1. 41% of students (n=149) identified themselves as 'Didactic Individuals' (students who preferred traditional teaching methods and to work on their own);

2. 24% as 'Didactic Group workers';
3. 24% as 'Creative Individuals' (students who preferred social media and autonomous learning via creative projects);
4. 11% as 'Creative Group workers'.

Interestingly, student choice of learning style had a significant effect on module performance with didactic individuals performing on average 9% more poorly than the three other groups ($F_{3,341}$ = 16.41, P<0.001). This group of individuals also contained all students who failed the module and all students who dropped out of University in their first year and raises interesting questions about how students learn and how we can best support them.

How students used social media and mobile technologies

During the course of the study students posted 3,088 comments to their Facebook groups of which 1,164 (39%) were from mobile devices. Time stamps were available for 3,012 (97.5%) of these posts and so we were able to use these to gauge the extent to which students used technology off-campus to engage in their learning. 56% of comments were posted outside of 'University hours' (9am-5pm, Monday-Friday) with 90% of these occurring during week days and 10% occurring over weekends. Most Facebook activity occurred between 6pm and midnight, but some students posted comments into the early hours of the morning (1am-5am). Not only did students mostly comment 'out of hours' but they also posted from various locations outside of the city (although not all posts on Facebook are tagged with a location) and 29% of these comments were flagged as being via mobile phones or Blackberries.

In addition to comments, students 'liked' posts (n=1,400) and regularly uploaded material to their Facebook groups. These uploads were interesting. Of the 1,300 student uploads 611 (47%) were text files (mostly Microsoft Word documents but occasionally ODT, RTF, PDF, PUB files), 7% were graphs (almost exclusively Excel files and only occasionally CRT files), but surprising 46% were images or video (JPG, PNG, BMP, WMV, AVI, MPG). Almost half of all uploads (46%) were from mobile devices with a clear preference among students for taking photos (72% of all image/video uploads) and posting them from their mobile phones (66% of image/video uploads).

What have we learned?

The study raises, we believe, some fundamental questions about the way we teach and the way students wish to learn.

All too often HE uses a 'one-size fits all' teaching and assessment model, where all students are taught the same way on a module and all given the same assignments to do. This is made worse in the sciences by the predominance of REPS assessments (Reports Essay Posters Seminars) in most undergraduate programmes. Whilst some students want the structure, formality and direction that such traditional teaching and assessment methods offer, others want flexibility, variety and autonomy. Some want to work in groups, whilst others do not. Students do not all learn the same way. Students do not all *want* to learn the same way, and they do not all want to be assessed the same way. What our study shows is that what students really want is choice. Choice in how they learn, choice in when they learn and choice in where they learn. If we truly wish to inspire students to develop their full potential, it is our firm belief that we need to design and embed new flexible pedagogies within our curricula with student choice at their core. Using social media in combination with mobile technologies provides one means by which such choice can be delivered.

What the students said

> *"I have really enjoyed it. It makes you more independent and also using Facebook is a lot quicker with regards feedback*

> *"It was awesome! Working in a group was fun as we were able to use each other's skills to our advantage."*

> *"I really enjoyed having the freedom to work on my stats in my own time... the task set was more of a fun activity than an assignment! I feel I learned a lot more than I would have done from lectures at 9am."*

> *"I have loved how it's given more scope to take charge of my own work and work under my own steam"*

> *"The Facebook module made life and the way the work needed completing a lot easier! Relaxing, stress free and the future of university learning!"*

"You have brains in your head. You have feet in your shoes. You can steer yourself any direction you choose. You're on your own. And you know what you know. And YOU are the one who'll decide where to go".
Dr Seuss

References

Barniskis, S.C. (2014). STEAM: Science and Art meet in rural library makerspaces. In: *iConference 2014 Proceedings*. University of Illinois at Urbana-Champaign, USA: iSchools, 834 – 837.

Crosling, G., Heagney, M. & Thomas, L., (2009). Improving student retention in higher education: Improving teaching and learning. *The Australian Universities' Review*, 51(2), 9 – 18.

Gordon, N. (2014). *Flexible pedagogies: Technology-enhanced learning*. York: Higher Education Academy.

Hammersley, A., Tallantyre, F & Le Cornu, A. (2013) *Flexible learning: A practical guide for academic staff*. York: Higher Education Academy.

JISC (2011). *Transforming Curriculum Delivery through technology: Stories of challenge, benefit and change*. Online at: http://www.jisc.ac.uk/media/documents/programmes/curriculumdelivery/Transforming%20curriculum%20delivery_accessible2.pdf

JISC (2009). *Effective practice in a digital age: A guide to technology-enhanced learning*. Online at: http://www.jisc.ac.uk/media/documents/publications/effectivepracticedigitalage.pdf

Littlejohn, A., & Pegler, C. (2007). *Preparing for blended e-Learning*. London: Routledge.

Ryan, A. & Tilbury, D. (2013) *Flexible pedagogies: new pedagogical ideas*. York: Higher Education Academy.

Scenario: Keeping it short and sweet

Rebecca Sellers

Jon's students often provide arguments in their writing that are long and the key points become diluted. To get them to think about the key points of their arguments he sets them a statement and asks whether they are for or against the statement. Rather than setting a word limit he asks them to record a 2 minute video or audio recording of their argument and states anything longer than 2 minutes will not be considered. The clips are then played in class and the students discuss what makes a good argument and the difficulties they have in keeping to the time limit. Jon also provides an example. The students are then asked to continue using this technique in their work to help them keep their arguments clear, precise and well-formed particularly when they are preparing presentations.

Making it personal
— a case study of personal smart device usage by higher education art and design students

Elaine Garcia and Martial Bugliolo

Introduction

This case study provides an overview of the lessons learnt from a project undertaken during the academic year 2013/2014 as part of the Higher Education Academy (HEA) Changing the Learning Landscape programme. This project provided eight students with personal smart tablet devices for the academic year for their personal use.

The aim of this case study is to share the lessons learnt from a small number of students as a pilot and investigative study before undertaking further research with higher student numbers. This project therefore aims to provide a deeper understanding of the views of eight students using qualitative data rather than a quantitative approach with larger numbers of students. Learning from this project will be shared with others who may be considering the roll out of smart tablet devices for learning within their institution or for their student group. This study seeks to provide guidance in how smart devices may be best utilized within education according to the experience students had within this project.

Student experiences were captured directly through both monthly updates of usage and an end of year presentation which students were asked to complete.

Background

In October 2013 as part of a Higher Education Academy (HEA) Changing the Learning Landscape project (DLinD CLL, 2014), a number of students at Plymouth College of Art (PCA) were given smart tablet devices for their personal and educational use throughout the remainder of the academic year. The project had a number of aims including to:

- gather learner perspectives and engage students with utilising mobile devices within their learning and daily lives;
- enable staff to better understand how technology can aid student learning;
- gain an understanding of smart device usage within an Art and Design discipline context;
- provide an opportunity for students to utilise smart devices and provide feedback to the institution on their effectiveness for learning and in everyday life.

Overall this project aimed to determine if personal smart tablet devices would be useful for students within both their education and their daily lives, and whether there were particular devices and platforms that students appeared to favour due to functionality and ease of use. It is important to note that this project did not seek to deal with potential issues that would be created from introducing institution-wide smart tablet devices, but rather aimed to determine the student views on the usefulness of such devices. For these reasons this project was intended as a small scale qualitative project which would focus on specific student experiences as a result of long term smart tablet ownership.

Course Tutors were asked to nominate students who were interested in undertaking the project, who did not already own a smart tablet device and who would be expected to commit fully to the project. Ownership of smartphones by students would not exclude them from this study as this was considered to be a different type of device due to the size and nature of the devices and because smartphone usage is almost 100% amongst these student groups. Students were chosen from a range of disciplines (Games Design, Illustration, Costume Design and Photography) and were given a range of devices (Kindle Fire, iPad mini, Google Nexus, Kobo Arc) in order that the experiences of students within different disciplines and utilising different devices could be measured.

For the purposes of this project students were not given a choice of device and those within the same courses were all given a device which ran either the Android or iOS platform so that daily comparisons were not made between the differing platforms by students. Making direct side-by-side comparison is considered to be unreliable partly due to the way in which manufacturers such as Apple and Google continue to introduce new revisions and features which are instantly compared and coveted by those with other types of smart tablets (Savov, 2014). Furthermore, the manner in which companies such as Google and Apple are building brand loyalty, which is based not only on emotional attachment but also the practicality of which devices you already own, results in an allegiance which Savov considers to be akin to a religion. For these reasons it was hoped that students would focus on the device they were using and their functionality.

Methodology

This project adopted a qualitative approach and utilised a case study methodology. A qualitative approach is appropriate in this case as it allows the collection of data within a naturalistic setting allows researchers to gain an understanding of participants. (Saunders, Lewis & Thornhill, 2012).

According to Creswell and Clark (2011) the advantages of such an approach include:

- It aims to describe and interpret participant's personal experiences of a phenomena;
- It allows participants to share their view;
- It provides a way of understanding complex phenomena;
- It tries to understand the interactions between people.

This therefore helps to ensure that the validity of the results is relatively high (Creswell, 2009).

In order to collect data and enable analysis in relation to student use of the smart tablet devices, students were asked to provide monthly written feedback on their use of the device during the preceding month and also information relating to any apps they had found to be particularly useful or work they had produced using the smart tablet. Students were given flexibility in relation to how this was provided. Some students elected to provide monthly feedback via a word document which they emailed to the project managers. Other students created blogs and updated these with posts on a monthly basis. Students were asked to provide feedback in relation to the following:

- The use of the device for learning both within and outside of the classroom;
- The use of the device for personal purposes;
- The apps students found useful (particularly free apps);
- Any comments made by staff or other students about the device and its use by students;
- Any other comments or thoughts students had in relation to the device and its use.

In addition to the monthly feedback at the end of the project students were asked to undertake a final presentation detailing their experiences during the year with their smart tablet after which, if all aspects of the project had been successfully completed, the students would be allowed to keep the smart tablet. Following the presentation a discussion session was undertaken with each student where further questions could be asked by the project team and any additional thoughts or themes could be explored in more detail. During these presentations the academic member of staff who nominated the student for the project was invited and in all cases chose to attend the presentation, being involved in the discussion about the use of the device by the student during the project. In addition at this point students were also asked whether they thought the institution should provide students with devices, whether they would recommend fellow students purchase the specific device they had and the degree to which they felt smart tablet devices could be useful to students within their studies.

Following the completion of the student presentations students were asked to provide a copy of their presentation to the project team and this and all other feedback given by students and staff throughout the length of the project was collated. Content analysis was undertaken by the members of the project team in order to identify the key themes which emerged from the project. The themes that emerged were presented to the College's senior management team and the project funders in the form of a final project report. This report was well received by College managers and the success of this project resulted in student smart tablet devices becoming a key area for further development in the future through incorporation in the institutions blended learning and IT strategy.

Lessons learnt

Different devices

When considering purchasing smart tablet devices it is important to firstly become acquainted with the number of differing devices that are available on the market. According to Gartner (2014) Android accounted for 62% of the smart tablet market in 2013 whilst Apple accounted for 36% of the market. Third place for smart tablet market share is held by Windows devices; however, this is only at 2% of the market. As Android and Apple devices account for 98% of the smart tablet market only these platforms were used within this project.

When considering the use of Android or Apple devices there are several issues to consider when deciding between platforms.

Android

An Android smart tablet will almost certainly represent a better option than an Apple iOS device in terms of price (Siegel, 2014). There are also a huge range of Android devices, with over 18,796 distinct devices (Sawers, 2014) available at a range of price points, all providing different features, specifications and build quality. A range of Android devices were chosen for this project, all having a similar price point at the time of purchase. These included the Google Nexus 7, the Kobo Arc and the Kindle Fire.

In this case study it appears that the Android platform is preferred by those students who have existing devices which run on the Android platform and/or who are generally more interested in digital technology. Smart tablets operating the Android platform are generally preferred amongst young people (18 or under) in contrast to over 18s preferring the Apple iOS (Phone Arena, 2012; Faw, 2013).

Students who preferred using these devices were, in general, willing to spend more time customizing the device by downloading items such as new keyboards. The students who preferred these devices also indicated features such as additional storage through an SD card slot were useful to them.

However, this case study suggests that for those students, who had already invested in Apple products such as the iPhone or MacBook, an Android device seemed difficult to use and they clearly indicated their preference for an Apple smart tablet.

Students appeared to be particularly frustrated when using devices such as the Kindle Fire where the full Android store was not available and therefore they were not able to download all the apps they wanted.

Apple iOS

Whilst the entry price point to Apple iOS products is considerably higher than Android, those students who were given Apple smart tablets stated a preference for these devices over the Android platform. Additionally a number of students who had been using Android devices also indicated a preference for Apple iOS smart tablets as opposed to Android devices. A number of students indicated that they would rather wait to save money in order to purchase an iOS product than to purchase an Android device earlier.

According to the students the main advantages of iOS when compared to Android was the ease of use from first use and the integration between the smart tablet and other existing devices or computers. These comments largely came from students using iOS devices who also have access to Apple Mac computers or other iOS devices (iPhone, iPod) already either on a personal basis or via the institution.

In reality much of the functionality students indicated they used on the iOS smart tablet could be replicated on the Android smart tablet, but this appeared to students to be a more complicated process to undertake or they were not aware that this functionality was available.

Subjects and disciplines

Whilst all of the students in this case study were taking Art and Design courses, a range of subject areas were chosen for this project. Students were selected from subjects classed as "high digital" (Games Design), "mid digital" (Photography and Illustration) and "low digital" (Costume Design). It was not anticipated that these students would have very differing views of the usefulness of smart tablet devices when the project was commenced, but it quickly became apparent that subject related differences did exist.

Students studying digital subjects (High Digital)

When considering use by differing disciplines it is interesting to note that students who have higher digital and computer usage within their course (i.e. Games Design) were less likely to consider the smart devices to be useful to them for either their personal or educational lives. Students within the Games Design subject area actually considered that smart tablet devices were not really of great use to them. These students did however consider that those courses with lower usage of digital technology or computers within their subject would be more likely to find such devices useful.

Students in "high digital" technology subjects stated that as they were in front of a computer for much of the day and all had smartphones; the addition of a smart tablet device didn't really add anything to their learning or personal lives. For these students an institutional investment in high specification computers was of higher importance than the purchase of smart tablet devices.

Students studying subjects with some digital aspects (Mid Digital)

For students "mid digital" subjects (Photography and Illustration) the use of smart tablet devices appeared to have more usefulness than those within the "high digital" subjects.

For "mid digital" students the use of a smart tablet device cannot replace the use of the computer, however it can provide advantages in undertaking some activities. "Mid digital" students found the devices particularly useful when working in an external environment such as visiting potential clients and displaying portfolios.

Unlike the "high digital" students, "mid digital" learners are still likely to use computers regularly as part of their course but would not necessarily be in front of a computer at all times.

Whilst these students considered that high end activities such as image manipulation still need to occur on a computer, they felt that the smart tablet devices were useful for everyday productivity activities such as email and taking notes. Even though these students were also likely to have a mobile phone they said that the size of the smart tablet was more useful for taking notes or photographs than a smartphone. The tablets were not too big to create difficulty in terms of transport; something that would create a barrier to using a computer.

These students considered that a personal smart tablet device would be useful for their studies and everyday lives but that it could not be a replacement for a computer for all aspects of their work.

Students studying subjects with low digital aspects (Low Digital)

It is perhaps somewhat surprising that students who were studying "low digital" subjects found the smart tablet device to be most useful to their studies and personal lives.

Whilst students undertaking "low digital" subjects would have access to computers, they stated that these would rarely be removed from storage within lessons due to the lack of need for their usage.

Therefore, in these situations the smart tablet device allowed students to access digital technology easily and quickly without the need to get a computer from storage or go to another room in order to gain access. It appears that "low digital" students generally would use the device to improve their productivity (i.e. taking notes) or would use the device on an *ad hoc* basis where it would be useful to quickly undertake an Internet search or take a photograph.

The *ad hoc* use of the smart functionality of the devices was used equally by students in high and low digital subjects. Whilst "high digital" students were able to browse the Internet easily on a computer (often their main tool within the classroom) these computers would not usually include the smart functionality provided by tablet device.

Students in "low digital" subjects report to have also found more uses for the smart tablet device in relation to both their study and personal lives than the students from mid and high digital subjects.

It appears, therefore, that the smart tablet devices provide a useful way for students studying "low digital" subjects to be introduced to digital technology and it is likely to be most useful for students within these subjects.

Personal ownership

One of the key aims of this project was to consider the personal nature of smart tablet devices and the significance of personal ownership of smart tablet devices.

This case study found that the personal nature of the smart tablet device does indicate the benefit of students owning their device and being able to manage it as they wish. This should include the ability for individual students to choose and download apps, to keep documents, images, books and music on the device and also to be able to personalize the device with reminders, calendars and email.

By comparison when devices have previously been provided as a group or classroom based resource within the institution these have resulted in minimal take up and the devices have therefore been largely unused. The problems associated with sharing smart tablet devices amongst students have been widely discussed amongst academic staff who have noted that the sharing of iPads can be undertaken successfully within the classroom but that it requires some time consuming workarounds (Gleeson, 2014).

Students also reported that a number of their peers had already invested in purchasing a personal smart tablet device and their usage is increasingly being seen within the classroom. This appears to be something which is accepted by academic staff who reportedly do not prevent students from using the devices in taught sessions.

This case study shows that there are clear benefits to found in accommodating the personal nature of smart tablet devices. The use of such devices is limited without a sense of personal ownership.

Institutional purchase

There were mixed responses when students were asked if they felt the institution should invest in personal smart devices for students as would be expected given their different opinions about the usefulness of devices.

The majority of students felt that the device was useful to them and would like to continue to use such a device for both their studies and personal lives. However, the students did not consider it should be a priority for the institution to purchase devices for students.

Generally students felt that devices should be purchased by individual students who wished to use them with the institution seeking to provide discounts from suppliers which could be passed on or providing apps for use by students who had purchased a device.

Some students felt that the institution could provide devices but only to those students who had demonstrated their commitment to their course through high levels of achievement or attendance.

Conclusions

This case study has provided an opportunity for student views about the personal use of smart tablet devices to be shared with a wider audience and has highlighted some of the complex issues that need to be considered when thinking about providing such devices to students.

It is clear from this case study that students cannot be treated as a homogenous group and views concerning the use of digital technology can be diverse and conflicting, even amongst students within a single institution and within similar discipline areas.

This case study only represents the experiences of eight students within one institution and differing results may be found within other institutions and other subject areas. Further research needs to be undertaken, particularly with larger number of students, to determine if these results do apply in other contexts and will undoubtedly change over time as digital technological changes and further innovations occur. Additionally research also needs to be undertaken to explore the views of academic staff towards the use of student smart tablets within teaching and learning. The implications of introducing such digital technology in relation to pedagogy, and teaching and learning in general, also need to be further explored.

Acknowledgements:

This project was funded by the Higher Education Academy as part of the Changing the Learning Landscape programme.

We would like to thank the students who contributed to this project: Jordan Ash, Joanne Cookney, Ryan Holder, Charmaine McDonough, John Mears, Sophie Pring, Ellen Sexton and Lewis Wain.

References

Creswell, J. (2009). Research design: Qualitative, quantitative, and mixed methods approaches, 3rd Edition. Thousand Oaks, CA: Sage Publications.

Creswell, J. & Clark, V. (2011). *Designing and conducting mixed methods research.* Thousand Oaks, CA: Sage Publications.

DLinD CLL (2014). Changing the Learning Landscape. Online at: http://dlind.referata.com/wiki/Changing_the_Learning_Landscape

Faw, L. (2013). Is Apple's iPhone no longer cool to teens? Online at: http://www.forbes.com/sites/larissafaw/2013/01/09/is-apples-iphone-no-longer-cool-to-teens/

Gartner (2014). Gartner says worldwide tablet sales grew 68 percent in 2013, with Android capturing 62 percent of the market. Online at: http://www.gartner.com/newsroom/id/2674215

Gleeson, M. (2014). *Pain and remedies of sharing iPads in schools.* Online at: http://mgleeson.edublogs.org/2012/11/02/pain-and-remedies-of-sharing-ipads-in-schools/

Phone Arena (2012). *New survey shows Android is "hot" among younger people while iOS gets the nod from the elderly.* Online at: http://www.phonearena.com/news/New-survey-shows-Android-is-Hot-among-younger-people-while-iOS-gets-the-nod-from-the-elderly_id35985

Saunders, M., Lewis, P. & Thornhill, A. (2012). *Research methods for business students, 6th edition.* Harlow: Pearson Education.

Savov, V. (2014) *iPhone or Android: It's time to choose your religion.* Online at: http://www.theverge.com/2014/6/26/5845138/choose-your-religion-iphone-or-android

Sawers, P. (2014). *There are 18,796 distinct Android devices, according to OpenSignal's latest fragmentation report.* Online at: http://thenextweb.com/mobile/2014/08/21/18796-different-android-devices-according-opensignals-latest-fragmentation-report/

Siegel, J. (2014). *The average Android phone costs just half of the average iPhone.* Online at: http://bgr.com/2014/02/18/android-iphone-price-comparison/

Scenario: Voice recognition

"What do you do with a hundred ideas... on Post-It notes?"

Beth had run a fantastic research activity for her dissertation. Her idea was to get people brainstorming; keeping the activity flowing. She used Post-It Notes to capture ideas that came out of her well-orchestrated discussion. So far, so good. When she got home, and the buzz of adrenalin had faded, she stared at all the Post-Its she had stuffed in her bag. "The trouble is, when people are rushing to generate ideas the last thing they think about is good handwriting!" But she read a few and realised she had a gold mine. Then she remembered Pete saying how he'd used the Dragon Dictate app to record inventories in his stock taking job. Having installed the app, Beth sat there for an hour reading back the Post Its. It was much more enjoyable and as she spoke she seemed to re-engage with the ideas and the activity.

Key tool: Dragon Dictate

Bringing well-established pedagogies into interactive lectures

Dave Kennedy and Daphne Robson

Introduction

In 2008 we started using tablet PCs and Classroom Presenter to teach a first year computing degree discrete mathematics paper. Our aim was to replace the traditional lecture delivery with an active learning approach (Anderson, Anderson *et al.*, 2007) and incorporate peer instruction ideas (Mazur, 1997). Mostly we were looking for student engagement.

We had 22 tablet PCs and classes of up to 40 students so from the start students were required to share a tablet PC. This proved to have many advantages. From 2014 we have used a suite of large touch screen PCs and DyKnow software to enable our active learning approach. The students no longer share a PC.

Our use of technology to enable interactive lectures has evolved to incorporate well established pedagogies such as:

- Active learning and engagement;
- Peer instruction;
- Immediate feedback;
- Concept tests.

Our teaching model

We have replaced the traditional lecture model with an active learning approach. A typical teaching session consists of a number of cycles of:

- Teacher introduces and explains a new concept and then works through one or two examples;
- Teacher sends a question to the students from a touch screen device;
- Students answer it using their touch screen device;
- Teacher retrieves all answers from students electronically;
- Teacher selects, displays and discusses students' answers with the class.

Students receive feedback for several different answers, and their own or similar answers will often be chosen. Students comment that they like seeing other students' answers as it helps them to avoid mistakes. They learn from seeing alternative strategies for solving problems and from the teacher-led discussion of why an answer is wrong.

Prior preparation

Our approach requires the teacher to think about each topic as a sequence of concepts where each is taught and tested and underlying concepts are covered before moving to higher order concepts (Anderson *et al.*, 2007) – all good teaching practice. The questions for each concept need to be developed and checked. Our philosophy was that the questions should:

- Be easy rather than hard;
- Aim for success and encouragement for all/most students;
- Take about 4 to 5 minutes to answer;
- Reinforce the concept just taught;
- Engage all students.

When writing questions we were also guided by Anderson's suggestions (Anderson, Anderson *et al.*, 2005):

- Leave enough room for the answer;
- Test just one concept;
- Use diagrams and tables.

We found that different topics naturally lent themselves to different types of questions e.g. diagrams, completing a table, writing and solving an

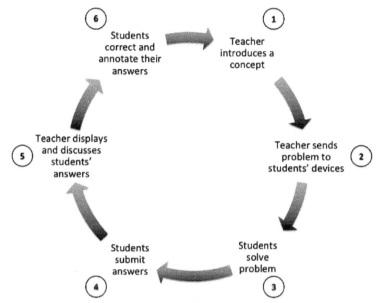

equation, open ended, etc. As we used the questions (and especially for the first time) we continued to modify them to make them clearer, make it easier for students to get started, make more room for the answer etc.

A large percentage of our questions are now of the "complete the table" type as this provides a structure for the answer and makes discussion of

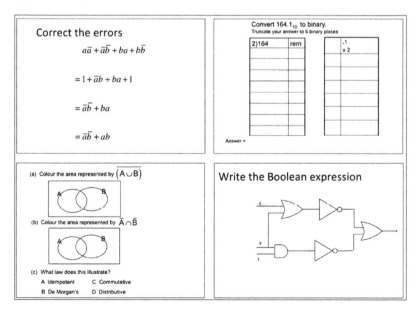

right/wrong answers easier for the teacher and for the students. We have also written additional questions that the faster students can do if they are waiting for others to finish. Examples of questions are shown below.

Advantages for the teacher

Engagement

Our aim was engagement and we got it! All students reported that the tablet PC activities were enjoyable and useful for learning. As maths teachers we were thrilled with the response from students. When a question was sent out there was a buzz of conversations as students worked in their pairs, consulted their notes and textbook, and compared their answer with those around them.

Feedback to the teacher

While students were answering a question the teacher could move around the room and check on progress. When the answers were received, the teacher scanned all answers and gauged the students' understanding of the concept. This helped the teacher adjust the length and nature of the subsequent discussion. If there were many incorrect answers then a more thorough discussion and explanation was warranted and could be followed by another similar question.

Discussion of common mistakes

When selecting answers for discussion there is more value in selecting incorrect answers. The incorrect answers often highlight common mistakes and of course they are examples of real errors made by students. Asking "Why is this answer wrong?" is a challenge for all (and especially the more able students) and is an opportunity for deeper learning.

Contributions from students

A major advantage of the active learning approach is that all students can contribute to the lesson. It is possible to ask questions in a lecture presentation, and wait for answers, but it is typically only the more able, more confident students who will answer. Our approach enables all students (especially the less confident and those who speak English as their second language) to contribute – right answers, wrong answers, different strategies, a comment or drawing (often humorous). And their contribution is recognised and valued.

More than just the answer

Mazur's peer instruction approach, using clickers, requires students to explain their reasoning to their neighbour. We found, as described by Draper, that an important component of peer instruction is providing an explanation for the answer (Draper 2004). A major advantage of using Tablet PCs or touch screens is that the questions are not limited to multi-choice. For us, most importantly, the answers include an indication of the thinking involved. This is useful feedback for the teacher but also, as Mazur argues, it is when students explain their answer that learning occurs.

Advantages for the students

Peer instruction

Mazur's idea of peer instruction (1997) involved students answering a challenging multi-choice concept question, sending in their answer, and then discussing and justifying their answer to their neighbour. Our active learning sequence was different from this and we didn't expect any peer instruction. So we were surprised when student comments emphasised this as a major advantage.

They learnt from each other and by explaining to their partner:

> *"Working with a partner meant if one did not follow as well, the other could help out."*

> *"As I explained concepts, I understood more clearly what I was learning."*

> *"Opportunity for students to problem solve co-operatively."*

Seeing others' answers

Students learnt from seeing others' answers and from the teacher led discussion. They learnt from the mistakes that others made, the alternative strategies they saw, and the realisation that they were not the only ones to make mistakes. They discovered that there is a lot of learning in making a mistake – and then understanding why it is a mistake. Nearly half the students described advantages of seeing other students' answers and the associated lecturer led discussion, for example:

> *"Going through the answers let me see both my mistakes, and other possible mistakes and problems, and how to correct them."*

> *"Often you learn more from understanding mistakes."*

> *"Can see, share, and learn from other's answers"*

> *"Anonymity – not worried about being wrong."*

Immediate feedback

We know from Hattie that a feature of excellent teaching and learning is providing feedback to students on their progress (Hattie & Gan, 2011). Providing feedback to all students is not an easy task. The immediate and frequent feedback on their answers was seen by the students as another major positive.

> *"Easy for teachers to check our answers."*

> *"Easy for the tutor to go over everyone's work individually without interrupting the class."*

> *"Feedback while practising in class."*

> *"Immediate feedback to students without great cost of tutor's time."*

Limitations

As well as the many advantages of interactive teaching, there are limitations.

Learning is not just about the classroom experience – even if it is an enjoyable, active learning experience. Learning and success still requires students to study, revise, and practice until they understand.

We have found the touch screens to be only just adequate for writing compared with tablet PCs.

Some students will find a question too easy, others will say it is too hard. Some students will finish a question while others have hardly started. Our solution is to provide additional questions and this has become easier with the DyKnow software.

Conclusion

This use of technology has enabled active learning, immediate feedback to the students and to the teacher, peer instruction, engagement, and contributions from all students. The technologies we have used include Classroom Presenter with tablet PCs for 6 years, Ubiquitous Presenter with a browser, and DyKnow Vision with large touch screens. We are currently trialling browser-based software with tablets and smartphones. We will continue to use this methodology and can see it being used with: improved touch screens, browser-based software, BYOD, tablets, and maybe smart phones.

References

Anderson, R., Anderson, R., Davis, K.M., Linnell, N., Prince, C., & Razmov, V. (2007). Supporting active learning and example based instruction with classroom technology. *SIGCSE'07*, Covington, USA. Online at: https://courses.cs.washington.edu/courses/cse421/06au/buaa/docs/uwalgs.pdf

Anderson, R., Anderson, R. & McDowell, L. (2005). *Best Practices for Lecturing with Digital Ink*. Online at: http://www.citidel.org/bitstream/10117/7021/1/papers/2005/papers/2005/AAM_2005.pdf.

Draper, S. W. (2004). From active learning to interactive teaching: Individual activity and interpersonal interaction. Online at: http://www.psy.gla.ac.uk/~steve/hongkong.html

Hattie, J. & Gan, M., eds. (2011). Instruction based on feedback. Handbook of research on learning and instruction. New York: Routledge.

Mazur, E. (1997). *Peer Instruction*. New Jersey: Prentice Hall Inc.

Scenario: Inverted keynote - cacophon(e)y of the crowd

Three hundred, possibly more, were sitting ready to be entertained by the keynote. An easy start to the day. The lecture theatre was warm, clean and comfortable. "This beats being at work," I said to my colleague, who looked as weary as me. I had Evernote ready. "I do like the way it adds the title to your notes automatically," I mused. "You use Penultimate then?" I asked Jim, only to be rudely awakened by the keynote.

"OK. So, take a look at the question. Create a 15 second video response using Instagram and this hashtag. Go!"

We had been forewarned, but I hadn't expected such an abrupt start! The rest of the 'keynote' session was spent listening to the responses and discussing them.

"Are my students ready for this?" I wondered. "At least as ready as me," I responded.

Key tool: Instagram.

Based on a technique used by Helen Keegan.
See: http://www.slideshare.net/heloukee/ple-u-nkeynote

Voices from 'the other side' — using Personal Response Systems to support student engagement

Michelle Blackburn and Joanna Stroud

Introduction

We approach the challenge of engaging students in lectures from different perspectives: that of the academic, Michelle, and the learning technologist, Joanna, and yet we find that we each speak with the same voice or passion. Having wanted to create a space in which students work with each other and a lecturer can effect a dynamic and interactive learning experience, we considered the idea of active learning. Active learning is defined by Freeman *et al.*'s 2014 meta-analysis (p.4) as "activities and/or discussion in class, as opposed to passively listening to an expert. It emphasizes higher-order thinking and often involves group work". In light of the study's finding that active learning techniques positively impact upon attainment and course performance, Eric Mazur, physicist at Harvard University and pioneer of the active and involving 'peer instruction' method, notes that "it's almost unethical to be lecturing" when data proves that didactic delivery is less effective than active learning techniques (Bajak, 2014). It has become increasingly apparent that we are not lone voices in advocating this approach in lectures.

Our challenge, therefore, is how to quickly and simply give students an opportunity to engage in active learning opportunities in a lecture environment. First, we needed to find a way to give students a voice, moving from a one-way system of knowledge transmission to two-way interaction. Secondly, we wanted to offer engaging activities that not only presented the opportunity to interact with a tutor, but also peers. A show of hands to questions is certainly one way of doing this, but we weren't sure that this encouraged interaction and frequently proved clumsy, making it difficult for a lecturer to collate results and ensure that everyone had equal opportunity to ask a question.

Technology has offered us a solution to these challenges. We already recognise that students are using smartphones in more creative ways: to make notes in lectures, to take photos of flip chart presentations, and to connect their learning experience with each other, for example by asking questions about assessments to their Facebook friends. They are also known to informally 'Google Jockey' (ELI, 2006); that is, search the web for key themes, topics, and resources while a class is ongoing, in some cases with students' search results displayed onscreen at the same time as lecture slides. We wanted to capture this energy and initiative and provide a framework to use it in teaching. At the simplest level, Personal Response Systems (PRS) enable tutors to pose questions to groups of students in a classroom environment, with the results collated automatically and displayed in real time. The technology supports the shift in pedagogical focus from passive to active learning (West, 2005; Martyn, 2007), and research suggests that it can help to promote positive affective benefits, such as student engagement and improved understanding through formative assessment tasks and deeper discussion (Carnaghan & Webb, 2006; Habel & Stubbs, 2014).

Although the technology is not particularly new, approaches to its use are becoming increasingly sophisticated. At their inception, PRS were expensive and cumbersome. Tutors had to book, carry, set up, issue, and collect handsets in the mêlée at the end of a class, and tools were often limited to basic multiple choice questions. A move from hardware-based PRS to more lightweight, flexible, and mobile platforms, such as Socrative, Nearpod, and Poll Everywhere, can appease concerns about resourcing that may have deterred a busy academic. They can also give tutors greater opportunity to focus on the pedagogy of their practice, spending more time on activity design and being responsive and spontaneous in the classroom. This is still hard work, and it takes time and effort to design appropriate and engaging learning interventions, in addition to becoming comfortable enough with a tool to use it in a live setting. However, staff should remember that support is always available from learning technology teams, and if an approach helps to deliver a more active and involving learning experience and, by extension, yields the suggested improvement in student attainment, it's got to be worth it (Samson, 2010).

We wanted to illustrate how we have used PRS technology in teaching large classes. Michelle is a Senior Lecturer with particular responsibility for designing and teaching employability skills for Business School students during their placement seeking year. The following case study illustrates how she has used Socrative, a free, online PRS that can be accessed from any 'smart' or Internet-connected device and has been used to produce a more active learning experience.

Using Socrative to teach employability

I am an academic with responsibility for teaching approximately 440 second-year undergraduates about employability skills in the year during which they apply for and secure an industrial work placement. I believe that students have a significant amount of expertise to share with me and their course colleagues given that they are either currently in work or active in the placement marketplace. Indeed, figures (Thompson, 2013) suggest that over 30% of students are working alongside their studies, and for me this means that they have direct experience of the fundamentals of employability, the current jobs market, and a range of insights around the recruitment practices of employers to whom I have no access.

Broad factors have impacted upon my efforts to provide a high quality learning experience, with the first being that "higher tuition fees mean higher student expectations across all aspects of the teaching and learning experience" (Universities UK, 2013: p12). Another is that my institution wants to be known for the quality of its teaching and commitment to education for employment (Sheffield Hallam University, 2011). I regularly consider what I can do to provide an experience that my students value and has a positive impact on their understanding and application of learning.

One way in which I wanted to enhance their experience was by opening up my lectures, giving greater opportunity for dialogue and interaction. The 'traditional' lecture requires, on the whole, that students are passive, and even when a lecturer wants to encourage discussion, the sheer number of learners and the consequent degree of peer pressure keeps all but the most confident students from speaking up. I wanted to remove these pressures, giving each student a voice and an opportunity to participate, and decided to explore how technology could help me achieve this.

However, I am not a technological expert. My mobile is rarely charged and I have never owned an 'i' anything. I needed inspiration and it came during an academic conference, when a presenter polled the attendees with an audience response tool called 'Socrative'. The context made an immediate impact on me: this was an audience of academics happily using the technology, rather than allegedly tech-savvy students. I decided I could try it too.

Socrative is very simple, offering multiple choice and free text questions. Both question-setting and answering are free, and it is accessed via the Internet, most often with university Wi-Fi. It works comfortably across a range of devices, including laptops, tablets, and smartphones, which the majority, but not all, of my students own and have to hand. The following headings identify the ways in which I employ Socrative in my employability teaching.

To gauge understanding

Rather than simply stand and decree that a C.V. should be roughly two pages long, I broadcast a multiple choice question with different page lengths as options. Students respond, but no one is singled out for having got the 'wrong' answer. The students seem engaged, and really enjoy seeing how their responses match up with others.

To make learning fun

I ask students this question about the email address they include on their C.V.:

> My email address…
>
> 1. Used to be cool
> 2. Is slightly rude
> 3. Is short and professional in tone
> 4. Takes 3 weeks to type
> 5. Doesn't matter as I never check it!

They tend to view the options as informal and amusing, but each makes a clear point without reading as a list of 'don't dos' on a slide. When the results have been collated we discuss the potential impact of each answer as a group. Questions like these can break the ice, leaving students more willing to verbally respond to more critically-focused follow-up questions. For me, this is really key to securing student engagement. From anecdotal student feedback I also think it encourages attendance.

To encourage deeper discussion

In order to both promote equity and encourage debate, I sometimes ask students to form groups and share a device to give their answer. This represents an opportunity for them to debate and convince each other of points of learning before sharing their joint decision with their peers using the technology. Be advised that this can make for a periodically noisy lecture theatre!

To promote collaboration

The technology's facilitation of interactivity enables the students and lecturer to collaborate in a more sophisticated way. If I am talking about application forms, for example, the range of questions about various aspects of the process might alter my delivery, meaning that we've worked together to set the direction and content of the session.

To deliver feedback at speed

Gibbs, Simpson and MacDonald (2003) suggest that the timeliness of feedback is essential to students' success. Socrative enables me to provide instantaneous feedback on the student's device once they have made their selection. The flexibility of the platform enables me to provide as much detail as is necessary; this could simply be the correct answer, an explanation of why their answer is wrong, or a question which implicitly directs them to the right one.

To give everyone a voice

Technology can empower students who are shy, whether due to social phobia or a lack of confidence in their spoken English, by making contributions anonymous. Their voices are heard and this is really important to me. Guest lecturers from industry can provide valuable insight into graduate recruitment practices, and Socrative is used to gather questions from the audience for a facilitated Q&A session. Everyone gets a chance, and when I ask for questions I have found I am less likely to experience a 'tumbleweed' when students are unwilling to speak up in front of peers or ask challenging questions.

In addition to the on-screen display I read out questions for the benefit of dyslexic students, and the anonymous nature of responses means that their standard of written English cannot be vilified by others, as can be the case with a flip chart!

To gather data

Socrative automatically produces spreadsheet reports around the responses I receive in lectures. On one hand, quantitative reports from multiple choice items can give me an immediate indication of areas in which students are comfortable or experiencing difficulty, while qualitative data from open-ended questions can be more revealing and inform future teaching choices.

To evaluate my practice

At the start, during, and at the end of each lecture I can ask students for feedback on my delivery, e.g. 'have I got the objectives right?', 'is there anything you think I ought to cover again?' and 'how was the lecture for you?' I use the feedback I receive to evaluate and reflect upon aspects of my own practice.

Conclusions and tips

Overall, I really enjoy using a mobile PRS in my lectures. The adaptive, flexible nature of Socrative means that it is highly customisable within a classroom setting and I can respond to needs and reactions as they arise, maintaining students' engagement and promoting a sense of empowerment over the direction of their learning.

My students have also responded positively, making statements such as "this is the only lecture I don't fall asleep in", and "everyone has their own opinion to each question." There are some, however, who find that the "use of [their] phone is slightly distracting…" so it is important to remember that not everyone will find the change a positive one. My personal tips for those considering use of Socrative or a similar PRS in future include:

- Tell students you will be using the technology and encourage them to bring a fully-charged device with them;
- Be honest if it is your first time, students can be very supportive. Tell them about the potential benefits, such as greater opportunities to interact, and more control of the way the lecture progresses;
- Supply access instructions, e.g. Wi-Fi, download, and any registration information via the VLE (Virtual Learning Environment) and, in addition, list the instructions onscreen as they enter the lecture theatre. Give a quick reminder before the first question.

- Send the questions to devices, but keep the question available on onscreen too, so that those without a device can still engage.
- Establish ground rules around use of devices outside of answering questions and what constitutes an 'appropriate' free text answer. Anonymity can sometimes encourage immaturity. It is possible to hide on-screen responses so that the tutor can share the appropriate answers and avoid the inappropriate ones. Exercise this control!
- Consider using the technology in other situations, for example as a short quiz before a lecture (or even outside of the timetabled lecture), or as part of a game in revision sessions.
- Consider accessibility if you change location. These platforms may not be suitable abroad, where device access and Wi-Fi may be limited and different charges exist for use of mobile data and SMS.

In conclusion, we are convinced that PRS technology can help to improve our students' learning experience. However, although we believe that lectures are enhanced through the use of these tools, we also acknowledge that there is a great deal more that could be done to make learning in a lecture environment truly active and participatory, and tasks must be carefully designed to be effective.

The lecture is a long-established format, and those which rely too heavily upon peer interaction may lead to frustration amongst those students who are unable to attend or are uncomfortable with a more participatory learning experience. As such, we feel it is best to mediate the two forms and identify where the greatest benefits can be found. The concept of the 'flipped' classroom, whereby learning materials traditionally delivered with a lecture are made available prior to the scheduled contact time is one such way to employ active learning techniques. The time that might otherwise have been spent on instruction is instead used for structured discussion, collaboration, and problem-solving activities, enabling students to share ideas with each other and the tutor to move freely through the room, scaffolding learning by participating in discussion. While many papers advocate the flipped classroom technique, Berrett (2012) outlines the concept and provides some useful examples; a good starting point for those who are not familiar with it.

References

Bajak, A. (2014). Lectures aren't just boring, they're ineffective, too, study finds. *Science Insider*. Online at: http://news.sciencemag.org/education/2014/05/lectures-arent-just-boring-theyre-ineffective-too-study-finds.

Berrett, D. (2012). How 'flipping' the classroom can improve the traditional lecture. *The Chronicle of Higher Education*. Online at: http://moodle.technion.ac.il/file.php/1298/Announce/How_Flipping_the_Classroom_Can_Improve_the_Traditional_Lecture.pdf

Carnaghan, C. & Webb, A. (2007). Investigating the effects of group response systems on student satisfaction, learning, and engagement in accounting education. *Issues in Accounting Education*, 22(3), 391–409.

Cox, S. & King, D. (2006). Skill sets: An approach to embed employability in course design. *Education & Training*, 48(4), 262–274.

ELI (2006). 7 things you should know about... Google Jockeying. *EDUCAUSE Learning Initiative*. Online at: https://net.educause.edu/ir/library/pdf/ELI7014.pdf

Freeman, S., Eddy, S.L., McDonough, M., Smith, M.K., Okoroafor, N., Jordt, H., & Wenderoth, M.P. (2014). Active learning increases student performance in science, engineering, and mathematics. *Proceedings of the National Academy of Sciences*. Online at: http://dx.doi.org/10.1073/pnas.1319030111.

Gibbs, G., Simpson, C. & Macdonald, R. (2003). Improving student learning through changing assessment: A conceptual and practical framework. *EARLI Conference, Padova*. Online at: http://www.open.ac.uk/fast/pdfs/Earli-2003.pdf.

Habel, C., & Stubbs, M. (2014). Mobile phone voting for participation and engagement in a large compulsory law course. *Research In Learning Technology*, 22. doi:http://dx.doi.org/10.3402/rlt.v22.19537.

Martyn, M. (2007). Clickers in the classroom: An active learning approach. EDUCAUSE Quarterly. 30(2), 71. Online at: http://www.educause.edu/ero/article/clickers-classroom-active-learning-approach

Samson, P. (2010). Deliberate engagement of laptops in large lecture classes to improve attentiveness and engagement. *Computers in Education*, (20)2, 22-37.

Sheffield Hallam University (2011). University vision statement and corporate plan. Online at: http://www.shu.ac.uk.

Thompson, S. (2013). *States of uncertainty: youth unemployment in Europe*. Institute of Public Policy Research. Online at: http://www.ippr.org/publications/states-of-uncertainty-youth-unemployment-in-europe

Universities UK (2013). Where student fees go. Online at: http://www.universitiesuk.ac.uk/highereducation/Pages/WhereStudentFeesGo.aspx.

West, J. (2005). Learning outcomes related to the use of personal response systems in large science courses. *The Academic Commons*. Online at: http://www.academiccommons.org/2005/12/learning-outcomes-related-to-the-use-of-personal-response-systems-in-large-science-courses/

Scenario: Twitter for learning

Rebecca Sellers

Susie wants to use Twitter to encourage her students to look beyond the set texts and websites for information about the subject and be able to communicate their findings quickly and easily. She decides to set up a hashtag rather than an account as this will allow everyone to see what is being shared and she is not solely responsible for the content. Using Twitter she envisions the students will use their mobile devices to upload things as they find them, rather than having to remember to add it later. She hopes the ease of using a mobile device will increase the frequency of the tweets. The favouriting button is identified as a way students can gather relevant resources together for later and further reading. The feed is also visible on the module's Virtual Learning Environment if they do not have a Twitter account.

Key tool: Twitter

Un-pop quiz
— a case study of motivating student engagement through smart games

Juliette Wilson

Introduction

Socrative is described as a 'smart student response system' (Socrative, 2013) and is a web tool which enables teachers to create teaching games/quizzes, or to ask students questions, via the use of mobile phones and smart devices. Socrative then produces immediate results which the teacher can view on their own device. This not only enables the teacher to receive swift feedback from groups of students large and small, but also gives students instant feedback on their answers; the feedback process is quick and symbiotic.

I was first introduced to Socrative on an academic development course aimed at developing the teaching skills of academics. It was used to check that the cohort had read and understood the module handbook and assessment criteria. For me, the use of the smart game motivated me to complete an otherwise mundane but necessary task which I might not have done. This experience made me consider the use of Socrative to stimulate undergraduate student engagement with the necessary, but often neglected, task of preparatory reading. Indeed, Burchfield and Sappington (2000) found that student compliance with preparatory reading had declined over a 16 year period. From personal and collegial anecdotal experience, undergraduate students' lack of preparatory reading often restricts the progress that can be made during class time. Thus to motivate undergraduate sociology students' engagement with preparatory reading I decided to trial the use of Socrative, under the rationale that the immediate feedback and a game like experience would be beneficial.

Background

In researching the effect of personal response systems on active learning in undergraduate science students Jordan and Mitchell (2009) found that they increased student engagement in lectures. Further, research has demonstrated improved test results due to the use of classroom response systems, and a positive reception by students (Jordan & Mitchell, 2009; El-Rady, 2006). Therefore, my only apprehensions in introducing Socrative to students, was firstly that some students may be excluded from the exercise due to lack of access to the technology. However, even in 2011 the University of Sheffield (2011) found that 99.6% of students owned a mobile phone, and Wang *et al.* (2008) introduced a web-based game to students and found that 100% of their students had laptops with Wi-Fi access, and 75% had the necessary technology on their mobiles. Secondly, students may be excluded due to an inability to use the application. However, in my own work I found Socrative very simple to set up and use on my phone, even though I am not adept at using smart mobile technologies and I have never, for example, downloaded an 'app'. Further, in my case I found that in the event of a student not owning the technology, or, as was more likely, the technology not working, students were happy to share devices and the activity worked just as well. In light of this I proceeded to trial the use of Socrative to motivate preparatory reading, based upon a realistic consideration of its possible exclusionary nature, and research which demonstrated positive pedagogical outcomes.

Implementation

Based upon research which demonstrated positive effects on the learning of undergraduate students through the implementation of quizzes and formative assessment (Jordan & Mitchell., 2009; El-Rady, 2006; Hatteberg & Steffy, 2013; Sappington *et al.*, 2002; Bell & Cowie, 2001) I enthusiastically announced to students:

> *'There will be a quiz on Tuesday.......*
> *Hello all, there will be a short quiz on Tuesday based on*
> *your reading for this week. So make sure you have all*
> *read Foucault's Carceral [...]'*

The next week more than half of the students failed to turn up for that class. Sappington *et al.* (2011) argue that whilst quizzes are unpopular with both students and teachers, they are a necessary medium through which to motivate the beneficial preparatory work of students. Thus, short quizzes based upon preparatory reading may function as formative assessment, which has been shown to enhance student learning effectiveness (Bell & Cowie, 2001). Further, Wang (2007) found that in terms of formative assessment, students more actively participated in web-based quiz games which could better facilitate their learning effectiveness. However, if quizzes are so unpopular that they mean students will not attend it is important to understand more about the implementation of quizzes in relation to the learning environment. On the positive side the students who did turn up said that they found the use of mobile technology and the fast interactive response format appealing; they enjoyed the novelty of it. Something which was similarly found by Wang *et al.* (2008) who reported that half of their students said they would attend more lectures if interactive lecture quizzes were used.

In my case students were asked to participate by using their own devices, and initially many looked at me for a while before slowly taking out their phones, and occasionally tablets. It has to be said that a few quite quickly got out their phones and logged on enthusiastically, but the majority were obviously unused to this sort of activity within their educational setting and seemed to need further encouragement before taking out their devices. A few did complain that their devices did not support this type of activity, but others readily shared their phones with these students so that they could participate collaboratively. I also observed that this activity tended to engage students who had otherwise been quiet during the course, and thus gave me as the tutor an opportunity to receive their input when I otherwise had not.

In the undergraduate courses taught in our department students can often feel unable to participate for fear of embarrassment, and the use of the smart game seemed to dispel some of that atmosphere and aided student input into the sessions. This is interesting in relation to findings by Cortez *et al.* (2004) and Soloway *et al.* (2001) who found that wireless technology in educational settings can increase social activity and interactivity respectively. Therefore wireless technological applications can create an environment where students can participate without fear of embarrassment.

Thus, the use of the smart game had benefits when the students participated, but the way in which the activity was introduced may have been a barrier to participation. This was confirmed by students themselves when I questioned them in later sessions. It transpired that the 'quiz' terminology reminded them of assessments and made them feel unprepared and nervous to attend. These anxieties may indeed be founded if students have experienced assessment as a judgment activity designed to reward superficial crammed learning, as opposed to an activity designed to motivate deep learning. However, if the concept of formative assessment is properly understood by students, and the activities are designed with specific aims in mind there should be no reason for students to fear such activities, indeed given an informed choice students may be very supportive of such a teaching approach. Thus the smart game was a useful tool, but it was the way in which the activity was introduced which seemed to have a negative impact on its use.

Discussion

I was therefore required to reconsider the manner in which activity was communicated, and thought back to my own experience. I had found the format appealing and motivating due to the game like qualities. When asked if I had completed the activity with my learning partner I remember saying "Yes, we won!" The sense of fun and competition which a game evokes, as opposed to the judgement and fear that a quiz seemed to instil, is important for understanding how best to utilise smart games in a learning environment. Indeed, Johnson *et al.* (2012) argue that games provide a safe environment for learning and Coco *et al.* (2001, p.493) state, "A core benefit of using games in sociology is linking enjoyable and memorable experiences to important sociological content…" This would coincide with my experience in that the use of the smart game provided a safe interactive learning-environment for less vocal students, and students found the experience enjoyable and memorable. Indeed, when using Socrative this year, one student commented with a smile, "We've heard about you and your 'games!'" However, Saltman (1988) found the need to reduce some of the relaxed and fun atmosphere of quizzes for the reason of better outcomes on end of term tests. When students took the ongoing quizzes more seriously they achieved better grades. Thus it may be about finding a balance between the two approaches, 'quizlike' and 'gamelike', which is the key to enhancing student participation *and* learning.

Based upon this experience I have continued to use smart games in my seminars to motivate student engagement with preparatory material such as pre-session reading.

However, despite student enjoyment and research which demonstrates the benefits of such use, there are certainly manly critics of this approach and it is by no means accepted by all university teaching staff. One critique of game-based learning–techniques is that they can promote surface or superficial learning if they do not manage to engage students deeply with the material. Indeed, in Sociology there are rarely short right or wrong answers, and usually longer answers are required which are difficult to input and check in the Socrative system. Thus again, considerations need to be made about how Socrative is to be best used. Wang *et al.* (2008) posit that lecture quizzes can be used to test how much students learn from a lecture. However, in the context of Sociology I believe this usage would contribute to more surface learning because, as Ramsden (2003) argues, testing learning can often lead to surface learning approaches and, despite doing well in such tests, students may have no deep understanding of the subject. I would argue that smart games such as Socrative are best used in a Sociology context to motivate and engage students at the beginning of a session for example, by encouraging them with some small success, and by using the rest of the session to enable students to discuss errors and search out answers for themselves; this approach could contribute to deep levels of learning as students actively and interactively participate with the content of the session.

A further consideration is that there are potential weaknesses of the technology to prepare for when using smart games. For example, I had planned to use Socrative during one session and when I logged onto the site it was updating and was not available for use. Therefore when using technology it is essential to have a back-up, and in this instance I used post-it notes for students to respond to the questions. Socrative, whilst not the only way of managing interactive motivational games, provides a free and readily usable format which does not require registration and the input of personal details. The interface is attractive and user-friendly, and it is easily accessed via smart phones and other devices. I do not suggest that Socrative is the only way to achieve the aims I seek to achieve in engaging students with preparatory class material, and I would, and do, use other techniques, but as a tool in the teacher's toolkit I have found smart games to be useful.

I introduced the Socrative smart game with the aim of engaging students in preparatory reading, something which is an issue in higher education Sociology contexts, and to an extent as part of a wider tutor's toolkit I have found that smart games can be an engaging and useful tool for teaching undergraduate Sociology students. I have continued to use smart games in my teaching, as despite occasional technological issues it is something which is quick and easy to set up for large or small groups which can have a beneficial effect on student engagement and learning.

Conclusion

While this is not a scientific study of using smart games to motivate undergraduate Sociology student engagement with preparatory reading, it does indicate that smart games can be beneficial to students' learning and that the framing of the activity is an important consideration. Thus further research is needed into how smart games might be used to enhance student's learning, and how exactly this can be done to best effect. I never announced the activity as a 'quiz' again, and in future sessions it was often not communicated prior to the session, and was introduced as a game which has the result of a lot more students turning up to participate!

References

Bell, B. & Cowie, B. (2001). The characteristics of formative assessment in science education. *Science Education,* 85 (5), pp.536-553. DOI: 10.1002/sce.1022.

Burchfield, C. M., & Sappington, J. (2000). Compliance with required reading assignments. *Teaching of Psychology,* 27, 58-60.

Coco, A., Woodward, I., Shaw, K., Cody, A., Lupton, G., & Peake, A. (2001). Bingo for beginners: A game strategy for facilitating active learning. *Teaching Sociology.* 29 (1), pp. 492-503. Online at: http://www.jstor.org/stable/1318950

Cortez, C.. Nussbaum, M., Santelices, R., Rodriguez, P., Zurita, G., Correa, M. & Cautivo, R. (2004). Teaching science with mobile computer supported collaborative learning (MCSCL). In: *WMTE '04: Proceedings of the 2nd IEEE International Workshop on Wireless and Mobile Technologies in Education (WMTE'04),* 67–74, Washington, DC, USA, 2004. IEEE Computer Society.

El-Rady, J. (2006). To click or not to click: That's the question. Innovate Journal of Online Education, 2(4).

Hatteberg, S. J. & Steffy, K. (2013). Increasing reading compliance of undergraduates: An evaluation of compliance methods. *Teaching Sociology,* 41(4), 346-352.

Johnson, L., Adams, S. & Cummins, M. (2012). The NMC horizon report: 2012 Higher Education Edition. Austin, Texas: *The New Media Consortium.* Online at: http://nct.cducause.edu/ir/library/pdf/HR2012.pdf.

Jordan, S. & Mitchell, T. (2009). E-assessment for learning? The potential of short free-text questions with tailored feedback. *British Journal of Educational Technology,* 40(2), 371-385.

Ramsden, P. (2003) *Learning to teach in higher education,* 2nd edition. London: Routledge Falmer.

Saltman. J. (1988). Mastering introductory Sociology: A teaching innovation. *Teaching Sociology.* 16(1), 284-288.

Sappington, J., Kinsey, K. & Munsayac, K. (2002). Two studies of reading compliance among college students. *Teaching of Psychology,* 29 (4), 274-272. Online at: http://orgs.bloomu.edu/tale/documents/reading_sappington _twostudies.pdf

Socrative (2013). Engage the class using any device. Website. Online at: http://www.socrative.com

Soloway, E., Norris, C., Blumenfeld, P., Fishman, B., Krajcik, J. & Marx, R. (2001). *Log on education: Handheld devices are ready-at-hand.* Online at: http://140.115.126.240/mediawiki/images/d/da/P15-soloway.pdf.

University of Sheffield (2011). CiCS student mobile device survey 2011. Online at: https://www.sheffield.ac.uk/polopoly_fs/1.103665!/file/ mobilesurvey2011.pdf.

Wang, A.I., Ofsdahl, T., & Morch-Storstein, O.K. (2008). An evaluation of a mobile game concept for lectures. *21st Conference on Software Engineering Education and Training.* Online at: http://www.researchgate.net/publication/228353090 _Lecture_quiz-a_mobile_game_concept_for_lectures.

Wang, T-H. (2007). Web-based quiz-game-like formative assessment: Development and evaluation. *Computers and Education,* 51, 1247-1263.

Scenario: Visual structures, spoken texts

The students were struggling to understand how to produce written assignments and Nicky was running out of ideas. "They don't seem to accept there's a problem, but the essays are consistently poorly structured and lacking evidence. As soon as I start to talk about writing skills they freeze up and deny there's any problem." This was not new to Jo, the writing tutor. "I have an idea. We'll stop writing for a while, and we'll start talking and taking pictures instead. That way we can work on structure and evidence in different media and come back to writing later. We'll create 'digital posters.'"

The students were asked to work in groups using their smart device camera to grab some 'visual evidence' in response to a challenge Nicky had set. She said the visuals could be actual photographs, metaphorical ideas or even graphs or drawings. In the workshop the students opened the 30hands app. It allowed them to order their images and record a voiceover for each one. They discussed which images would work best to structure their piece. Once they had chosen these they recorded a spoken account of the research they had conducted using the most useful pictures to structure their narrative. Each group published their 'digital poster' video presentation to the class wiki.

The class compared their presentations and considered their different use of structure and evidence to strengthen the presentations. Taking on board the feedback from the discussion they went away and produced a written report incorporating the same images, the same structure and feeling more confident about making an academic argument.

Key tool: 30hands or Explain Everything

Based on the idea of Digital Posters by Diane Rushton and Cathy Malone in Digital Voices (see next chapter)

Using social video to capture reflective voices

Diane Rushton, Natalie Wilmot, Andrew Middleton and Simon Warwick

Introduction

Cross Cultural Management is a compulsory second year module for students studying BA (Hons) International Business at Sheffield Hallam University. The aim of the module was to support home and Chinese top-up students to develop the cross cultural competencies required for employment in multicultural organisations as described by Catteeuw (2013, p.265), "Nowadays it is beyond doubt that there is a high need of professionals with intercultural competence". In order to achieve this, the module leader's approach was to introduce the students to reflective practice.

Background

The value and role of reflection in education is well documented in the literature (Boud *et al.*, 1985; Dewey, 1991; Moon, 1999; Mann, 2009). Since then UK Higher Education has increasingly adopted reflective practices to learning, teaching and assessment as advocated by Francis and Cowan (2008), Hedberg (2009) and Bolton (2010); most specifically in the context of skills development and employability agendas. Within this context and agreeing with Quinton and Smallbone (2010, p.125) who posit "that engaging in reflection is a vital part of learning for university students and its practice should be embedded in course design", a 3000 word reflective report on the development of their knowledge, skills and competencies relevant to a career in cross cultural management forms the main (60%) assessment task. Our previous experience of using reflective journals with students was that they need to learn how to reflect. As Usher (1985) discusses, they need to know how to select from their current external experiences and draw on their own internal experiences in order to learn.

While the value of reflective practice is widely accepted in educational circles, a critical issue is that reflective writing is complex and has high rhetorical demands (Ryan, 2011). Dyment *et al.* (2010) identify a series of factors that may limit or enable high quality reflection in student journals. Such factors are clarity of expectations, training, responses, assessments, relationships with the lecturer and developing the practice. In our previous work with Digital Posters (Rushton *et al.*, 2014) we brought speech into the service of writing to develop students' academic writing "as one of their owned voices" (Elbow 1995, p. xlvi) and this was the catalyst for us to use the spoken word for weekly self-reflection that would feed into the summative written assessment.

In order to support the students with this substantive piece, we required them to make a weekly audio/video reflection using YouTube, for which they have university accounts. Ubiquitous access to audio and video technologies allowed us to explore the potential for innovative media interventions in the curriculum in which user-generated media was pedagogically integrated in order to motivate, orientate, challenge and support the reflective learner rather than simply convey knowledge (Middleton, 2009).

Agreeing with Campión and Navaridas Nalda (2012) that the applications of Web 2.0 enable more independent, creative, participatory and co-operative learning and with Sethi (2013, p.5) that "implementation of technology in enhancing higher business management education is not an option but a requirement" we, as module leaders, took the innovative approach of using of mobile devices in the Cross Cultural Management module. As our previous experience showed that students were intrigued by the innovative use of technology, and engaged positively with it (Rushton *et al.*, 2014). We therefore focused on the use of Google Apps (primarily YouTube) for student self-reflection.

Reflection via YouTube on smart devices

Personal learning through personal technology

Given that 82% of new students at universities in the UK own a smartphone (UCAS, 2013), we wanted to use their technology as a pedagogical tool. As well as being pragmatic and ensuring technology was seamlessly integrated into the activity, the shift to the use of personal, ubiquitous technology seemed to reinforce the idea of reflection as being a personal construction and one that makes connections beyond and impacts on learning outside of the specific module (Siemens, 2003). As Middleton and Nortcliffe (2009) point out "students needed to be encouraged to think beyond their expectations of a traditional learning environment." This use of students' own technology was, therefore, symbolic of our expectations about their personal commitment to learning through reflection.

As our previous experience showed that students were intrigued by the innovative use of technology, and engaged positively with it (Rushton *et al.*, 2014), we were not innovating for the sake of it; but rather in order to enhance the learning experience and promote student engagement. As Rushton and Lahlafi discuss (2014), the impact of mobile technology on student engagement is a growing area of debate in the literature (Kukulska-Hulme, 2005; Lindquist *et al.*, 2007; Dyson *et al.*, 2009; Cobb *et al.*, 2010; Gokhale & Bhakare, 2011). The aptly titled "Mobile phones in the classroom: if you can't beat them, join them" (Scornovacca *et al.*, 2009, p.145) concludes that mobile phones, "…increased class interactivity, increased their interest level… and [to a somewhat lesser extent] the subject material, and overall was a useful and enjoyable addition." Woodcock *et al.* (2012) also found that students are interested and open to the potential of using mobile phones to support learning. However, if technology is to be used to enhance the quality of HE business education, it must be "blended with educational decisions like content" (Sethi, 2013, p.16). With a view to this, we focused on the use of Google Apps (primarily YouTube) for student self-reflection.

Deciding to use YouTube as a suitable space for reflection

After a consultation process in which several different apps were considered, YouTube (for Android OS users) and YouTube Capture (for Apple iOS users) were chosen as the apps to record the learner reflections. This was for a number of reasons. First and foremost YouTube is a format that is familiar to most of the technology friendly population with more than 1 billion unique visitors a month (YouTube website). The students had active Google and YouTube accounts as part of their Apps for Education accounts in the University, so minimal setup was required. The app is free and takes up very little space (24mb) on the students' personal devices. Finally the app used the native camera and sound recorder of the students' device to create a good quality output that upon uploading to YouTube is automatically converted into a universal format.

The uploaded videos were set up to be private and were then shared by the students with the module tutors to maintain the integrity of the students' thoughts and reflections.

We also considered other apps including AudioBoo, the native recorder app on students' devices and QuickVoice. AudioBoo seemed to meet most of the requirements and the fact that you were time limited was seen as an advantage as the student reflections needed to be succinct; however, there were ethical considerations to take into account as any sound bites recorded in AudioBoo are shared freely and it was felt this could put off some students from participating.

The native recording app on smart phones was looked at but discarded mainly due to the format that the recordings are captured in and the size of files that would need to be shared. We wanted to ensure that there would be minimal work to share and access the files for both the teaching team and the students. Converting and sharing large files did not match our criteria to minimise technical barriers to staff and students.

We also decided against QuickVoice as, although this was free for Apple users, there was a charge for the Android version and at present our institution is not ready for the Bring Your Own Device Managed Service that would be able to subsidise such apps for students to deploy to their own devices.

Looking forward to the next academic year, there is an app called Adobe Voice that is in its infancy at the moment, but could offer us more flexibility and a more robust method of sharing these reflections in the future. Due the constantly changing nature of the app market, there will always be new apps available, and we will be mindful of that.

What we did

A number of learning activities were developed and jointly delivered by the tutors, the Head of the University's Innovation and Professional Development team and an E-Learning Advisor in the first workshop of the module. The requirements of the students were that each week in the last 15 minutes of the workshop, in pairs, they would record their reflective discussions on their learning and development of their cross cultural management competencies. To do this they would use the YouTube Capture app on their personal smart devices. Their three minute-long recording would then be uploaded to YouTube under a setting which required the URL in order to be able to view the video, and this URL was emailed to the tutor so they could listen to the reflective account.

Prior to the first two hour-long workshop students had been sent an email to ask them to download the YouTube Capture app onto their smart devices (iOS or Android). The workshop was then structured as follows:

- The rationale for reflective practice was briefly outlined in terms of reflective practice and the assessment;
- The students were paired so that they could support each other in reflective discussion;
- The tutor and the Head of Innovation and Professional Development demonstrated a discussion and recording of it with the seminar tutor;
- The E-Learning Advisor, with reference to a one-sided illustrated handout, demonstrated how to upload the recordings to YouTube;
- The students had a go.

The outcome of the first workshop was that all students were ready to engage in their weekly peer reflection activity.

Each week, at the beginning of the next workshop, the tutor would give formative feedback on an anonymous sample in order to support the development of their self-reflection.

Training students how to think and write reflectively impacts on their summative reflective written assessment (Dyment *et al.*, 2010). In our previous work we have learnt the persuasive benefits of modelling new techniques.

Further, support was given by the tutors who posted a weekly video discussion and reflection of an article or experience about that week's topic on the virtual learning environment (VLE), so the students were able to see that the tutors involved were also engaging with the technology and process of reflection.

Observations

We observed the initial enthusiasm and excitement of the students being able to use their mobile devices in the classroom. Student reflections on the experience in their summative assessment indicate that they valued the experience, even if somewhat late in the day.

Many of the students did experience some feelings of nervousness related to making the recordings. However, it is interesting that this appears to have been experienced at different times during the module. Some felt embarrassed at the beginning of the module:

> Weekly reflective recording followed the workshops,
> initially this made me feel uncomfortable and
> nervous.....those nerves began to go away after my first
> few recordings and as my knowledge of reflection grew.

Other students, on the other hand, became more uncomfortable as the module progressed:

> The first few weeks went well as I have video recordings
> for the first few seminars which helped me with my
> reflection; however I struggled on completing further
> video clips due to nervousness and self-confidence issues.

Despite this nervousness, the majority of the students did value the experience:

> This is a tool which initially I didn't think would work
> for me, but I have since used it for different pieces of work
> and I find it really does help.

They also understood the value of self-reflection in developing their cross cultural skills and competencies:

> The recordings are a useful tool to use when trying to
> reflect on key learnings and identify what skills I need to
> work on for the future.

This validates our innovative use of mobile technology to engage and motivate students in recognising and developing their cross-cultural skills and competencies. "If I were to improve, I would have made more voice recordings as it would have helped in the reflection process of my learning even more so."

Discussion and conclusion

Following our first experience with the use of the YouTube Capture app in the module, we offer guidelines and reflect on the changes we will make:

- Don't underestimate the time required in finding appropriate mobile technologies and supporting the activities;
- Ensure good Wi-Fi in teaching rooms;
- Allow plenty of time in the initial workshop for scaffolding, making sure students understand what is being asked of them. As we run the approach for a second time we will have an introductory lecture where we introduce the concept and value of self-reflection;
- Allow plenty of time in the weekly workshops for students to carry out their reflective conversations, record and upload. We will remain vigilant to support those students who have lapses of confidence in having reflective conversations and recording them;
- Direct the students each week to the weekly recordings by the tutors on the Blackboard VLE site.

References

Bolton, G. (2010). Reflective practice: Writing and Professional Development. London: Sage Publications Ltd.

Boud, D., Keogh, R., & Walker, D. (1985). *Reflection: Turning experience into learning*. London: Kogan Page.

Catteeuw, P. (2013). Portfolio assessment and intercultural competence. *The 9th International Scientific Conference eLearning and software for Education*, Bucharest, April 25-26-2013.

Campión, R.S. & Navaridas Nalda, F. (2012). Web 2.0 and higher education: Its educational use in the university environment. *European Journal of Open, Distance and E-Learning*, 2.

Cobb, S., Heaney, R., Corcoran, O. & Henderson-Begg, S. (2010). Using mobile phones to increase classroom interaction. *Journal of Educational Multimedia and Hypermedia*, 19(2), 147-157.

Dewey, J. (1991). *How we think*. Buffalo, NY: Prometheus Books (Originally published: Lexington, MA:D.C. Heath, 1910).

Dyment, J.E. & O'Connell, T.S. (2010). The quality of reflection in student journals: A review of limiting and enabling factors. *Innovative Higher Education*, 35, 233-244.

Dyson, L.E., Litchfield, A., Lawrence, E., Raban, R. & Leijdekkers, P. (2009). Advancing the m-learning research agenda for active, experiential learning: Four case studies. *Australasian Journal of Educational Technology*, 25 (2), 250-26.

Elbow, P. (1995). *Landmark essays on voice and writing*. New Jersey: Lawrence Erlbaum Associates.

Francis, H. & Cowan, J. (2009). Fostering an action-reflection dynamic amongst student practitioners. *Journal of European Industrial Training*, 32, 336-346.

Gokhale, R. & Bhakare, S. (2011). New learning paradigms: The SMS way and student to student learning with mobile technology. *International Journal of Arts & Sciences*, 4(8), 275-283.

Hedberg, P. (2009). Learning through reflective classroom practice: Applications to educate the reflective manager. *Journal of Management Education*, 33, 16-36.

Kukulska-Hulme, A. (2005). Current uses of wireless and mobile learning: Landscape study on the use of mobile and wireless technologies for teaching and learning in the post-16 sector. JISC-funded project. Online at: http://www.hefce.ac.uk/pubs/rdreports/2010/rd18_10/

Lindquist, D., Denning, T., Kelly, M., Malani, R., Griswold, W.G. & Simon, B. (2007). Exploring the potential of mobile phones for active learning in the classroom. *SIGCSE '07 conference proceedings*, 384-388.

Mann, K., Gordon, J. & MacLeod A. (2009). Reflection and reflective practice in health professions education: A systematic review. *Advances in Health Sciences Education*, 14(4), 595-621.

Middleton, A. (2009). Beyond podcasting: Creative approaches to designing educational audio. *ALT-J, Research in Learning Technology*, 17(2), 143 - 155.

Middleton, A. & Nortcliffe, A. (2009). Audio, autonomy and authenticity: constructive comments and conversation captured by the learner. *ALT-C 2009 "In dreams begins responsibility"- choice, evidence and change*, Manchester, UK, 8-10 September.

Moon, J. A. (1999). A handbook of reflective and experiential learning. London: Routledge.

Quinton, S. & Smallbone,T. (2010). Feeding forward: using feedback to promote student reflection and learning: A teaching model. *Innovations in Education and Teaching Innovations*, 47(1), 125-135.

Rushton, D., and Lahlafi, A. (2014). Mobile phones: Not a distraction in the classroom but a means of engagement? *EDINEB 2014 Conference Innovative Business Education Design for 21st Century Living.*

Rushton, D., Middleton, A., & Malone, C. (2014). Digital posters: Talking cycles for academic literacy. In: Lillis, T., Harrington, K., Lea, M. and Mitchell, S. (eds.) *Working With Academic Literacies: Case Studies Towards Transformative Practice.* Perspectives on Writing Series. Fort Collins, CO: The WAC Clearinghouse and Parlor Press.

Ryan, M. (2011). Improving reflective writing in higher education: A social semiotic perspective. *Teaching in Higher Education*, 16(1), February 2011, 9-111.

Scornavacca, E., Huff, S. & Marshall, S. (2009). Mobile phones in the classroom: If you can't beat them, join them. *Communications of the ACM*, 52(4), 142-148.

Sethi, R.S. (2013). Role of technology in enhancing the quality of higher business management education: A description. *International Journal of Management Excellence*, 1(1), 13-17.

Siemens, G. (2003). Learning ecology, communities and networks: extending the classroom. Elearnspace, 17th October 2003. Online at: http://www.elearnspace.org/Articles/learning_communities.htm

UCAS (2013). Eight out of ten freshers have smart phones. Online at: http://www.ucasmedia.com/2014/eight-out-of-ten-freshers-have-smartphones

Usher, R. (1985). Beyond the anecdotal: Adult learning and the use of experience. *Studies in the Education of Adults*, 17(1), 59-74.

YouTube website (2014). Statistics. Online at: https://www.youtube.com/yt/press/en-GB/statistics.html

Scenario: Tutorial action notes

"Tell you what," Gill said to her student, "why don't you record the tutorial. Send me a copy back for my records and include a few written action notes to outline the main points as you see them."

This was a sudden change of plan for Gill. A couple of years ago she'd realised her students were either not making notes in tutorials or were too busy concentrating on making their notes to take in everything she was saying. She had decided to use her phone voice recorder to capture the conversation instead and had been emailing her students the recordings ever since. But today she'd looked at her student as he watched her dig into her bag for her phone and wondered why it was *her* doing the recording.

Pleased with herself, the next student she met sat down and put his iPad on the desk and said, "Do you mind if I record this using Notability? It really helps me to record conversations and scribble notes at the same time. I save all my notes on Google Drive." Later Gill received a copy of the tutorial and a link to the Google Drive folder.

Key tools: student's phone! Or Voice Record app, Notability

Based on the work of Anne Nortcliffe, Sheffield Hallam University. See: Nortcliffe, A. (2014) "My story and My solutions as A Dyslexic Academic", The Dyslexic Academic Symposium 2014, London Metropolitan University, 8th November 2014, [Online] http://prezi.com/mgqgay4xbu0j/

Collaborative curation in the classroom

Catherine Hack

Background

Since bioethics was identified in the Subject Benchmark statements for Bioscience students (QAA, 2002), course teams have attempted to incorporate it into undergraduate programmes (Wilmott, 2004). However, questions remain about how it should be taught and who should teach it (Downie & Clarkburn, 2005). Bioethics encompasses both philosophy and science, and requires skills in evaluating and developing arguments, communication and collaboration. All first year students in the School of Biomedical Sciences at the University of Ulster are provided with an introduction to bioethics. In the short introductory class it was important to capture some of the ethos of why it is important to study bioethics, without overwhelming students with philosophical frameworks. The approach taken was to start with a bioethical question in the public domain, support students as they collate and evaluate the evidence, and conclude by identifying the stakeholders and the key ethical issues.

Activity

Prior to the class, an email was sent inviting the students to bring a mobile device to class; 44% brought smart phones, 33% laptops and 22% tablets. At the start of the class, the students were presented with a question: "Do you think UK media is biased against GM crops?" Two spreadsheets had been prepared in Google Docs, one for the evidence in favour of GM crops (PRO-GMO) and one for articles which were negative towards GM (NO-GMO). The spreadsheets were formatted to support students in curating and evaluating the evidence they collected. The columns included titles and prompts to identify the source and article type (e.g. online site for traditional newspapers or news broadcasters, social media, website, blog), to rank the evidence provided and to comment on how well balanced and/or informative they considered the article.

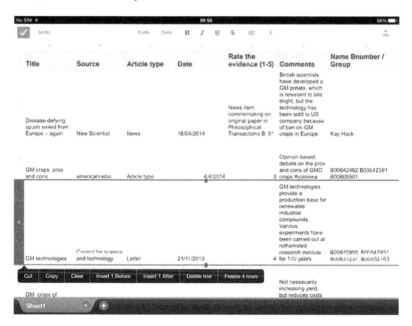

Figure 1: Google Docs Spreadsheet to capture evidence from UK media that supports the growth of GM crops.

Evidence, findings, analysis or reflection

Observation of the classroom indicated that the majority of the students were enthusiastically involved in the activity. A small number of individuals and groups that appeared unsure of the task were quickly identified and support provided. The students were allowed to form their own groups, and they quickly assigned roles, with those with a laptop taking responsibility for recording the information, whilst those with other devices searched and scoped the information. Whilst everyone had a device and there was Wi-Fi available in the classroom, those with phones with small screens were at a disadvantage. The use of the Google Docs spreadsheet was a familiar and accessible environment. Students were asked to tag their contributions with their student identification number, and it was clear that small groups of 2-3 students were much more productive than larger groups.

Analysis of the data indicated that 90% of the enrolled cohort made a contribution to one of the spreadsheets, 75 students contributed 48 articles to the 'PRO-GMO' spreadsheet, and 123 students contributed 78 articles to the 'NO-GMO' spreadsheet. Approximately 38% of the articles were from the online presence of traditional media (newspapers and broadcasters), with 48% from websites. Only 5% of the articles were identified via social media (Twitter and Facebook). Less than 12% of the returned articles did not meet the criteria of the question, because they were not aimed at a UK audience (4.5%) or because they were a peer-reviewed scientific paper, i.e. not part of the 'mainstream' media as requested (7.5%). Articles that did not meet the question criteria were posted early on in the class, once the message that the articles should be from mainstream media was reinforced, compliance with the question criteria improved. The opportunity to 'tweet' progress throughout the task, contributed to student engagement and interaction within the large classroom.

> **Fab class, thanks bby #BMS104**
> 10:22 AM - 3 Apr 2014   ♀ unknown, United Kingdom

Figure 2: Feedback at the end of the class via Twitter

The task was supported with Twitter, which encouraged interaction and promoted some competition between the groups as well the opportunity to provide real time feedback, from peers and the tutor. Whilst the use of Twitter was voluntary, it did provide an opportunity for students to ask questions and give their opinions; the type of interaction that can be difficult to initiate with large groups of first year students (Tyma, 2011).

Discussion and Conclusion

This activity was designed to raise students' awareness of bioethics and the importance of giving consideration to alternative, evidence-based arguments to resolve difficult ethical dilemmas. However, the task also provided students with information and skills on:

- **Developing an effective Google search strategy** - Whilst students typically consider themselves 'expert' at using search engines such as Google, the evidence indicates that they are not using its features effectively. This task supported students in developing advanced search strategies that provided distinct results which met the question criteria.

- **Evaluating sources** - The structure of the spreadsheet supported students as they identified and evaluated credible sources of information in the mainstream media

- **Evaluating communication strategies** - The task was focussed on exploring the messages in the mainstream media on an important bioethical issue, which encouraged students to consider how information from scientific research (peer reviewed journals) is communicated to the general public.

- **Using social media** - The task raised students' awareness of how social media can be used to disseminate scientific information or misinformation.

- **Raising awareness of digital identity** - The use of Twitter and Tweet Beam to broadcast tweets to the class, promoted awareness of the risks of 'over-honesty' in the public domain

This class will be run again, with a couple of slight modifications to the activity. The group size will be limited to a maximum size of three and students will be encouraged to follow up on the activity to draw out key ethical principles, identify the stakeholders, and the risks and benefits of the technology. The activity will continue to be supported with Twitter. Whilst it is recognised that this does exclude non-Twitter users, this was outweighed by the benefits of receiving authentic real-time feedback and engagement with the class. The approach, whilst applied to bioethics, could be used in a wide range of subject domains.

References

Downie, R., & Clarkeburn, H. (2005). Approaches to the teaching of bioethics and professional ethics in undergraduate courses. *Bioscience Education e-journal*, 5(2). Online at: http://www.bioscience.heacademy.ac.uk/journal/vol5/Beej-5-2.aspx

Tyma, A. (2011). Connecting with what is out there! : Using twitter in the large lecture. *Communication Teacher*, 25(3), 175-181.

Willmott, C. J., Bond, A. N., Bryant, J. A., Maw, S. J., Sears, H. J., & Wilson, J. M. (2004). Teaching ethics to bioscience students: a survey of undergraduate provision. *Bioscience Education e-journal*, 3(9). Online at: www.bioscience.heacademy.ac.uk/journal/vol3/Beej-3-9.aspx

Quality Assurance Agency (2007). Subject benchmarks statement biosciences. Online at: http://www.qaa.ac.uk/

Scenario: Excursion to the smart city data mine

"So, what is data?" Perhaps a fairly standard question in a standard Research Methods module, but Rebecca was introducing the debriefing workshop for her 30 students. Her only instruction last week had been, "Take your smartphones and using their multimedia functionality and whatever apps you have or can find. Go into the city and research 'Cars'! Be imaginative!"

"Cars?!"

That was last week, and this week the students were sharing their photographs, their videos, audio, web pages, spreadsheets of traffic counts, artwork made from road sign graphics... The list of rich data went on.

"Today we are going to look at a few key ideas that come from last week's excursion and by the end of the semester you will have crafted this work into the best report you never dreamed of writing!... By the way, did anyone devise a research question before you set off..? Did you write it down? Did this change? ...Let's hear about the methods you used and how well they worked?"

Key tools: smartphone and numerous apps including camera, recorder, SoundCloud, YouTube Capture, Google Drive, Grafio

Using smart devices to enhance learning
— the use of Twitter and blogging in nurse education

Neil Withnell

Introduction

Student nurses are different to other higher education students as they spend half of their nurse training in clinical placements. Students can easily feel left out when away from the university. This case study describes how a staff and student collaboration was established to enhance communication and foster belonging using a shared Twitter account and an accompanying blog site.

Background

The use of social media to enhance student engagement in teaching and learning is an area that is growing and has the potential to become a crucial element of student nurse education in the future. Whilst there has been some suspicion and apprehension about the use of social media in education (Jisc, 2014) this is a growing area in education that can be highly effective in developing learning. Nursing students are understandably suspicious of social media as they are aware of the regulatory body Code of Conduct and the need to be professional at all times. Nursing students are educated regarding the Code and are made aware of the numbers of qualified practitioners that have been removed from the profession as a result of inappropriate use of social media. However, there are many nursing students that are using social media professionally and recognise the benefits of the educational nature of this platform.

In the UK, 53% of smartphone users access social media platforms on a daily basis using their mobile devices with 9 in 10 Twitter users now accessing the platform via their smartphone (Ipsos, 2014). It is clear that the student population is diverse and that the increase in social media is an area that educators need to explore.

Development

The use of Twitter in higher education is growing exponentially (Megele, 2014) and the undergraduate Nursing course at Salford University felt it could be used locally as part of the whole teaching and learning experience for undergraduate nursing students to develop a greater sense of belonging.

Ideas began to form about how to complement and develop this new way of working. It was felt that there were so many potential benefits to using social media in an educational context including: the opportunity to follow key people and organisations, the sharing of information and the contacts that can be made. Therefore, in December 2013 a small team of nursing lecturers met up to look at the formation and implementation of a dedicated undergraduate nursing Twitter account (@nursingSUni) and an accompanying blog site. (http://salforduniversitynursing.wordpress.com/)

The discussion about setting this up was extremely convincing and, although there were concerns about the use of social media, it was felt that there were far more advantages than disadvantages. The use of a shared Twitter account with staff and students would only enhance communication and give the students a shared ownership and sense of belonging.

Experience

This initiate went live in January 2014 with a strong emphasis on engaging students interactively and through collaborative partnerships. Students are seen as equal partners in their educational experience (Higher Education Academy, 2014) and it was felt that this innovation could be crucial for developing professionalism, communication and engagement with an emphasis on the enhancement of their education.

The Twitter account and blog site are managed by staff and curated on a weekly basis by students and staff. When the Twitter account was first set up the call went out to all students asking if they would like to curate the account with support from staff members. The first few weeks were curated by staff and this enabled students to observe what was happening before deciding whether they wanted to become involved. Within a very short space of time several students were asking about how to curate the account and to date there have been more students than staff doing this. The account is 'manned' on a weekly basis from Monday and there are always staff members available for support if the student is unsure of how to respond or if unavailable for any reason.

Curating the Twitter account is additional to an academic or student workload, and it is testimony to the students that they are very keen to commit their time and energy to curating it. Many students who are juggling motherhood, assessments, examinations, and placements continue to be committed to engaging with this initiative.

Students are fully supported in this role and are able to contact staff at any time for advice. In all cases so far one of the staff members has remained logged into the account supporting from a distance. Students are seeing the benefits of the Twitter account and this approach is gaining momentum. For example in Welcome Week alone there were 17,900 views of the Twitter account amongst the March starters. To date (September 2014) there are currently over 2,500 followers to the Twitter account and these are increasing on a daily basis.

The blog site was set up as an area to provide guidance and advice for nursing students and also features guest blogs. Students, and staff, are becoming more involved in 'blogging' having seen other blogs and recognising how reflection can help with education. Following a week of curating the Twitter account the curator writes or videos a short blog entry to summarise and reflect on their week. From this several students have set up their own blog. To date there have been over 3,200 views of the blog site with many positive comments on the blogs by students.

Reflecting on the experience and its benefits

The Twitter account and blog offer flexibility for our students as this can be accessed from anywhere at any time. Opportunities to link with others are clearly evident in the Twitter feed. Students are supporting and collaborating with other students, qualified practitioners, NHS providers and many partners across the UK. Feedback from students, within their blogs and through discussion, indicates that they feel part of the School and express their satisfaction with this 'belongingness'. Students want to fit in and this can increase a student's willingness to connect with other students, both near and far, in their field of study. Information and digital literacy and technology-enhanced learning are incidental benefits of this initiative.

There are key players in the field of nursing, midwifery, pharmacy, mental health and more on Twitter who are at the forefront of academic practice and information. For example, Jane Cummings, the Chief Nursing Officer for England, has over 17,000 followers on Twitter. There are many others, the governing body, and leaders in the field and students are able to ask questions, keep up-to-date and share best practice. There are weekly Twitter chats and students are joining in with these and debating topics, which in turn assists with their studies. This information is being shared on Twitter and students are discussing and sharing best practice through this medium. They are also knocking on and entering doors 'virtually' where social media is creating new opportunities for networking. A lot of events have taken place through the use of the Twitter account, key speakers, and new developments within the school and this has been an important area of growth within the school and in the education of student nurses.

Feedback from the students highlights that they see the benefits of curating the Twitter account. They are behaving professionally, sharing best practice and engaging in Twitter chats on important areas. This in turn leads to input into their reflective accounts and their own studies.

Students access the Twitter account on their smart devices, making it accessible from wherever they are.

Concluding thoughts

Students are bringing their own devices to the classroom now, and are being actively encouraged to use social media to enhance their learning. It is recognised that education of student nurses must embrace the use of new technologies and there is a commitment within the school to engage with social media.

Engaging with social media helps to keep the students 'in-touch' with what is happening on their nursing course, wherever they are. Students can see what is happening within the school through the Twitter account and can remain connected with staff and peers. Within placements there is often limited access to computer systems within local hospitals and communities, so it is easy to keep up-to-date with the Twitter account by using their smart devices. Now, however, students are able to use their own devices to take notes, look up policies and procedures, or find out some information for a particular disease or treatment, and this can only improve patient care. Furthermore, it is anticipated that students can increase their employability through their networking and can enhance their CV. The use of personal smart devices and social media, for the nursing students, demonstrably strengthens their connections and sense of belonging.

References

Higher Education Academy (2014). Engagement through partnership: students as partners in learning and teaching in higher education. Available from http://www.heacademy.ac.uk/resources/detail/students_as_partners/Engagement_through_partnership

Ipsos (2014). Social media trends: The culture of now. Online at: http://www.ipsos-mori.com/researchpublications/Trends-and-Futures.aspx

Jisc (2014). Listen, understand, act: Social media for engagement. Online at: http://www.jisc.ac.uk/inform/inform39/ListenUnderstandAct.html#.U7VM 65RSbig

Megele, C. (2014). Theorising Twitter chat. *Journal of Perspectives in Applied Academic Practice*, 2 (2), 46−51.

Scenario: YouTube VLE

Last year Jo's students had stepped forward to manage the class Twitter Channel. Enough had volunteered to make regular posts, develop their peer network and foster connections to other people and professional groups. She wanted to develop things a bit this year, building on this momentum and also upon the increased use of visual media she had noticed in recent posts. She put out a further course invitation. This time to form a course YouTube Channel. "What we'll do is find videos to illustrate some of the concepts were discussing each week. If we can't find anything suitable, then I would like to think about how we can make videos. I'd like to start the lecture each week by showing one of our videos and writing responses to it on Twitter. We'll create a course playlist of selected videos and our challenge is to build up our viewing figures over the semester."

Key tool: YouTube

Based on: Trier, J. (2007b). "Cool" engagements with YouTube: Part 2. Journal of Adolescent and Adult Literacy, 50, 598–603.

SECTION 3 APPS FOR LEARNING

In this section the role of smart apps and their significance to learning are discussed. In the first chapter, *Approaching apps for learning, teaching and research,* Fiona MacNeill discusses effective, time efficient strategies for discovering and integrating useful apps into the academic workflow and offers some teaching scenarios where an app can be used to solve a specific problem or to fill a new niche.

In the second chapter, *Being smart: using apps lifewide,* Andrew Middleton looks at a selection of apps used by educators and identifies how, for many, the most important apps are those that are used 'lifewide'.

Approaching apps for learning, teaching and research

Fiona Macneill

Introduction

This chapter looks at discovery techniques and strategies for approaching the use of apps in support of learning, teaching and research. Example scenarios are included to help illustrate situations where apps can solve a problem or augment existing teaching practice.

This chapter has a pragmatic tone and is based upon my own experience working with apps and smart devices in higher education for over five years. Your own path of discovery with your device will be granular and accumulative and it is my hope that the suggested strategies outlined herein will help you to make the most of the functionality afforded by apps and will give you the confidence to expand upon your current use of your smart device.

App discovery

Something that I have found through experience is that the respective App Stores themselves are not always the best places to discover apps. This is something that Apple's App Store has tried to address through the compilation of thematic

The Google for Education blog announced the introduction of the Google Play for Education store in January of 2015 (Sproat, 2015), however access to this specially tailored store is contingent on an institutional management contract for Chomebooks and/or Android tablets (Google, 2015b). This can be viewed alongside news on the MacRumors site from March of 2015 that Apple plans to make changes to their iPad in Education programme (Rossignol, 2015). Although both of these initiatives offer potential rewards in terms of Mobile Device Management and app selection, the lone educator who endeavours to learn more may not have access to these resources due the level of institutional buy-in required for access

Box 1. Google Play for Education

collections, for example their "Education Collections" which are grouped by subject relevance (Apple, 2014a). Google's app store, Google Play, has also attempted to achieve similar goals through the use of Educational sub-categories such as "Apps for Students" and "Maths & Science Made Fun" (Google, 2014a). These collections and category groupings can be helpful when searching for apps, which are suitable for your students, but when using store search functions more broadly, unless you have a specific app in mind you can receive a vast and overwhelming array of results. For example a search for the word "writing" without using filters in the Apple's App Store will bring back everything from: handwriting practise apps, word games, to note-taking apps and a only a smattering of apps which are appropriate for academic writing. When searching in the Apple App Store, if the "productivity" drop-down filter is selected the results are more useful. At this point the apps, which I use for writing started to be listed, but still, a large number of apps lacked relevance which has a tint of irony, when the default search option is "By Relevance". To pinpoint the broader issues with app stores: there is a lack of helpful reviews, you cannot exclude children's apps and games from search, and the non-linear relationships between functionality in apps make discovery difficult.

Apps may not fit comfortably functionality-wise within a 'productivity' definition in the same way as a piece of desktop software like Microsoft Word. If we take a moment to think about this it seems obvious, as a large part of how we perceive 'productivity' is flavoured by our prior experience using desktop applications like Microsoft Word; a veritable do-it-all word processor. An app might package a small selection of functions, similar to those that Microsoft Word offers us, such as writing tools, spell-check and formatting tools, but the app might also traverse other genres of functionality or may be deliberately minimalist in order to promote focus while writing. Examples of apps which fall into a more minimalist niche for writing are Index Card (Denvog, 2013) and OmmWriter for iPad (Herraiz Soto & Co., 2013).

My key recommendation is to use web search engines, such as Google, Bing, Yahoo and DuckDuckGo, in the first instance to search for the desired task or a function of a prospective app. The aforementioned task or function that you want to see is what will lead you to prospective apps, "apps" that you can subsequently identify in the relevant app store for your smart device. This need not be time-consuming, as an experiment and a way to get started use a built-in Clock app or get yourself a timer app like Timer+ and set 10 minutes aside (Minima Software, 2014). Think about the thing that you would like an app to do or a way that you would like it to work, for example "make notes on my iPad, app" and see what comes up in your chosen search engine. In the search engine DuckDuckGo (duckduckgo.com), an app-specific category will be included on your search page due to the inclusion of the word "app". DuckDuckGo also enables the use of Quixey, the app-only search engine, which you can access by putting "!Quixey" at the end of your search. The exclamation mark in this context, is called a "!bang command", and uses DuckDuckGo's search tools to access Quixley (DuckDuckGo, n.d.).

Sharing opinions and practice

Searching for online opinions is only one way that you can tap into collective knowledge around apps. In-person discussions, whether in the corridor at work or with friends and family, can be great sources for app recommendations. Furthermore consider sitting down for a coffee with fellow smart device owners. Try to resist the temptation to discuss what these devices don't do as that can derail the dialogue, instead focus on what you do with your device and what you aspire to do with your device. You may be surprised to learn that others have discovered different apps for completing similar tasks. Several higher educational institutions in the UK now run events focused on the use of these devices and discussion of apps, which can support teaching and learning (Aiyegbayo, 2014). Consider attending events like this at your institution or establishing your own. These events can be very informal or have a thematic basis for focus on specific outcomes (MacNeill, Webber & Hewitt, 2014). For example you might have a session around an app which a few of you agree is useful for in-class teaching, such as Doceri Interactive Whiteboard (SP Controls, 2014) or Explain Everything (MorrisCooke, 2014) and then you can use the session to explore the app in more detail together and discuss the things that you like about it and questions which you have come across.

Support of your teaching and research

A key aspect of personalising your device and thus confirming its value is to make use of apps for support of teaching and research. The most effective way to integrate this personalisation into your existing workflow is to consider the search for apps as not dissimilar to the search for literature. In your academic sphere you are likely to have keystone literature, a cadre of works, which you have found to be integral to your research and/or teaching practice. A cadre of apps can also take on these properties over time, however just like your keystone texts it is worth interrogating their usefulness from time-to-time. Do they remain relevant, do they continue to serve the desired task or purpose, has something new emerged which does a better job, is there a free option which your students could use that would do something similar? These questions may seem familiar when applied to literature and over time as with research sources, favourite apps will emerge.

WebDAV is an acronym for "Web Distributed Authoring and Versioning" as an extension of HTTP; "Hyper Text Transfer Protocol". Was defined by a Working Group of the Internet Engineering Task Force (IETF) as a "set of methods" which can be used as a means for "management of resource collections" (Internet Engineering Task Force Trust, 2007).

Box 2. *Webdav*

You will find that unlike desktop software, which in some cases has a historical legacy reaching back 20 years or more, such as the likes Microsoft Office or Adobe products, your 'favourite' app may be superseded by something that does the job better in the near future. This may sound like a stress inducing notion and can present challenges in terms of moving your content from one app to another. These challenges are lessening due to improvements in cloud-based storage services associated with smart device operating systems, for example iCloud drive and Google drive, and also through the emergence of what I like to term as third-party connective apps (Apple, 2014b; Google, 2014c). The criteria for "third-party connective apps" is that they must be listed as sharing/saving/transfer mechanisms from a wide variety of apps, typically they also have a web-based service element. Examples include Dropbox, Box, OneDrive, Evernote, Instapaper and Feedly (Box, 2014; DevHD, 2014; Dropbox, 2014; Evernote, 2014a; Instapaper Holdings, 2014; Microsoft, 2014a). Some of these services are content specific, for instance web content bookmarking in the cases of Feedly and Instapaper and others allow a variety of content in the cases of Dropbox, CloudOn, OneDrive and Box. In addition to third-party solutions, increasingly WebDAV (see Box 2.) connections are offered within apps allowing access to institutional repositories for storage, backup and retrieval. For example Microsoft Sharepoint can be used through a WebDAV connection in productivity apps such as, Apple's Pages, Numbers and Keynote, and also iAnnotatePDF, Notability and GoodReader (Branchfire, 2014; Ginger Labs,

2014; iTunes, 2014a, 2014b, 2014c; Microsoft, 2014b; Selukoff, 2014). We are not quite there yet in the case of all apps, particularly those which produce media artefacts such as audio or video files, but increasingly your data will be independent of the apps themselves therefore allowing you the flexibility to try out alternative apps.

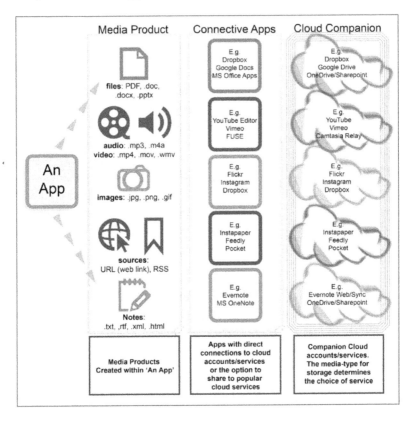

Figure 1. Third-party connective apps. This figure illustrates the relationship between media products created within an app and intermediary apps which liaise directly with cloud-based accounts and services

A very quick way to check the status of an app is to review the features list when an update is released through your respective App Store. What functions have the developers introduced? You may be surprised by new and helpful additions to the functionality that can make your favourite apps even more useful. Also if there is a piece of functionality which you would like to see in your favourite app, try writing to the developers to suggest it prior to switching to a new app. One of the excellent things about customerto-developer relationships, when it comes to apps specifically, is that it is a far more direct relationship than some traditional desktop software. Many apps have integrated feedback functions where you can provide the developers with direct suggestions so that they can actively improve the app and introduce new functionality. I have found developers to be very responsive and a quick message is all it takes. Also if you like an app and you are finding it helpful, consider leaving a review, recommending it via social media or writing a blog post about the pros and cons. To return to my prior point about app stores, if we share our reviews as educators, it will help to make searching for apps more fruitful in the future.

Example scenario 1

You plan to create a slide in your PowerPoint presentation displaying data from the United Nations related to a specific country, but before you create the slide you decide to search for "United Nations, app". Many International organisations and governmental bodies now have apps, including the United Nations (UN) which have several apps for different purposes (United Nations Digital, 2014). In this case you find an app from the UN, which will not only allow you to show data but comparative data between countries. Instead of a static slide you could use the app as a tool to question your students, for example students could ask a question like "what is the comparative level of education between country x and country y?" and the live answer to that question as well as a visualisation of that data will be live at your fingertips (United Nations, 2014).

The British Government are not actively pursuing app development, instead focusing on mobile accessibility for the re-designed gov.uk site (Loosemore, T., 2013). The data.gov.uk project overseen by the Transparency Board aims to create "a network of re-usable government data" this includes 3rd party apps which use "non-personal, non-sensitive data" (data.gov.uk, n.d., para. 1) for example: crime statistics, council information, etc.

Box 3. British Government's use of apps

Personalisation for teaching

Another way to approach the use of apps in a live teaching situation is to consider the personalisation of your device as an advantage and think about how that might aid you. For example in your teaching spaces a desktop computer may be provided, connected to the projection system. This desktop is designed to serve the needs of the masses and as a consequence it will likely have a restricted ecosystem of software applications. Depending upon the situation and your familiarity with the classroom computer it may not be possible to confidently use anything beyond Microsoft PowerPoint. Provided you have a reliable Wi-Fi connection and a video adapter for connection to the projection system your device can be your personalised teaching tool. This point is largely restricted to iOS devices and Windows touch screen devices, as Android devices have varying levels of compatibility with projection systems unless the room is specifically setup for that purpose; for example a Chromecast box could be made available for presentation from Android devices. At schools, colleges and universities where the choice has been made to install Apple TVs, AirPlay compatible software or Chromecast boxes in teaching spaces, wireless display has the potential to not only be beneficial for students in terms of sharing in-class activities, but also presents advantages such as ease of use and freedom of movement in the room for teaching staff. These benefits are supported by JISC Regional Support Centres' report on the experience of staff using Apple TVs in conjunction with iPads at West Suffolk College (Jisc Regional Support Centres, 2013).

Example scenario 2

As a means of teaching anatomy you plan to use the website Zygote Body to display aspects of the human skeleton. However, the site is only compatible with Google Chrome and you are unsure of whether Chrome is installed on the classroom computer. As an alternative you install 3D for Medical's free app Essential Skeleton and display this in-class using the app's built-in annotation tools. If this were a frequent need you may choose to install the paid apps, Essential Anatomy or Zygote Body 3D Anatomy Atlas (3D4Medical.com, 2014; Zygote Media Group, 2014b). Apps like Essential Anatomy can also be used to provide quick annotated diagrams that can be saved as images for addition to the Virtual Learning Environment (VLE) for out of class study.

Beyond the classroom

Many apps have the potential to be powerful resource creation tools, helping to support your students beyond the classroom. For example instead of sending a written email in response to a student question you may choose to use an audio recording app to send them a quick verbal response as an email attachment, or to use an app like TechSmith Fuse to provide a quick video reply (TechSmith, 2014a). Apps like Explain Everything or Doceri can be used to explain concepts through video in real-time, providing similar qualities as an in-class demonstration on the board (MacNeill, 2013b). The app, Explain Everything is used to great effect by Dr. Keith Turvey in his "Narrative Ecology Explained" video, in which he uses to the app to visually explain his Narrative Ecology theoretical framework (Turvey, 2013). As a way of integrating these practices into your workflow, next time you receive an email question from a student, ask yourself the following questions: can this question be answered visually and would the other students benefit from the answer as well?

Example scenario 3

> A student has sent you an email asking where to find certain materials in your course or module within the VLE. Instead of writing an email back you take a quick screenshot of your course module and then use an app such as Skitch (Evernote, 2014b) to annotate the screenshot with arrows and labels, showing the visual location of the materials in question. This screenshot would be complete in a matter of minutes, could be emailed directly to the student from within the app and then also quickly uploaded to your course or module as a class forum entry or as an attachment to a course/module announcement. In this example your time-saving is two-fold: on the one hand you saved yourself from writing a description of the location of the materials and on the other you answered a question which other students may have potentially asked or felt unsure about asking.

The creation of resources outside of the classroom and possibly outside of work-time brings me to the concept of division between work and home life. As the popularity of smart devices has grown, in my own experience as a learning technologist, instructors have frequently come to me with concerns that the use of these devices has blurred the lines between work and home life. This is a view which was investigated by Jennifer J. Deal

(Deal, 2014) in a recent article in the Wall Street Journal. The article posited that the technology can make users feel like they need to respond to emails outside of work-time; however, as the article also suggested, the technology can also minimise the need for this through consideration of how we configure and use these tools. This is not a new problem, any technology that introduces portability changes the rules of the game. For example there are likely to be times when you choose to turn off your mobile phone or mute it, so you are not disturbed by its ringing. Even though the aforementioned mobile phone is likely to be a smart device now, it offers similar yet more sophisticated functionality. You can quickly turn on a "do not disturb" function, or even schedule that function during periods when you plan to research or you are at home. Furthermore there is a lot that you can do with customisation in terms of the kind of notifications you receive, so if you have an important email thread which you are following you can choose be notified of those crucial email replies with an onscreen badge instead of feeling the compulsion to keep checking your inbox. The key to all of this is to set the rules of engagement, let others know how you operate and stick to your rules as far you are able.

As for use of your device at home, utilitarian non-work apps can present some truly rewarding discoveries resulting in benefits within your work as well. For example, I have used my smart devices to measure the width of my front door to see if I could fit a new sofa through it, LINEA (Critec, 2014); edit photos which I have taken, Aviary Photo Editor (Aviary, 2014); scan documents, TinyScan (Appxy Information Technology, 2014); and create short videos about trips I have taken, iMovie (iTunes, 2014d). All of these experiences have resulted in immensely fulfilling digital products and then subsequently I used these skills to create resources for teaching and also passed on app recommendations to others. The point is if you view this only as a work device then you may only realise your device's potential as a word processor.

Retreat

As a means of gaining familiarity with your device I recommend taking a retreat with it and decide if this is a work retreat or home life retreat. Load up any materials that you think you might need on the device, for example that word document you are working on, or those photos from a recent holiday you are planning to tweak. Search for and download some apps based on what you want to do, you may choose more than one; use this as an excuse to see what works best. Then dissuade yourself from packing your laptop and you're away! As a result of these sorts of experiments in my own experience, I now use my device for all my writing projects, as I can maintain my focus more intently in an app rather than within desktop/laptop software where I find the windowed layout to be a distraction (I have planned and written this document on an iPad, with the exception of the references). My most surprising use of an app during a day when I had decided to be iPad-exclusive was during a student event when I used a free app to help some students to take high quality passport-style photos for their student cards. I never needed the ID PhotoPrint app again, but it solved an immediate problem perfectly (Tinkertanker, 2013).

Cloud services and when is Free is not free

In the *Support of your teaching research* section above, I mentioned the use of cloud services in conjunction with apps. I recommend exercising caution when considering your options for data storage in the 'cloud' and in this area I defer to the advice provided by your institution's IT department. At my own institution we have a provided cloud-based solution, which can be used in conjunction with a number of apps, but many device users choose to use 3rd party services like Dropbox for both personal and work related uses. The key question to ask yourself is, who does this data belong to? If the data belongs to your institution and is privileged to your position within the institution then that data needs to be stored on the solution provided by your institution. Also when working on research projects and materials consider the intellectual property rights for those materials and works. For example, if you plan to use online collaboration tools or cloud-based storage solutions to work on projects with colleagues, make sure that you have checked the Terms of Service (TOS) as well as the End User Licence Agreement (EULA) prior to selecting the tool to ensure that the service provider or developer does not assume any ownership rights over your work in the fine print. You may find that your institution advocates the use of certain tools over others due to these considerations. If you are unsure about your use of an app or service, seek guidance from IT support professionals at your institution.

In short, most apps, whether they interface with a cloud service or not, have a Privacy Policy. For instance in the Apple App Store you will find this information below the app description. When considering your privacy, in non-work related use of apps, think about what the app's purpose is, and whether it needs the data it is requesting. So for example, if you install an app, which is for accessing a social media platform, and it requests access to your contacts, ask yourself why does it need access to your contacts? It is likely that this app wants to use your contacts data to find matches between your contacts and your activity on the social media platform, but you have lots of people in your contacts who are not members of that social media platform, why does the app need that data? This particular request has caused me to uninstall apps more than once, or manually enter only the people who I wish to contact using the app.

On the other side of the scale a photo app will need access to the photos on your device in order to be useful. To help you make decisions with regards to your personal privacy on both iOS and Android devices you can review which data sources your apps have access to within the settings (Apple, 2014c, "Basics: Privacy"; Google, 2015a).

To summarise: as one does with the use of certain websites and software applications you have to make trust-based decisions and if there isn't enough information to go on, then reconsider whether you want to go ahead with installing the app.

Recommending apps to your students

Within the context of post-secondary education, many of the apps that you discover over the course of using your device could offer potential benefits for your students. Also encouraging the use of smart devices' web capabilities to access resources, for example through your VLE can be of great benefit. These approaches present tangible value in terms of inclusivity. Ofcom figures from the first quarter of 2014 showed that ownership of smartphones in DE (low-income) households now outnumbers ownership of laptops at 47% as compared to 44% (Ofcom, 2014a). This suggests that for students in this socio-economic group, smartphones may be their most readily available option for accessing the Internet. Data from Ofcom's 2014 Internet use and attitudes bulletin also supports this with 57% of UK adults saying that they access the Internet from their smartphone, 86% of that '57%' response group were identified as being of typical post-compulsory education age; 16-24 year olds (Ofcom, 2014b, p. 3). The use of apps and the devices' web access capabilities is particularly beneficial in the areas of: personal organisation, written work, research, and revision. When recommending apps and device use to students it is worth considering the following issues:

1. **App costs:** a free app, low cost or free web-based app may be more enticing to students than apps you may personally choose to purchase.

2. **Access to data:** apps which do not require any disclosure of information for their use, for example no service-specific account needed and do not request an email to be entered are preferred; both for ease of use and data protection.

3. **Clearly define how the app is useful:** what is it about this app, which makes it really compelling? Why do you use it and in what context? In her book, *Best Practices for Teaching with Emerging Technologies*, M. Pacansky-Brock suggests listing all technology tools, including "supplemental mobile apps" that will be used during the course of study. Pacansky-Brock recommends creating a "list of tools that will be used and your reason(s) for using each" and making this list available to students prior to the start of the course as, "it empowers students to be able to register for classes that meet their own learning styles and overall preferences" (Pacansky-Brock, 2013, Chapter 1, Section A, para. 2).

4. **Inclusivity:** are there options available, possibly as web resources, for those students who do not have smart devices, but do have laptops/desktops? Conversely any software or web application, such as the VLE or an online reference tool should ideally be smart device accessible. To define a web application in this context, D. Nations, writing on about.com's tech trends website explains the concept very succinctly as, "any application that uses a web browser as a client" (Nations, n.d., para. 1). The difference being that when we choose to use such applications on a smart device they must also be responsive, meaning that the layout and functionality actively adjusts to access from the device's web browser as well as being accessible from a within conventional desktop/laptop web browsers such as Mozilla Firefox, Microsoft Internet Explorer, or Apple's Safari.

5. **Signposting:** another idea that Pacansky-Brock introduces in *Best Practices for Teaching with Emerging Technologies* is the idea of visually or descriptively signposting mobile accessible assignments and activities to students. As she writes, "consider using a small icon to designate 'mobile worthy' activities, "your

students will appreciates your efforts to make their everyday tools part of their college learning experience..." (Pacansky-Brock, 2013, Chapter 6, Section 7: "Which Activities Are Appropriate for Mobile", para. 4).

I was recently asked about whether it is appropriate for academic staff to recommend certain apps as they are commercial products which may or may not be supported by the institution's IT department. This is a legitimate concern and to play it safe you may wish to recommend only apps that are related to institutional services or are provided by approved vendors. Although apps can provide a cost and time effective solutions to academic challenges, I think that there is a case to be made for couching recommendations in terms of personal use and personal choice. You might choose to give a recommendation like this, 'I have personally used apps for editing short videos in slow motion, for example x app, it costs y amount and other similar apps might be available'. For students who do not have access to smart devices there may be web-based alternatives, for the slow-motion video example, YouTube's free web-based video editor could be an option (Google, 2014e). I like to follow a rule of three when providing technical solutions, so in addition I might also suggest that the students could book a video editing computer station at the institution's media centre where they could get technical help with the project. The point is any of the three approaches to the project will have similar results and it may not be possible for all the students to use the institutional editing facilities at the same time, so apps provide a greater level of flexibility for completing this project. The Swiss Army Knife-like power of apps to solve situations like this should not be underestimated and in this example recommending an app is not that dissimilar to recommending an article, book or selection of online resources, which might aid the completion of a given assignment. You also don't necessarily have to recommend a specific app, but could suggest more generally that students consider using their smart devices for the project. It is possible that your students' current scope of device-use is restricted to a small number of apps, they may not be aware of the potential of their device.

If you work with students who have specific educational needs, take a bit of time to investigate the accessibility options available within an app; are there any integrated options within the app for type-size or style adjustments, does the app respect the operating system accessibility options? For example, a popular app like Evernote, might be helpful to students with Dyslexia for collecting and storing notes but accessibility-wise it does not offer in-app adjustment of background colour/contrast and typeface style of notes so it may not be as suitable as alternative note-taking apps (MacNeill, 2014). Furthermore device operating systems can offer some very helpful built-in accessibility tools. For example the Speak Selection and VoiceOver functions on Apple's iOS devices are incredibly helpful for text to speech and these tools have developed at a rapid pace with operating system updates (Apple, 2014c, "Accessibility: Speak Selection & VoiceOver"). The recent iOS8 update introduced Speak Screen, a two fingered top-to-bottom screen swipe to read out the contents of the page shown on screen (Apple, 2014c, "Accessibility: Speak Screen"). This function also brings up a collapsible on-screen controller allowing the user to control the speed of the voice and to skip ahead or rewind.

A further recommendation is that if you undertake any induction activities with your students, consider auditing your students' device ownership (Chen & Denoyelles, 2013). A good way of doing this is through use of an audience response tool, which allows students to use their smart devices to answer the 'device ownership' question interactively for example, using Poll Everywhere or Socrative (MasteryConnect, 2014; Poll Everywhere, 2014). With an accurate indication of device type ownership you can think about potential app sharing and class-based activities based on this information.

Steps for use of smart devices with your students

The next step after gaining familiarity with apps to support your teaching delivery and research practices is to implement the use of appropriate apps in the classroom with your students; where each student or group of students uses an app for an in-class activity or project. When considering apps for in-class use there is a simple list of rules, which you can follow, inspired by the "Mobile learning practitioner's checklist" developed in the Higher Education Academy's *Making mobile learning work* publication, the concepts are updated due to changes in mobile technologies since publication in 2011 (Traxler & Wishart, 2011).

Checklist for in-class use of smart devices

1. **Learning outcomes:** how is using smart devices going to achieve your learning outcomes and what is the added value? Particularly does the use of this app in the classroom introduce the students to

a skill or tool they could make use of elsewhere in their studies and more broadly? Sometimes the added value is something as simple as not having to book a computer room, which necessitates communication of a room change, in order to allow students to look up or access materials on the web briefly during a class session.

2. **Wi-Fi and mobile network coverage:** ensure that there is adequate Wi-Fi in the area where you plan to use the devices. In the case of location-based activities where you might be relying on 3G or 4G coverage, ensure that the area has coverage and discuss this with your students to ensure that they are happy to use their data plans for this purpose.

3. **Devices:** do you plan to ask the students to use their own devices or devices you provide?

    o   **Devices are provided:** if you have a bank of devices, which the students can use you can pre-install a paid app for completion of a specific task; this can still work well if you only have a small number of devices. A ratio of one device per three students can be very effective. In contrast, one device to one student can be isolating in a classroom situation as it creates a situation where students can enter their own individual virtual zones. So to explain, if you would like the students to take a test where you wish to measure individual responses, then one to one is the correct ratio, but for most other activities a more collaborative or team approach can be successful.

    o   **Student owned devices:** if asking students to install an app on a personal device, free apps are the ideal for take-up, but if only a paid app with do it must have added value beyond the classroom in the same way that buying a textbook offers study value. For example you may ask student teachers to mark-up a sample paper to indicate mistakes, using a PDF annotation app; a very worthy exercise which I must credit to Dr. Nadia Edmond (MacNeill, 2013a). In this case it may be useful to install a paid app for this as the students can go on to use that app in their teaching practice. Conversely in this situation you may wish to use a free app that offers a smaller toolset, providing the students with a taster of paper annotation and then suggesting apps, which offer more advanced functions.

4. **Presentation and sharing:** how will the students share the work that they have created on the devices with the rest of the class? This can be as simple as passing the devices around, although students may be less inclined to do this with personally owned devices. Solutions that allow you to show collective responses on the classroom projection system, such as Poll Everywhere, Socrative and Nearpod (Kovalskys, 2015) can be helpful here. Technical solutions can also provide sharing functionality. Solutions include, as mentioned in the personalisation for teaching delivery section, Apple TV, Chromecast and software for Mac/PC that allow the computer to act as an AirPlay receiver; over Wi-Fi broadcast of Apple device screens to the enabled computer (Apple, n.d.).

5. **"Contingency" (Traxler & Wishart, 2011):** With the best will in the world sometimes things will happen which are beyond your control. For example if the Wi-Fi connection becomes unavailable, that can derail a session when using a mobile responsive website, a web application or an app with web contingent functionality. I recommend testing beforehand in the room you plan to use, with the equipment you plan to use such as an Apple TV. Also having the main classroom or presentation laptop on a wired connection is helpful so that you can circumvent the Wi-Fi for presentation purposes. If you are planning to use an online presentation tool, it is also worth having a basic version of the same material as a PowerPoint presentation or PDF file. For example a polling activity could still be completed using questions shown on the classroom projection system and a show of hands in the room.

6. **"Student Autonomy" (Traxler & Wishart, 2011):** This concept was explained effectively in the *Making mobile learning work* publication: "the need to work with students to enable them to choose the best ways of using their personal devices to support their learning" (Traxler & Wishart, 2011). Use of the students' own devices speaks to this point, as you providing an educational experience which they can take with them and revisit, not something which remains on the loaner device which exists only within the confines of the classroom. You are empowering students to begin their own journey into the personalisation of learning.

Device neutrality and BYOD is the future

On an individual basis we may find ourselves predisposed to a certain corporation's hardware ecosystem due to a variety of factors, including but not limited to compatibility with existing hardware/devices, data and SMS plans and employer supported or purchased hardware. Your students will also have their own preferences and may prefer to use their own equipment due to familiarity and accessibility, to access centralised web-based services (Johnson & Adams, 2011, p.17). The emerging apps and web applications of the future are compatible with multiple operating systems and multiple device types and facilitate live sharing with a strong web-based component. Also the prevailing apps will allow created content to be accessible from a variety of platforms, as Fang explains in *EDUCAUSEreview Online* this "content must be produced to be accessible via various devices and platforms, using not what is "leading edge" or "bleeding edge" in the market but rather the more generic protocols or formats that most, if not all, devices accept" (Fang, 2014, para. 18).

The aforementioned points are becoming increasingly important considerations when choosing which apps you want to use for in-class collaboration or when recommending apps to your students. In my own work I try follow a device neutral rule as far as possible, seeking apps which are available for both Apple and Android operating systems, unfortunately Windows compatible apps are still a rarity. As the Horizon Report stated in the 2013 edition (Johnson *et al.*, 2013, p.16) and the Open University's Innovating Pedagogy report (Sharples, *et al.*, 2014) recently validated from a UK perspective, that Bring Your Own Device or BYOD is the overwhelming trend in education and will affect the nature of apps which succeed in the market. This results in both benefits and challenges in terms of adoption and support, but I for one am excited about the possibilities which will arise as smart device ownership becomes unanimous.

Practical examples

Learning: assignment and activity ideas

- **In-class activity:** place students in groups, with a smart device per group, and ask them to create a visual comic strip to explain a narrative idea. This is an idea which I must credit to Dr. Ruben R. Puentedura at his workshop as part of the 2011 New Media Consortium conference where he introduced the idea of using the app, Strip Designer for this purpose (Egeblad, 2014; Puentedura, 2011). Potential apps: Comic Life (Plasq, 2014), Strip Designer.

- **In-class or group assignment:** use of video apps to demonstrate correct practice to other students, particularly relevant to clinical skills in health subjects as evidenced by A. Monaghan's use of video apps (University of Brighton, n.d.). Potential apps: Coach's Eye (TechSmith, 2014b), Ubersense Coach (UberSense, 2014).

- **Group or individual assignment:** ask students to create short videos from photographs with voice-overs to explain a historic event or narrative. Potential apps: generic camera app available in iOS, iMovie, YouTube Capture (Google, 2014d)

- **Group assignment activity:** ask students to create a location-based mobile activity, this may be created on a desktop/laptop for eventual use on a mobile device. Potential apps: Aurasma (Aurasma, 2014), Scramboo Playmaker (Scramboo, 2014)

- **Individual or Group activity:** ask students to annotate an image, for example an advertisement or art work for critical evaluation purposes. Potential apps: Skitch, Notability, BaiBoard (Lightplaces, 2014), Explain Everything, Doceri Interactive Whiteboard.

- **Online group activity:** collaborative lecture notes - ask your students to keep notes which mean something to them (minimalist or in-depth) and then request that they add the notes to a blog or group discussion board in the VLE. This is helpful for students who struggle to take notes and a source for potential online discussion. Potential apps: Blackboard Mobile Learn (Blackboard, 2014), web access to the VLE via smart device, Evernote, Notes Plus (Tran, 2015) and other note-taking apps currently available.

Teaching: presenting, marking and formative feedback ideas

o **In-class presentation:** using a conventional presentation format (slides and verbal delivery), apps that feature remote control options can be helpful. Such as Keynote, where an iPhone/iPad can be used to remotely control the presentation on a Mac or iPad connected to the projection system. Or apps such as BaiBoard or SlideShark (Brainshark, 2014), which allow you to broadcast a presentation or a virtual whiteboard (which can in-turn be shared on the desktop computer hooked up to the projection system).

o **Interactive audience response options:** for flexible presentations including audience response tools Nearpod is a multi-platform tool and companion app which can be controlled in-class through the app. Two additional apps for audience response are Socrative, Poll Everywhere and there are others.

- o **eMarking options:** these are largely VLE platform and eSubmission dependent, two contemporary examples are Bb Grader (Blackboard, 2015) and Turnitin for iPad (iParadigms, 2014).
- o **Formative feedback:** there is vast array of apps, which can be used to provide formative feedback, here are just a few ideas.
  - o **Audio feedback:** generic iOS Voice Memos app, SoundNote (Estes, 2014), Recordium (Divband, 2014), iAnnotatePDF, Notability, Turnitin for iPad;
  - o **PDF annotation:** iAnnotatePDF, Notability, Adobe Reader (Adobe Systems, 2014), Notes Plus;
  - o **Video feedback:** TechSmith Fuse, iMovie, generic video app.
- • **Note-taking during meetings with students:** Evernote, Notes Plus, Notability and others.

Research: research and personal organisation ideas

- • **Source discovery and filtration:** use apps like Feedly, Instapaper, Newsify (Alexander, 2014), Flipboard (Flipboard, 2014) to discover and subscribe to blogs and news sources (using RSS feeds – *see Box 4*). Each of these apps allows you customise and categorise your sources for easy

RSS is an Internet protocol and is an acronym for Really Simple Syndication (RSS 2.0 Specification, n.d.). It is a method by which users of web-based content, including written blog posts, online articles and audio/visual materials such as audio or video podcasts can be acquiring via subscription.

Box 4. Using RSS feeds

reading and organisation of your research and personal interests. If you use this category of app in tandem with social media it will help to highlight topic and research related news which you can share amongst your network

- • **Bookmarking:** Feedly, Flipboard and Instapaper have companion plugins for desktop web browsers, which can be used to bookmark pages for later consumption within the mobile apps. Furthermore the multi-platform app Pocket runs the gamut from bookmarklet tool to RSS curator and has, according to the Pocket website, compatibility with "500+" apps in order save a variety of sources for later review (Read It Later, 2015). Alternative mobile web browsers, rather than browsers provided through the operating system, such as Mercury (iLegendSoft, 2014) and iCabMobile (Clauss, 2014) allow for customisation of sharing and saving to a variety of online bookmarking services.

- **Social networking:** the mobile app iterations of social media networks are often far more efficient and pleasurable to use than in their desktop forms. Twitter (2015), LinkedIn (2015), Pinterest (2014), Learnist (2015), Facebook (2015) and Google+ (Google, 2014f) all have companion apps. From a work perspective I have found Twitter, LinkedIn and Pinterest to be most useful in support of research, for seeking teaching resources and professional networking.

- **Compilation of materials for research:** there are a number of apps that allow for the import and management of multiple file types, in the case of Notes Plus different files can be compiled in a virtual notebook. Recommended apps: iAnnotatePDF, Notes Plus, Notability.

- **Simple apps for focused reasons:** for getting initial thoughts on paper there are apps which can be helpful to aid focus. Recommended apps: Index Card, Paper (FiftyThree, 2014), Ommwriter, Evernote.

- **Reference management apps:** EndNote for iPad (Thomson Reuters, 2015), Mendeley (2014), PaperShip for Mendeley and Zotero (Shazino, 2014); each interacts with companion online services. There are also apps such as RefME and Thomson Reuters RefScan which use barcode recognition technology with images taken using the smart device camera to produce formatted reference information (ReferenceME, 2015; Thomson Reuters, 2013).

References

Adobe Systems. (2014). *Adobe Reader (Version 11.6.4)* [Mobile application software]. Retrieved from https://itunes.apple.com/gb/app/adobe-reader/id469337564?mt=8

Aiyegbayo, O. (2014). How and why academics do and do not use iPads for academic teaching? *British Journal of Educational Technology*. doi: 10.1111/bjet.12202

Alexander, B. (2014). *Newsify: Your news, blog & RSS Feed Reader* (Version 3.5.1) [Mobile Application software]. Retrieved from https://itunes.apple.com/gb/app/newsify-your-news-blog-rss/id510153374?mt=8

Apple. (n.d.). Play content from your iPhone, iPad, iPod touch or Mac on your HDTV. Retrieved from: https://www.apple.com/uk/airplay/

Apple. (2014a). *Apple Store: Education Collections*. Retrieved from https://itunes.apple.com/WebObjects/MZStore.woa/wa/viewRoom?fcId=569575321&mt=8

Apple. (2014b). *iCloud Drive* (Version iOS 8, OS X 10.10) [Software]. Retrieved from: https://www.icloud.com/#iclouddrive

Apple. (2014c). *iPhone User Guide iOS8*. Retrieved from: https://help.apple.com/iphone/8/#/

Appxy Information Technology Co. (2014). *TinyScan – PDF scanner to scan document, receipt & notes (Version 3.4.1)*. [Mobile application software]. Retrieved from https://itunes.apple.com/gb/app/tinyscan-pdf-scanner-to-scan/id595563753?mt=8

Aurasma. (2014). *Aurasma (Version 3.5.0)* [Mobile application software]. Retrieved from https://itunes.apple.com/gb/app/aurasma/id432526396?mt=8

Aviary. (2014). *Photo Editor by Aviary (Version 3.5.2)* [Mobile application software]. Retrieved from https://itunes.apple.com/gb/app/photo-editor-by-aviary/id527445936?mt=8

Box. (2014). *Box for iPhone and iPad (Version 3.5.2)* [Mobile application software]. Retrieved from https://itunes.apple.com/gb/app/box-for-iphone-and-ipad/id290853822?mt=8

Blackboard. (2014). *Blackboard Mobile LearnTM (Version 4.1.2)* [Mobile application software]. Retrieved from https://itunes.apple.com/gb/app/blackboard-mobile-learn/id376413870?mt=8

Blackboard. (2015). *Bb Grader (Version 1.0.2)* [Mobile application software]. Retrieved from https://itunes.apple.com/gb/app/bb-grader/id897611355?mt=8

Brainshark. (2014). *SlideShark Presentation App (Version 4.0)* [Mobile application software]. Retrieved from https://itunes.apple.com/gb/app/slideshark-presentation-app/id471369684?mt=8

Branchfire. (2014). *iAnnotatePDF (Version 3.1.1)* [Mobile application software]. Retrieved from https://itunes.apple.com/gb/app/iannotate-pdf/id363998953?mt=8

Chen, B. & Denoyelles, A. (2013). Exploring students' mobile learning practices in higher education. *EDUCAUSEreview*, October 7 2013. Retrieved from: http://www.educause.edu/ero/article/exploring-students-mobile-learning-practices-higher-education

Clauss, A. (2014). *iCab Mobile (Web Browser) (Version 8.6)* [Mobile application software]. Retrieved from https://itunes.apple.com/gb/app/icab-mobile-web-browser/id308111628?mt=8

Critec. (2014). *Measure Tools – LINEA (Version 1.0.4)* [Mobile application software]. Retrieved from https://itunes.apple.com/gb/app/measure-tools-linea/id537639632?mt=8

Deal, J. J. (2014, October 27). How to fix the work/life imbalance. *The Wall Street Journal*. Retrieved from: http://www.wsj.com/articles/how-technology-can-help-work-life-balance-1414382688

Denvog. (2013). *Index Card (Version 3.4.1)* [Mobile application software]. Retrieved from https://itunes.apple.com/gb/app/index-card/id389358786?mt=8

DevHD. (2011). *Feedly (Version 24.4)* [Mobile application software]. Retrieved from https://itunes.apple.com/gb/app/feedly.-free-blog-tumblr-youtube/id396069556?mt=8

Divband, M. (2014). *Recordium - voice recorder, audio editor and notetaker (Version 3.2)* [Mobile application software]. Retrieved from https://itunes.apple.com/gb/app/recordium-voice-recorder-audio/id718873886?mt=8

Dropbox. (2014). *Dropbox (Version 3.6.1)* [Mobile application software]. Retrieved from https://itunes.apple.com/gb/app/dropbox/id327630330?mt=8

DuckDuckGo. (n.d.). !Bang. Retrieved January 5, 2015, from https://duckduckgo.com/bang.html

Egeblad, J. (2014). *Strip Designer (Version 1.15.1)* [Mobile application software]. Retrieved from https://itunes.apple.com/gb/app/strip-designer/id314780738?mt=8

Estes, D. (2014). *SoundNote (Version 2.5.2)* [Mobile application software]. Retrieved from https://itunes.apple.com/gb/app/soundnote/id364789577?mt=8

Evernote Corporation. (2014a). *Evernote (Version 7.6.3)* [Mobile application software]. Retrieved from https://itunes.apple.com/gb/app/evernote/id281796108?mt=8

Evernote Corporation. (2014b). *Skitch – Snap. Mark Up. Send. (Version 3.3)* [Mobile application software]. Retrieved from https://itunes.apple.com/gb/app/skitch-snap.-mark-up.-send./id490505997?mt=8

Facebook. (2015). *Facebook (Version 22.0)* [Mobile application software]. Retrieved from https://itunes.apple.com/gb/app/facebook/id284882215?mt=8

Fang, B. (2014, October 13). Creating a Fluid Learning Environment. *EDUCAUSEreview Online*. Retrieved from: http://www.educause.edu/ero/article/creating-fluid-learning-environment

FAQ page. (n.d.). Retrieved January 5, 2015, from http://data.gov.uk/faq#q1

FiftyThree. (2014). *Paper by FiftyThree (Version 2.2.2)* [Mobile application software]. Retrieved from https://itunes.apple.com/gb/app/paper-by-fiftythree/id506003812?mt=8

Flipboard. (2014). *Flipboard: Your Social News Magazine (Version 3.1)* [Mobile application software]. Retrieved from https://itunes.apple.com/gb/app/flipboard-your-social-news/id358801284?mt=8

Ginger Labs. (2014). *Notability (Version 5.33)* [Mobile application software]. Retrieved from https://itunes.apple.com/gb/app/notability/id360593530?mt=8

Google. (2014a). *Google Play: Education Category*. Retrieved from https://play.google.com/store/apps/category/EDUCATION

Google. (2014b). *Google Chrome (Version 39.0.2171.95)* [Software]. Available from https://www.google.com/chrome/browser/desktop/

Google. (2014c). *Google Drive (Version Windows and OS X 1.18.7821.2489)* [Software]. Available from https://support.google.com/drive

Google. (2014d). *YouTube Capture (Version 2.0.2)* [Mobile Application software] Retrieved from https://itunes.apple.com/gb/app/youtube-capture/ id576941441?mt=8

Google. (2014e). *YouTube Editor* [Software]. Available from https://www.youtube.com/editor

Google. (2014f). *Google+ (Version 4.8.0)* [Mobile application software]. Retrieved from https://itunes.apple.com/gb/app/google+/id447119634?mt=8

Google. (2015a). *Review app permissions.* Retrieved January 11, 2015, from https://support.google.com/googleplay/answer/6014972?hl=en

Google. (2015b). Google for Education. Retrieved from: https://www.google.com/ edu/products/class-content/

Herraiz Soto & Co. (2013). *OmmWriter for iPad (Version 1.3)* [Mobile application software]. Retrieved from https://itunes.apple.com/gb/app/ommwriter-for- ipad/id438878854?mt=8

iLegendSoft. (2014). *Mercury Web Browser (Version 8.9.4)* [Mobile application software]. Retrieved from https://itunes.apple.com/gb/app/mercury-web- browser-powerful/id331012646?mt=8

Instapaper Holdings. (2014). *Instapaper (Version 6.1)* [Mobile application software]. Retrieved from https://itunes.apple.com/gb/app/instapaper/ id288545208?mt=8

Internet Engineering Task Force Trust. (2007). HTTP extensions for web distributed authoring and versioning (WebDAV). Retrieved from: http://tools.ietf.org/ html/rfc4918

iParadigms. (2014). *Turnitin (Version 1.3.0)* [Mobile application software]. Retrieved from https://itunes.apple.com/gb/app/turnitin/id657602524?mt=8

iTunes. (2014a). *Keynote (Version 2.5.1)* [Mobile application software]. Retrieved from https://itunes.apple.com/gb/app/keynote/id361285480?mt=8

iTunes. (2014b). *Numbers (Version 2.5.1)* [Mobile application software]. Retrieved from https://itunes.apple.com/gb/app/numbers/id361304891?mt=8

iTunes. (2014c). *Pages (Version 2.5.1)* [Mobile application software]. Retrieved from https://itunes.apple.com/gb/app/pages/id361309726?mt=8

iTunes. (2014d). *iMovie (Version 2.1.1)* [Mobile application software]. Retrieved from https://itunes.apple.com/gb/app/imovie/id377298193?mt=8

Jisc Regional Support Centres. (2013, September 2). West Suffolk College: iPads and Apple TV: Transformational learning in the 21st century. Jisc Regional Support Centres UK, E53. Retrieved from: http://www.webarchive.org.uk/wayback/ archive/20140701102039/http://www.jiscrsc.ac.uk/case-studies/e/west- suffolk-college-e53.aspx

Johnson, L. & Adams, S. (2011). Technology outlook for UK tertiary education 2011- 2016: An NMC Horizon Report Regional Analysis. Austin, Texas: The New Media Consortium. Retrieved from: http://redarchive.nmc.org/publications/ technology-outlook-uk-tertiary-education

Johnson, L., Adams Becker, S., Cummins, M., Estrada, V., Freeman, A., & Ludgate, H. (2013). NMC Horizon Report: 2013 Higher Education Edition. Austin, Texas: The New Media Consortium. Retrieved from: http://redarchive.nmc.org/publications/2013-horizon-report-higher-ed

Kovalskys, G. (2015). *Nearpod (Version 6.0)* [Mobile application software]. Retrieved from https://itunes.apple.com/gb/app/nearpod/id523540409?mt=8

Learnist. (2015). *Learnist: Experts Curate Lessons to Share Their Knowledge (Version 1.3.4)* [Mobile application software]. Retrieved from https://itunes.apple.com/gb/app/learnist-experts-curate-lessons/id826591175?mt=8

Lightplaces. (2014). *BaiBoard – Collaborative Whiteboard (Version 2.9.4)* [Mobile application software]. Retrieved from https://itunes.apple.com/gb/app/baiboard-collaborative-whiteboard/id490534358?mt=8

LinkedIn Corporation. (2015). *LinkedIn (Version 8.3)* [Mobile application software]. Retrieved from https://itunes.apple.com/gb/app/linkedin/id288429040?mt=8

Loosemore, T. (2013, March 12). We're not 'appy. Not 'appy at all. [Blog post]. Retrieved from https://gds.blog.gov.uk/2013/03/12/were-not-appy-not-appy-at-all/

MacNeill, F. (2013a). Dr Nadia Edmond - iAnnotate PDF for iPad [Video File]. *eLearning Team, University of Brighton.* Retrieved from: http://youtu.be/aKfT8FzWrUs

MacNeill, F. (2013b). Dr Keith Turvey and Alan Monaghan - Explain Everything for iPad [Video File]. *eLearning Team, University of Brighton.* Retrieved from: http://youtu.be/TQj1U24i1Nw

MacNeill, F. (2014, September 7). The Adjustment Bureau: The case for adjustment in mobile apps [Blog post]. Retrieved from: http://blogs.brighton.ac.uk/fjm15/2014/09/07/the-adjustment-bureau/

MacNeill, F., Webber, J., & Hewitt, B. (2014). App Swap Breakfasts: Pedagogy, mobile devices and learning discourse over breakfast. Case study presented at *Changing Landscapes a meeting of the UCISA, Digital Skills and Development Group.* Retrieved from: https://www.ucisa.ac.uk/publications/changing_land.aspx

Martonik, A. (2014, July 2). Android L preview: Do Not Disturb mode. [Blog post]. Retrieved from http://www.androidcentral.com/android-l-preview-do-not-disturb-mode

MasteryConnect. (2014). *Socrative* [Software]. Available from http://www.socrative.com/

Mendeley. (2014). *Mendeley (Version 2.3.2)* [Mobile application software]. Retrieved from https://itunes.apple.com/gb/app/mendeley/id380669300?mt=8

Microsoft Corporation. (2014a). *OneDrive (Version 4.5.3)* [Mobile application software]. Retrieved from https://itunes.apple.com/gb/app/onedrive/id477537958?mt=8

Microsoft Corporation. (2014b). *SharePoint 2013 for business* [Software]. Available from http://www.microsoft.com/en-gb/business/products/sharepoint-2013

Minima Software. (2014). *Timer+ (Version 2.0.2)* [Mobile application software]. Retrieved from https://itunes.apple.com/gb/app/timer+/id391564049?mt=8

MorrisCooke. (2014). *Explain Everything ™ (Version 2.60)* [Mobile application software]. Retrieved from https://itunes.apple.com/gb/app/explain-everything/id431493086?mt=8

Nations, D. (n.d.). Web Applications. Retrieved from: http://webtrends.about.com/od/webapplications/a/web_application.htm

Ofcom. (2014a). Smartphones are more popular than laptops among DE households. Retrieved from http://stakeholders.ofcom.org.uk/market-data-research/market-data/communications-market-reports/cmr14/internet-web/uk-4.30

Ofcom. (2014b). Internet use and attitudes 2014 Metrics Bulletin. Retrieved from: http://stakeholders.ofcom.org.uk/market-data-research/market-data/communications-market-reports/cmr14/uk/

Pacansky-Brock, M. (2013). *Best Practices for Teaching with Emerging Technologies.* [Kindle Edition]. Retrieved from http://amzn.com/B009E3EHY4

Pinterest. (2014). *Pinterest (Version 4.1.2)* [Mobile application software]. Retrieved from https://itunes.apple.com/gb/app/pinterest/id429047995?mt=8

Plasq. (2014) *Comic Life (Version 2.1.11)* [Mobile application software]. Retrieved from https://itunes.apple.com/gb/app/comic-life/id432537882?mt=8

Poll Everywhere. (2014). *Poll Everywhere* [Software]. Available from http://www.polleverywhere.com/

Puentedura, R. R. (2011). The Lively Sketchbook Tells a Tale: Digital Storytelling and Mobile Devices. Presentation given at the *New Media Consortium Annual Conference, Madison, Wisconsin, U.S.A.* Retrieved from: http://www.hippasus.com/rrpweblog/archives/2011_06.html

Read It Later. (2015). *Pocket.* Retrieved January 17, 2015, from https://getpocket.com/

ReferenceME. (2015). *RefME (Version 3.1)* [Mobile software application]. Retrieved from https://itunes.apple.com/gb/app/refme/id553222694?mt=8

Rossignol, J. (2015, March 6). Apple overhauling iPad in education program to simplify sharing devices and apps [Blog post]. Retrieved from: http://www.macrumors.com/2015/03/06/ipad-education-deployment-changes/

RSS 2.0 Specification. (n.d.). Retrieved January 17, 2015, from http://www.rssboard.org/rss-specification

Scramboo. (2014). *Playmaker* [Software]. Available from http://platformhelp.scramboo.com/playmaker/

Selukoff, Y. (2014). *GoodReader (Version 4.7.0)* [Mobile application software]. Retrieved from https://itunes.apple.com/gb/app/goodreader/id777310222?mt=8

Sharples, M., Adams, A., Ferguson, R., Gaved, M., McAndrew, P., Rienties, B., Weller, M., & Whitelock, D. (2014). *Innovating pedagogy 2014: Open University Innovation Report 3.* Milton Keynes: The Open University. Retrieved from: http://www.open.ac.uk/blogs/innovating/?p=3

Shazino. (2014). *PaperShip for Mendeley & Zotero (Version 3.2.2)* [Mobile application software]. Retrieved from https://itunes.apple.com/gb/app/papership-for-mendeley-zotero/id631980748?mt=8

SP Controls. (2014). *Doceri Interactive Whiteboard (Version 2.1.4)* [Mobile application software]. Retrieved from https://itunes.apple.com/gb/app/doceri-interactive-whiteboard/id412443803?mt=8

Sproat, L. (2015, January 21). Android tablets with Google Play for Education come to schools in the UK [Blog post]. Retrieved from:

http://googleforeducation.blogspot.co.uk/2015/01/Android-tablets-with-Google-Play-for-Education-come-to-schools-in-the-UK.html

TechSmith Corporation. (2014a). *TechSmith Fuse (Version 1.5.1)* [Mobile application software]. Retrieved from https://itunes.apple.com/gb/app/techsmith-fuse/id725534683?mt=8

TechSmith Corporation. (2014b). *Coach's Eye – Instant Replay Video Analysis (Version 4.6)* [Mobile application software]. Retrieved from https://itunes.apple.com/gb/app/coachs-eye-instant-replay/id472006138?mt=8

Thomson Reuters. (2013). *Thomson Reuters RefScan (Version 1.0.1)* [Mobile application software]. Retrieved from https://itunes.apple.com/gb/app/thomson-reuters-refscan/id596094780?mt=8

Thomson Reuters. (2015). *EndNote for iPad (Version 1.2.4)* [Mobile application software]. Retrieved from https://itunes.apple.com/gb/app/endnote-for-ipad/id593994211?mt=8

Tinkertanker. (2013). *ID PhotoPrint: US passport photos, delivered (Version 1.4)* [Mobile application software] Retrieved from https://itunes.apple.com/gb/app/id-photoprint-us-passport/id558788006?mt=8

Tran, V. (2015). *Notes Plus (Version 4.5.2)* [Mobile application software] Retrieved from https://itunes.apple.com/gb/app/notes-plus/id374211477?mt=8

Traxler, J & Wishart, J. (Eds.). (2011). *Making mobile learning work: Case studies of practice*. Bristol: ESCalate, Higher Education Academy Subject Centre for Education. Retrieved from: http://escalate.ac.uk/8250

Turvey, K. (2014). *Narrative ecology explained*. [Video file]. Retrieved from: http://vimeo.com/67519846

Twitter. (2015). *Twitter (Version 6.19.1)* [Mobile application software]. Retrieved from https://itunes.apple.com/gb/app/twitter/id333903271?mt=8

UberSense. (2014). *Ubersense Coach: Slow Motion Video Analysis (Version 4.2.0)* [Mobile application software] Retrieved from https://itunes.apple.com/gb/app/ubersense-coach-slow-motion/id470428362?mt=8

United Nations Digital. (2014). *Apps*. Retrieved from: http://www.un.org/digital/#apps

United Nations. (2014). *UN CountryStats (Version 2.0)* [Mobile application software]. Retrieved from https://itunes.apple.com/gb/app/un-countrystats/id505192468?mt=8

University of Brighton. (n.d.). CLT Learning and Teaching Scholarships. Retrieved January 5, 2015, from http://about.brighton.ac.uk/clt/fellowships-and-awards/learning-and-teaching-fellowships/

Zygote Media Group. (2014a). *Zygote Body (Version Lite)* [Software]. Available from https://zygotebody.com/

Zygote Media Group. (2014b). *Zygote 3D Anatomy Atlas & Dissection Lab (Version 1.2)* [Software]. Available from https://itunes.apple.com/gb/app/zygote-3d-anatomy-atlas-dissection/id667678805?mt=8

3D4Medical.com. (2014). *Essential Anatomy 4 (Version 4.5)* [Mobile application software]. Retrieved from https://itunes.apple.com/gb/app/essential-anatomy-5/id596684220?mt=8

Scenario: Video assessment

Dave had just finished presenting at the faculty workshop on how he'd used the Coach's Eye app with his Sports students. He'd titled it "Instant Feedback" and described how he had used Coach's Eye on his iPad to video record and analyse student skills. He had added a voiceover commentary and drawn annotations onto the videos for each student to indicate ways in which they could improve. Angie was speaking to Dave excitedly describing how she could use it with her Nursing students as they learnt about lifting patients. "You can use it for making demonstration videos too. Add a commentary and post it to the VLE."

Later that week Angie had installed Coach's Eye for use in the role play she had planned for the students. Her colleague, Beth saw what she was doing and said, "I'm going to use that to record some patient-nurse interactions and then ask the patients to provide feedback to the nurses.

Beth's partner Simon is a lab technician and saw what Beth had done. He said "I can use that to give feedback in my student induction workshop 'Health and Safety in the Lab'. That'll save you a few patients! "

Simon's mate Pete taught in Education. "They do peer observation," he thought. "I wonder…"

Key tool: Coach's Eye

Being smart
— using apps lifewide

Andrew Middleton

Introduction

This chapter considers the range of smart apps being used by teachers and students and how they form a personalised technological environment which crosses and erodes previously established boundaries between leisure, study, work and home. Drawing on the results of a survey of academic app usage, it looks at a selection of key apps and how they support academic practice. It begins by situating app usage in a broader teaching and learning context.

The age of the app

The use of the word 'app' denotes a software application that is installed onto a smart device, be it phone, tablet or other form of personal smart technology. The apps mentioned here represent the thousands being used in post compulsory education, formally and informally. From the user's perspective, apps fall broadly into two categories:

- Generic apps - those most associated with the core functionality and general use of the device;
- Specific apps - those which have been selected, downloaded and installed by the user to support their more particular needs.

The significance of this simple grouping became apparent following the design and analysis of a small survey of academics which showed how some people personalise their device more than others. Many value the general functionality and characteristics of their device above its capacity to perform or support specialised tasks. This appreciation of personal, ubiquitous technology has a bearing on its homogenous, lifewide integration.

Personalised environments for teaching and learning

When academics, support staff or students select apps, they become involved in creating and continuously modifying a powerful, flexible and personal environment for teaching or learning. More than this, the ongoing selection of apps indicates the importance of *personalisation* as a process heightening the usefulness of the device and the way it can become integral to everything they do.

While there are some apps which are developed for specific disciplinary or professional needs, mostly the apps used in higher education are either generic and pre-installed apps that come with the device or they are apps selected by the user 'off the shelf' from app stores (MacNeill, 2015) to address a need which they have defined for themselves. It is these widely used apps which are discussed here.

Smart apps are in many cases used as 'lifewide' tools, applied to good effect at home, at university, at work, in leisure, or for general interest. The browser app, for example, is agnostic. Not caring what hat the user is wearing, it continues to deliver timely information in or out of the classroom, all day long. Its use is driven only by need, not prescription. This is true for most of the apps reported on by staff who completed the app usage survey for this chapter. They have a general purpose.

As discussed in the opening chapter, *Introducing Smart Learning*, the potency of smart learning comes from *crossing* the formal, informal divides; it is about user empowerment through the ubiquity of the device and its personalised functionality. In this intra-spatial view of mobile device usage, the technology accompanies the user throughout their day and so is always there to support them. In the case of education, the devices and the apps travel with the teacher or learner, individually and communally, extending their reach, thinking and activity. For students, apps mediate independent and social learning 'just-in-time' and 'just-in-place' as a lifewide and 'life-wise' learning environment. Learning no longer needs to be reserved for particular times and places. Neither does teaching.

This ubiquity is both empowering and, to some extent, demanding.

Promoting innovation, interactivity and inclusivity with students

Most of the apps here are either free or inexpensive - as in the price of a decent cup of coffee. That is, academics can download, install and use them, and can expect their students to do so too.

Installation involves little more than selecting them from the smart device's online store, although managing apps requires thought as discussed in the previous chapter by Fiona MacNeill.

Some students may be surprised at the suggestion they should use their own device and at the expectation that they should install apps on it to support their learning. They may respond badly if this is not introduced properly in advance (see Juliette Wilson's chapter *Un-pop quiz*). On the other hand the suggestion can go down well with students if they are given notice and support, especially if the academic models the expected behaviour (see Rushton *et al.'s* chapter).

Diffusion of innovation

Everett Rogers (2003) in his work on the diffusion of innovation said that "people are more likely to adopt an innovation if they see the advantage of the new strategy relative to what they currently use." This highlights how important it is to be clear about the benefits of an innovation: make sure there are benefits for everyone involved, even if these are indirect. Equally, do not adopt an empty vessel strategy: change that brings benefits to you may be just unwanted change to others, including your students. Change always comes with pain, therefore ensure that everyone involved buys into achieving the improvements you have in mind. If they are not interested, then perhaps you should not do it.

Beyond clarifying the relative advantages of an innovation, there are four other attributes, according to Rogers, that are useful to bear in mind when seeking successful innovation. In the context of app advocacy, *compatibility* highlights the importance of aligning the innovation with existing values and past experiences to enhance the meaning and familiarity of the app use. As an innovator you may have a vision for transforming your world, but as a change agent it may be wiser to bring others on board more incrementally. *Complexity* and app advocacy should usually go hand-in-hand given that the functionality of most apps is limited and their usability design kept simple, but bear in mind that complexity may be experienced beyond the actual app: its dependence on Wi-Fi connectivity, for example, may thwart an otherwise 'obvious' simple application. *Trialability* reminds the app innovator to test frequently and often, noting that apps are usually updated several times a year. Updates to functionality or pricing are not always helpful and can introduce unforeseen complexities. Trialability also suggests that it may be sensible to first use apps in non-critical situations with the target group to both test their suitability and to develop their familiarity with the students. *Observability* describes the visible benefits or evidence for adopting the new approach. This highlights the need to keep talking about what you are doing so that it remains present and valued in the minds of all those involved and so that seeds of doubt are properly addressed: a minor problem should be acknowledged and dealt with, and should not be allowed to distort and undermine the whole innovation.

Other attributes of innovation that can ensure a new technique goes well are *status* and *incentive*. If you are proud of something novel that you are doing it can help to involve your students in celebrating it: notoriety in newsletters, conference presentations and published papers can add to the warm glow and kudos, and can continue to fuel the progress of an innovation. Incentives, beyond the learning benefits, are more difficult to orchestrate in an educational setting, but it is worth considering the reasons students may wish to be associated with the innovation. There may be indirect benefits: using an app in one situation may have advantages elsewhere. For example, an association with innovation can enhance a student's employability.

Finally, in terms of thinking about innovation, consider innovation 'clustering'. Along with incremental development, innovative ways of thinking and change can help to foster other good ideas: once you and your students know that innovation is possible, you may realise that 'one thing leads to another'.

Actively valuing participation

The idea of using technology to make learning more interactive and inclusive can be helpful in communicating the benefits to students. Personal Response Systems like the Socrative app, for example, can really enliven the existing classroom, making it more interactive (see the chapters by Michelle Blackburn and Jo Stroud, Juliette Wilson, and Dave Kennedy and Daphne Robson). Similarly, ideas about collaboration using Project-Based Learning and group work can be transformative if students are prepared to use their own devices as discussed by Shelly Stevenson and Bianca Wright.

However, some students may not want to use their own technology and may need their university to provide them with what they need. This may require institutions to introduce loan schemes or even require institutions to give devices to students on arrival. The University of East London gave all new students a tablet device in 2014 to create "a level playing field" (Coughlan, S., 2014). Aiyegbayo (2014), reporting on an iPad project targeted at University of Huddersfield staff highlighted how many staff did not know how to make use of the device to support teaching and that uneven ownership of comparable devices by students at the time compounded the challenge. Elaine Garcia and Martial Bugliolo, in their chapter *Making it personal – a case study of personal smart device usage by higher education Art and Design students,* also discuss the intricacies of rolling out tablets to students, noting that tablets do not always fit easily onto a course and some students will reserve the right to determine what kind of technology meets their needs.

If hardware adoption is patchy and uneven, software app adoption will be at least as uneven.

Exclusive practice

The use of smart devices and some apps will exclude some students. Looking back ten years to Peter Rainger's chapter *Accessibility and mobile learning* (Rainger, 2005) it is encouraging to see what progress has been made with regard to applying Universal Design principles to mobile technologies towards increasing accessibility. The variable size, weight and attention to device portability, high screen resolution, care to user interface design, battery life and connectivity options, all improve accessibility. The ability to adapt and modify devices (by installing apps, for example) and to use multimedia and speech recognition or text-to-speech controls are further signs of good progress having been made. However a MELSIG event at the University of Sussex in 2014 looked at inclusivity in smart learning and several presenters demonstrated that diverse app developers brought with them diverse and often unpredictable practice. This means that the onus is on the end-users of the apps to evaluate their design (MacNeill, 2014).

The expectation for students to use specific technology needs to be introduced carefully. Students should be made aware at the earliest opportunity of proposals to introduce new technologies and should be involved in selecting them where this is feasible.

Because there are so many alternative apps available it may be better for academics to advocate the benefits of apps in general, where they exist, rather than always prescribing what students should use. One teaching strategy is to recognise how one-size may not fit all: for every app there is usually an alternative app that does something similar. Websites like AlternativeTo (http://alternativeto.net/) and other app comparison websites are useful in this respect. If, for example, students are asked to 'make notes', then the teacher's role is not necessarily to specify an app but to discuss the possible advantages of using smart technology and leave it to each student to decide whether they are going to use technology at all and which app to use. In general, teaching and learning should focus on how students learn, not on specific technology. This philosophy, in the age of personalised technology, is arguably a more viable way of enhancing learning with technology.

Alternative strategies for learner engagement should be ready and thought through too, but ultimately students need to decide for themselves whether it is beneficial to use their own devices and to install apps.

A survey of emerging practice

The rest of this chapter looks more closely at how apps are being used to support teaching and learning.

A survey was designed to establish a set of 'killer apps'; that is, a set of apps that most academics or students could use as the basis for a good 'apps for learning' collection. A shortlist of 20 apps was produced which drew upon those apps which had been discussed at MELSIG events in 2013-14 (see MELSIG website http://melsig.shu.ac.uk). As well as establishing a useful shortlist the research wanted to understand something about their purpose, particularly whether each of the apps were valued primarily as being helpful to academic life, or life in general.

A survey listing the 20 apps was circulated using a Google Form to some of the authors featured in this book who provide a useful representative small group of informed academics and developers demonstrably engaging with apps in their practice.

Following three short questions about the respondent (name, role and device used), 20 question pairs followed to discover the extent to which each respondent used the respective app, if at all, how they used it, and its strengths and its weaknesses. Respondents were asked to indicate whether a particular app was now important to them. Finally, the survey concluded with a comment field which asked the respondents to identify any other apps they felt should have been included in the list.

Results and analysis

The responses are listed in Table 1. *20 Apps for Learning*.

The initial analysis demonstrated how most of these respondents gravitated more towards the core general functionality of their device and how its presence changed the way they went about life: the responses, mostly, did not signal an appreciation of 'killer apps', rather an appreciation of important functional characteristics.

While some specific apps stand out as being exceptionally useful, in the main the survey results indicate a need for the data to be analysed according to the characteristics of smart apps, those characteristics that enhance or transform teaching and learning. It is important, therefore, for teachers and students to think about apps and smart devices in general and how they change the learning and teaching landscape. By and large they should not be concerned about specific apps, which may come, go and change.

Key characteristics of apps used in university life

This section highlights the key characteristics associated with smart apps by looking at the comments of respondents to specific apps in the survey. Apps most closely associated with the characteristic are listed.

Seamlessness — synchronising life and work across devices

Example apps: Evernote, Google Drive, Dropbox, Mendeley, Email, Calendar, Twitter, Facebook, Chrome, Pages, Keynote

Many of the 20 apps work across devices by storing data in the Cloud. They enable the user to access and update information whether they are sat at a PC or using their smart device. In some cases access to the information requires connectivity, although some apps generate local copies of data which can be used offline for later synchronisation.

In Evernote, for example, notes can be originated, edited, stored and retrieved whenever or wherever the learner accesses their technology. The smart device extends typical note taking functionality by making it easy to 'scan' and import whole documents, take photographic notes, make audio notes, and share any note with collaborators. This versatility, once it is widely understood, stands to change attitudes and approaches to note making. One of the respondents said,

This has grown to be indispensable. I use the free version though I am nervous about running out of space. I use it across devices and PCs. Started using it for citations too.

App	App description used	Users	Importance
1. Evernote	versatile multiple media note making and bookmarking tool	6	3
2. Dropbox	file management and sharing app and online service	7	4
3. Chrome	Google's web browser with synchronisation across devices	6	5
4. Mail	your device's native email app	8	6
5. Calendar	your device's native calendaring or scheduling app	7	6
6. Camera	your device's native camera app	6	6
7. Google Drive	Google's tools for managing and creating documents, spreadsheets, presentations, forms, etc	7	7
8. YouTube Capture	for making and sharing videos on YouTube	5	3
9. Dictionary	for looking up the meaning of words and finding alternative words	5	1
10. iBooks or Kindle	for reading eBooks and articles	5(1)	3
11. Dragon Dictation	for converting spoken word into text	2	1
12. Socrative	for promoting student interaction in class, etc	5	2

13. Twitter	for social networking	5	4
14. Facebook	for social networking	3(1)+2 personal only	2
15. Explain Everything	for screen capture and recording video presentations	3(1)	0
16. iPhoto (or equivalent for your OS)	browse, edit and share your photos	1(3)	0
17. Pages (or equivalent for your OS)	word processing app	1(1)	1
18. Keynote (or equivalent for your OS)	presentation app	1(2)	1
19. Mendeley	for managing citations	3	2
20. Voice Record	for recording, editing, managing and distributing audio	2(3)	1

Table 1. 20 Apps for Learning

While Evernote is an example of a recent technology, all but one of the respondents talked about how useful it is to be able to access and create email. The same was said of the generic calendar tools on devices. Respondents said,

> *I still live through my email. Life and work gets blurred though. Not healthy but it's how I manage.*

> *This is very important to me for both work and home mail which is on all my devices, so I can pick up email anywhere. I send things to myself via mail, which is great.*

Having more access is not always desirable however,

> *As a rule I do not look at and pick up emails outside of work time as I try and achieve a work-life balance.*

Most of the apps referred to here perform similar tasks to web versions of the same tool or extend that functionality to the smart device. Indeed analysing the "Top 100 Tools for Learning" in the C4PT 2014 survey "compiled from the votes of over 1,000 learning professionals from 61 countries worldwide" reveals that 75% (Apple iOS) and 69% (Google Android OS) of the key tools have an equivalent smart device app.

While seamless access to data is highly valued, it is associated with the breaking down of a demarcated view of life and work. Lifewide convenience comes at a cost and needs to be managed. It requires both academics and students to be proactive in negotiating the way they engage with their work and with each other. This need to negotiate expectations suggests a new dimension to digital literacy; one that puts staff and students on a level playing field. Confidently setting appropriate expectations of each other is a life skill and one that is important to student employability.

Communality — co-production and sharing

Example apps: Google Drive, Dropbox, Socrative, Twitter

Many of the apps are designed to support the co-production of information and in some cases support synchronous editing and communication. Applications in the Google Drive suite stand out as examples of established collaborative tools in this list: Google Docs, Spreadsheets and Google Hangouts support real time collaborative activity; however, nearly all of the apps in the short list support collaboration indirectly through their capacity to share information via email or file sharing services.

Dropbox is an example of a file storage and sharing service. Any files can be stored and later accessed from another device in any location. Both files and folders can be shared with collaborators. However, several respondents noted that they had moved from Dropbox and begun to use Google Drive instead. While becoming dependent upon a single provider is a concern, the suite of Google Apps make Google Drive a sensible place to store and share work.

> *I used Dropbox although I have now moved on to Google Drive. [Cloud storage] literally revolutionised my life. I went from constantly having to save things to disc/pen drive / portable drive, to being able to access my materials anywhere. I began with Dropbox, and moved to Google Drive when I moved to an institution that*

*supported the Google Apps suite. Being able to share
online as well as store is so valuable.*

One academic spoke of using a Google Spreadsheet as a tool to manage
Office Hours. Using this, students can sign up for a tutorial. The idea of 'co-
production', therefore, extends beyond collaborating on activities and
assignments into functioning effectively as a learning community.

Data rich — browsing, selecting and retrieving key materials and information

*Example apps: Evernote, Google Drive, Dropbox, Mendeley, Email, Chrome,
Twitter, e-Books, Facebook, Pages, Keynote*

Another way of being an organised learner, or teacher, is to make sure you
are ready to take part. Beyond co-editing documents, one respondent noted
that having all relevant documents to hand in Google Drive to support
meetings, tutorials and revision was highly beneficial. Having access to
information, especially pre-selected, tagged and sorted into folders means
that both academics and learners should be able to contribute more readily
and decisively in seminars and to pull in useful examples dynamically.

Mendeley is a citation management software; one of the few apps targeted
specifically at the academic user in this study. Mendeley indexes PDF
documents and research papers into a personal digital library, structured
using thematic folders and tags. It incorporates a powerful search tool
which scours not only papers saved by the user, but all papers that have
been indexed with the Mendeley service. Users can establish Mendeley
groups too which work well for group work or collaborative academic
writing in general. The app, however, does not have the range of
functionality of its desktop or its web-based service at the time of writing
and demonstrates how true seamlessness between different environments
is still developing.

The web browser (Google Chrome in the case of this survey) exemplifies
both seamlessness and data richness. The act of browsing, selecting and
retrieving key materials and information supports strategies like Google
Jockeying (EDUCAUSE, 2006) in which participants in a class search for
further information, such as definitions or citations, to clarify or develop
topics being presented.

Social presence and lifewide multilogues

Example apps: Twitter, Facebook, Evernote, Google Drive, Mendeley, Email, Chrome, e-Books, Facebook, Pages, Keynote

Megele (2014) conceptualises Twitter interactions as multilogue conversations and identifies how they collapse pre-existing understandings of formal and informal learning, spanning and blurring life and study.

Discourse happens in and across many media; not just those that are primarily dedicated to communication. This is where the strong connection between smart technology and social media establishes a paradigm shift for education, as it does for society in general. This socially mediated discourse, however, is dynamic and inclusive, unlike more traditional forms of academic discourse which are typically mediated by different and more formal conventions or protocols.

There is an evident informality associated with such media: the brevity and speed of communication and the nature of social commenting have emerged in contrast to traditional protocols for academic discourse. Social media is changing the form of academic discourse, if not its essential nature. While academia is still learning to define and assert good practice in socially mediated critical thinking, we are learning that new ways of networking and managing our social presence are able to improve our scholarly engagement. Many of the initial conversations that led to this book, for example, took place using social networking tools and, in the main, the chapters have been written and reviewed in a shared Google Drive folder.

The use of Twitter, for example, is now widely used. Its validity as an academic medium to promote 'good thinking' is still emerging, but as in the case of previous technologies like the telephone, it should not be unduly derided and dismissed due to its association with trivial, popular media. Respondents indicated how useful it can be for establishing communal presence and for promoting interactivity. There are many examples in this book, including Neil Withnell's Nursing case study, that prove its worth. As with any technology, Twitter's value is found in how we come to use it. Twitter, for example, does not 'dumb-down' discourse and it does not dispense with other forms of discourse; like other social media, it can add to the ways in which scholarship, teaching and learning thrive in a social context.

Twitter is personal, social, ubiquitous, pervasive, and rich. It is both instantaneous and long-lasting, and supports communication in and across spaces. It functions as an active learning space or as an underpinning space to inform learning and communal engagement. It fosters collaboration amongst co-located peers and facilitates connections with the outside world.

TweetChats structured around a few useful questions, for example, can engender commitment to a learning community and vibrant discussion - globally if that is useful (see Chrissi Nerantzi and Sue Beckingham's chapter). Other team-based activities and simulations can be organised and, if using a course hashtag, ideas and resources can be shared and aggregated.

While many respondents confirmed their use of Twitter, most did not see it as being central to their academic practice, though one or two noted how their account had remained "dormant" for a while until something "clicked." One said,

> It is amazing to have a very knowledgeable network when you need them though. I have devised several teaching activities using Twitter - it's quite versatile when you put your mind to it.

Facebook fared less well in this survey. Respondents said,

> It's not my preferred place, but I am involved in several Facebook groups so you end up taking part. I find Fb generally confusing though.

> I only use Facebook for Personal use.

As with many other social media, the appropriateness of the media to support learning in a particular context emerges with the conviction of the innovator to engage students in a better way than before. Mark Feltham and Caroline Keep, for example, in their chapter *Oh, the places you'll go – smart learning in the natural sciences* discuss how Facebook has worked well for their students. Mark Feltham (2014) demonstrated how powerful it can be when you understand how it works, particularly by using closed Facebook Groups: it's often familiar to students, quick and easy to use, social, and makes setting work fun. Activities can use a range of media and, because it is the learner's own space, they can be more relaxed and creative in the ways they respond. Feedback from both tutors and peers can be immediate, access to the learning environment is continuous, it supports group engagement by design, and it is mobile.

Facebook, more than Twitter, is a space often more associated with home and life outside of work. In both cases respondents and other commentators have noted how establishing an account for home and another for university is necessary and perhaps this management of dual identities is something that will become more prevalent as the 'early majority' and 'late majority' (Rogers, 2003) join the innovators and early adopters in using smart learning strategies.

Rich mediation

Example apps: Camera, YouTube Capture, Explain Everything, iPhoto, Pages, Keynote, Evernote, Voice Record, Dragon Dictation, Twitter, Facebook

Academia has always been closely associated with the written word. Working with rich digital media has never been a mainstream academic activity, requiring infrastructure, technical skills and time (Diamond & Middleton, 2013). It also requires a different way of thinking about, representing or engaging with knowledge. This difference leads to the idea of richness: it is not so much about accommodating learning styles, as about having more ways of communicating ideas, engaging and challenging the learner.

Mobile phones incorporated camera functionality at an early stage, helping to establish the idea of the multi-functional phone. Alongside the device's capacity to store large quantities of reasonably high quality images, the resolution quality and connectivity has continued to develop. Latterly the functionality of the still camera has been expanded to incorporate digital video. Making good use of the device's connectivity and inter-app functionalities, both still photographs and video have become commonplace applications for recording and sharing 'life'.

The native camera app was noted for its lifewide usefulness and exemplifies the idea of seamless interactivity. Respondents talked as much about how they used the camera at home as at work. That habit means that it is easier to 'lifeblog' through class too,

> *Great for note taking - whiteboards, flip charts, post-it notes etc Sometimes just to remind who was there and what was happening.*

This life-blogging habit, however, suggests how important it is to talk about digital literacy in relation to critical thinking and how notes, in whatever media they are made, are then processed.

Smart devices and smart apps remove many of the barriers to creating and integrating video, audio, photographs, animation and graphics. Taking digital photographs and shooting digital video with personal smartphones is commonplace in life beyond academia; Facebook, Twitter and YouTube presences are peppered with such found and generated media. However, it is not yet clear how easily and well academics and students are embracing this opportunity. At the time of writing academia is still a long way from being able to claim that teachers and students are confidently using rich media to enhance and transform the way they engage with each other. This comes down to cultural and procedural conventions and expectations (Diamond & Middleton, 2013). It is still not generally accepted practice, for example, for an academic to make their own video, on their own device, and then share it on their own YouTube channel. However, this is now changing as evidenced in this book and in this survey. If barriers remain in this area, it is likely that they are more to do with awareness of what can be done easily and to reasonably high levels of quality.

Video, audio, screencasting, presentations, photographs, diagrams, drawings and other graphical and time-based data are supported in numerous apps. This is an area in which people who use such media tend to search out apps that have features that appeal to their different needs and expectations. It seems the metaphorical interface design in this range of apps can be frustrating,

> *I can't stand iPhoto - have never understood how it*
> *organises photos and it is hard to export them.*

The apps supporting the use of multimedia tend to fall into two categories: those that involve finding and storing media, and those that involve making it. YouTube broaches this. Some respondents mentioned how they found YouTube videos to use in their teaching. The YouTube Capture app has gained some traction, for example,

> *Used to get students to capture ideas at outreach*
> *workshop. Video each other giving views on ethical*
> *issues, practice public speaking.*

> *I have used this to capture student interviews which are*
> *then brought back into my teaching. Typically it will be*
> *students talking about their experience of assessment and*
> *the advice they would give to students who will be*
> *experiencing a similar assessment to them 'next year.'*

Diane Rushton and colleagues in the chapter *Using social video to capture reflective voices* also talk about how their students are using the YouTube Capture app for making and sharing weekly video reflections, while noting that settling on the right app for the job took some thought.

While apps like Camera, YouTube Capture, iPhoto, Explain Everything and Voice Record were listed in the survey, respondents mostly preferred to talk about the rich media apps that they had found for themselves, for example,

> *I use Playback on my iPad to prepare screencasts for the*
> *students.*

Other apps in this rich mediation category were listed in response to the survey's catch all question "What apps should have been listed?" For example,

- Skitch - image annotation;
- Sketchbook Mobile - drawing;
- Pinterest - collecting visual ideas;
- Animoto - making videos from photographs;
- Flickr Studio - "finding images to use in presentations etc with cc licences"

Authentic and lifelong

The apps are not 'educational' in most cases; neither do they pertain specifically to other aspects of life in the main. This last section simply notes that as education is disrupted by the emergence of smart apps, so are other parts of our life. Change, indeed, is lifewide.

The app, and the need to manage the functionality of one's device, in this respect represents one's authentic engagement with the world.

Conclusions

It is important that more academics and students talk about how their use of apps is helping them to teach and learn and how new ways of thinking and working together can make the connections between university and the world beyond stronger.

The nature of the smart app ultimately determines the user's appreciation and experience of smart technology. Personalisation of technology, inclusive interactivity, seamless lifewide integration, communality, the increased authenticity of the learning environment, and the incorporation of rich digital mediation are highlighted as being important characteristics of smart learning and the integration of apps for learning.

The 'age of the app' is characterised by the user's fluency in customising their device to meet their lifewide needs by installing the apps that they judge to be useful. The findings from the small survey underpinning this chapter, and other accounts in this book, suggest that curricula and academic practice more generally are being enhanced, but that it is still too early to expect widespread transformation of practice: innovators are testing the water. App 'fluency' will be evidenced when all academics and students turn to their device first for information and when they use it interactively to develop knowledge, wherever they are.

References

Aiyegbayo, O. (2014). How and why academics do and do not use iPads for academic teaching? *British Journal of Educational Technology.*

C4PT (2014). The top 100 tools for learning 2014 list: the results of the 8th Annual Survey of Learning Tools. Online at: http://c4lpt.co.uk/top100tools/

Coughlan, S. (2014). *University gives free tablet computer to new students.* BBC News, Education & Family website, 25 September 2014. Online at: http://www.bbc.co.uk/news/education-29346992

Diamond, S. & Middleton, A. (2013). Sound infrastructure for academic innovation In: Middleton, A., (Ed.), Digital voices: A collaborative exploration of the recorded voice in post-compulsory education. MELSIG & Sheffield Hallam University, 107 − 117.

EDUCAUSE (2006). 7 things you should know about Google jockeying. *EDUCAUSE Learning Initiative (ELI).* Online at: http://www.educause.edu/library/resources/7-things-you-should-know-about-google-jockeying

Feltham, M. (2014). 10 reasons why you should use social media in your teaching. Presentation at '*Social Media for Learning #1', Media-Enhanced Learning Special*

Interest Group, John Moores University, 3rd April 2014. Online at: http://melsig.shu.ac.uk/?page_id=566

Macneill, F. (2014). App swap workshop: The Adjustment Bureau. Presentation at Digital Media Interaction and Inclusivity', Media-Enhanced Learning Special Interest Group, University of Sussex, 9th September 2014. Online at: http://melsig.shu.ac.uk/?page_id=645

Megele, C. (2014). Theorising Twitter chat. *Journal of Perspectives in Applied Academic Practice*, 2(2), 46 − 51.

MELSIG website: http://melsig.shu.ac.uk/

Rainger, P. (2005). Accessibility and mobile learning. In: A. Kukulska-Hulme and J. Traxler *Mobile learning: A handbook for educators and trainers*. Abingdon, Oxon: Routledge.

Roblyer, M.D., McDaniel, M., Webb, M., Herman, J., & Vince Witty, J. (2010). Findings on Facebook in higher education: A comparison of college faculty and student uses and perceptions of social networking sites. *Internet and Higher Education*, 13, 134 − 140.

Rogers, E.M. (2003). *Diffusion of innovations, fifth edition*. New York: Free Press.

Shen, J., Brdiczka, O., & Ruan, Y. (2013). A comparison study of user behavior on Facebook and Gmail. *Computers in Human Behavior*, 29(6), 2650 − 2655.

APPENDIX

About the smart learning scenarios

Andrew Middleton

The scenarios used in *Smart Learning* are presented between chapters as vignettes and are intended to inspire you. They come from both actual and imagined examples of practice.

They take a narrative form to 'concretise' (Carroll, 2000) or 'make real' the ideas. Carroll says a scenario is "a concrete description of activity that the user engages in when performing a specific task, description sufficiently detailed so that design implications can be inferred and reasoned about." Software engineers, like Carroll, use scenarios to reliably test ideas before development. In education our interest in scenarios is less about testing and more about imagining. Scenarios allow essential ideas to be considered in a realistic way so they can be easily abstracted and applied to the reader's own context: they are enlightened by contextual detail, but not obscured by it.

Scenarios can be used to work out, capture and communicate thinking, and review and compare existing practice. In *Smart Learning* they help to clarify ideas as pedagogic propositions.

Well-formed scenarios feature: goals, sub-goals or outcomes; settings; agents or actors playing primary or supporting roles (descriptions of who is involved, how and why); a plot - the sequences of actions and events done by or to the actors or changes to the setting.

Using a narrative voice helps to concretise the description of the idea and ensures a scenario focuses on essence, being or experience. This is the most useful way to consider emerging ideas for educational technology because ideas about learning interactivity are best when they are independent of specific technology which are fixed in time; academic innovation is always best focused on what people do and feel. Nevertheless, references to particular technologies such as smart apps are useful for inspiring innovators.

Scenarios can describe the past, present or future and are risk-free tools for imagining the future and for asking 'what if..?' Stylistically they are colourful narratives and 'good enough' representations of possibilities.

Scenarios are also brief and, in this respect, are different to academic case studies where accounts are carefully set out and loose ends need to be tidied so that they are robust and reliable. In contrast, some loose ends are helpful to the scenario reader who should be encouraged to imagine the idea in their own context. Educational scenario narratives infer much of their context and are often not explicit about the setting. Case studies are not generalisable; in contrast inspirational scenarios are written so that essential thinking, ideas and logics can be applied by the reader to their own context as with any interpretation of narrative.

To avoid unnecessary repetition, many of the scenarios describe students and tutors working 'in the open' using social media tools. It is common practice for pseudonyms to be used to protect the identity of those taking part. Equally, in some social media sites, it is possible to set access rights or limit commenting and rating. *YouTube*, for example, allows uploads to be publicly accessible, unlisted or private.

Attributions and acknowledgements

Some of the smart learning scenarios are specifically attributed, others include acknowledgements to specific workshop participants where that has been possible, otherwise I have constructed them, being inspired by a range of conversations, readings, observations and workshop activities.

Possibilities

The scenarios used here represent a small sample of ideas and are intended to add colour to punctuate the other chapters. I continue to generated other scenarios on the Smart Learning Scenarios website at: http://melsig-andrew-middleton.tumblr.com/

References

Carroll, J.M. (2000). Five reasons for scenario-based design. Interacting with Computers 13, 43 – 60.

About the authors

Sue Beckingham
Sheffield Hallam University, s.beckingham@shu.ac.uk, @suebecks

Sue is an Educational Developer, taking a Faculty lead role for technology enhanced learning (TEL) at Sheffield Hallam University. She is a Fellow of the Higher Education Academy and also a Fellow of the Staff and Educational Development Association where she is a member of the Executive Board and founding member of the SEDA SIG on TEL. Her teaching portfolio includes Professionalism and Communication; Digital Marketing; Web 2.0 in Business; Social Media Use in Organisations; and Information Design. She is also a course designer and facilitator of the cross institution open online course 'Bring Your Own Device for Learning' and co-lead of the weekly Learning and Teaching in Higher Education online chat #LTHEchat. She has published a number of book chapters, journal papers, and conference papers; and has keynoted both nationally and internationally on the use of social media in a higher education context. Sue's research interests alongside TEL include digital identity and connectedness, and the use of social media in higher education and business. As a lifelong learner she is currently taking a second Master's degree, an MSc in Technology Enhanced Learning, Innovation and Change.

Michelle Blackburn
Sheffield Hallam University, m.blackburn@shu.ac.uk, @MichSheff

Michelle Blackburn is a Principal Lecturer within Sheffield Business School at Sheffield Hallam University. She specialises in Student Engagement and Employability and has over 20 years' experience as a HR consultant before becoming a full-time academic in 2009. Michelle teaches both undergraduate and postgraduate students on areas of Organisational Behaviour and Human Resource Management. She has taught students within the UK and Internationally. Michelle is a Member of the British Psychological Society, a Senior Fellow of the Higher Education Academy and a Fellow of the Chartered Institute of Personnel and Development. Michelle has undertaken research in the areas of reflective learning, talent management and career development and has written on many aspects of pedagogy including assessment design, the use of technology in teaching and internationalisation of the curriculum.

Martial Bugliolo
Plymouth College of Art, mbugliolo@pca.ac.uk

Martial Bugliolo is Course Leader in Interactive Media at Plymouth College of Art, as an interactive practitioner and educator at Plymouth College of Art, Martial explores the potential of online technologies to map and evaluate the relationships of students with resources across online communities. Martial is researching, investigating and developing in areas, such as blended learning and e-Learning to identify future technologies and how to enhance them to suit the curriculum planning and delivery to support students' needs and experience.

Mark Feltham
Liverpool John Moores University, m.j.feltham@ljmu.ac.uk, @MarkFeltham666

Mark is a Principal Lecturer in Animal Ecology in the School of Natural Sciences and Psychology at Liverpool John Moores University. He is committed to innovation in teaching and learning and has recently led projects including 'The HEdWorks Project: bringing makerspaces, making and the maker ethos into HE' which has looked at the use of mobile technologies, social media and making to enhance the student learning experience and foster creative learning. He has developed 'Student stats EXPO: creative learning in action' to showcase the work of undergraduates learning about statistics through creative modes of study including through their use of Rube Goldberg Machines, ornithopters, statistics guides, videos, DIY experiments and independent data collection. Mark has been involved in the 'Creative learning and flexible learning pathways' project to develop new ways to enable students to choose how, when and where they learn, and in 2012 the 'Social Media and flexible pedagogy: promoting innovation and autonomous learning using Facebook' project' which considered how social media can be used to help students become flexible and autonomous learners in an environment that fosters collaboration, deep learning and encourages innovation.

Elaine Garcia
Plymouth University, elaine.garcia@plymouth.ac.uk, @ela1negarc1a

Elaine is a Freelance Educational Technology Consultant. She has worked in education for over 13 years and has led a number projects for funders including JISC, Janet and the HEA. She is in the final year of her PhD considering the use of social media in HE teaching and learning. Elaine has published a number of journal papers, book chapters and conference papers. Her research interests relate to social media, teaching and learning and information systems. Elaine is also a member of the Publications and Communications Committee of the ALT and is an Associate Fellow of the HEA.

Catherine Hack
Ulster University, cj.hack@ulster.ac.uk, @hack_kay

Kay has 20 years' experience of teaching and pedagogic research in higher education. She teaches bioethics on undergraduate and postgraduate degree programmes and for staff development. She has chaired both university and Health Research Authority Research Ethics Committees. Her experience provides a unique position from which to view the ethical issues that arise across the pedagogic research landscape.

Caroline Keep
Freelance educator, carolinekeep1@gmail.com, @Ka81

Caroline is currently working in science education, teaching secondary physics in which she develops science and practical skills using maker education projects. She also works in HE with Liverpool John Moores University as part of the Maker Education Working Group and has interests in the development of mobile technologies, social media for teaching and learning and flexible pedagogies. Caroline is co-founder of HEdSpaceUK, blogs for Liverpool Girl Geeks and is member of the Institute of Physics. She has a special interest in developing innovative teaching using maker education for the promotion of girls in STEM.

Dave Kennedy
Christchurch Polytechnic Institute of Technology (CPIT), New Zealand, dave.kennedy@cpit.ac.nz

Dave is a computing and mathematics lecturer at CPIT. The computing courses have an applied, industry focus and a "learning by doing" approach. It is this "learning by doing" interactive learning that was introduced to the discrete mathematics paper in 2008. Dave and Daphne Robson have published a number of research papers based on their use of technology to enable active learning.

Fiona MacNeill
University of Brighton, f.macneill@brighton.ac.uk, @fmacneill

Fiona is a Learning Technologies Adviser, as part of the eLearning team at the University of Brighton. She has worked in the Learning Technology field for the past five years in both the UK and the United States. Specialising in mobile pedagogy, Fiona has been running user groups based around mobile technologies since 2010; most recently in the form of #appswaps at the University of Brighton. Another area of her interest lies within User Experience Design with particular emphasis on inclusivity and enabling technologies. Fiona strives to understand and support the human factors in development and use of learning technologies.

Andrew Middleton
Sheffield Hallam University, a.j.middleton@shu.ac.uk, @andrewmid

Andrew is Head of Academic Practice & Learning Innovation at Sheffield Hallam University with 21 years of experience in higher educational development. He is best known for his work developing audio feedback and other digital voice pedagogies. He leads the UK Media-Enhanced Learning Special Interest Group (MELSIG), a pioneering group interested in enhancing and transforming learning with digital and social media. Andrew has edited books on media-enhanced learning, been a facilitator on the open learning event *Bring Your Own Devices for Learning*, and is Managing Editor of the open journal the *Student Engagement & Experience Journal*.

Chrissi Nerantzi
Manchester Metropolitan University, c.nerantzi@mmu.ac.uk, @chrissinerantzi

Chrissi Nerantzi is a Principal Lecturer in Academic CPD at Manchester Metropolitan University. She developed and leads the openly licensed FLEX CPD scheme, teaches on the Postgraduate Certificate and the MA in

Academic Practice and supports individuals and teams at MMU to enhance teaching practices. Chrissi is an open educator and has participated in and initiated open education initiatives with colleagues from her own and other institutions (examples include @openfdol, @byod4l, @lthechat, #creativeHE) and carries out research in this area with a special focus on collaboration in cross-institutional settings.

Anne Nortcliffe
Sheffield Hallam University, a.nortcliffe@shu.ac.uk, @anortcliffe

Anne is an academic in Engineering and Computing and leads the Industrial Collaborative Engineering Programme at Sheffield Hallam. Currently she is supporting the design and implementation of Aerospace, Food and Chemical Engineering courses. She is committed to inspiring and supporting and the education of next graduates in her subject areas. Anne is an active researcher and has been looking at ubiquitous technology and the impact it has on learning for many years. This interest ranges from audio technology for audio notes and feedback to the potential impact smart technology can make to enhance the academic and student experience of higher education.

Chris Rowell
Regent's University London, Rowellc@regents.ac.uk, @Chri5rowell

Chris works as the Deputy Learning Technology Manager where he organises and delivers all aspects of Technology Enhanced Learning (TEL) within the university. He also manages a number of projects setting up and promoting learning technology, as well as supporting academic teams to develop new courses. In his professional life he is a Certified Member of Association for Learning Technology (CMALT), member of the conference committee of SEDA, founding member of the SEDA SIG on TEL and Deputy Editor of the ALT's Online Newsletter.

Diane Rushton
Sheffield Hallam University, d.rushton@shu.ac.uk

Diane is Principal Lecturer, International Business and Assessment Lead, at Sheffield Business School. With over 25 years in Higher Education, she has always had a holistic approach to the support of students for both academic and employability success. Her research interests have been in the areas of feedback-feedforward, developing student academic and digital literacies. Most recently her focus has been in digital voice pedagogies and the impact of mobile devices and technologies on student engagement and learning.

Daphne Robson
Christchurch Polytechnic Institute of Technology (CPIT), New Zealand, Daphne.robson@cpit.ac.nz

Daphne Robson is Head of Mathematics and Statistics at CPIT and lectures mathematics on Computing and Engineering degrees. Her research focuses on the use of technology in education. She has used tablet PCs for interactive class activities for seven years and is involved in the development of software for helping students learn to solve linear equations.

Rebecca Sellers
Leeds Beckett University, r.sellers@leedsbeckett.ac.uk, *@becksell2001*

Rebecca is a Learning Technologist at Leeds Beckett University, with a particular interest in e-assessment. Prior to moving to Leeds Beckett University in 2015 she was a Blended Learning Officer at the University of Leeds in the Faculty of Environment. Rebecca holds a BSc in Environmental Geology and an MSc in Engineering Geology and has 3 years' experience as a geoenvironmental engineer prior to working in academia.

Jo Stroud
London School of Hygiene and Tropical Medicine, joanna.stroud@lshtm.ac.uk, @JoStroud

Joanna is an e-Learning Officer at the London School of Hygiene and Tropical Medicine, and Project Lead for its FutureLearn partnership. She has 8 years' experience in higher education and technology enhanced learning, having previously worked at Sheffield Hallam University and the London School of Economics. Joanna's specific areas of interest include e-assessment, open educational practices, and digital media. She is a Certified Member of the Association for Learning Technology (CMALT) and Fellow of the Higher Education Academy (FHEA)

Shelly Stevenson
Coventry University, aa4348@coventry.ac.uk, @shellystevenson

Shelly has been a radio broadcast journalist for 30 years. She began her career in a small radio station in California as a newsreader and assistant programme producer. From there she moved to Belgium where she produced and presented a news programme broadcast across the three countries in English. While at AFN she won the 1993 Communication of Excellence Award for American Red Cross. More recently Shelly has worked in the UK for BFBS, BBC, Imagine, and Heart FM. For the past 10 years, Shelly has assisted various youth organisations in developing community and web radio stations and developed the OCN programme, Radio Broadcasting Basics.

She has been researching the changes in journalism and teaching using mobile devices and was instrumental in the 3rd Year Cohort of Journalism and Media degree to win the top award for the Broadcast Journalism Training Council for Multi-Platform journalism in 2014. Shelly has an MA in Specialist Journalism from Coventry University and is currently undergoing her PhD in Digital Communities of Faith.

Simon Thomson
Leeds Beckett University, s.thomson@leedsbeckett.ac.uk, @digisim

Simon is a "flipped academic" (Bruton, 2012). He is Head of E-Learning at Leeds Beckett University, an academic post working in the Centre for Learning & Teaching. His current work includes the development of a conversational framework for technology use, with a focus on its ability to enable, enhance, enrich and empower learning & teaching. Simon was recently awarded a HEA National Teaching Fellow and is a Senior Fellow of the Higher Education Academy.

Denise Turner
University of Sussex, D.M.Turner@sussex.ac.uk, @DeniseT01

Dr Denise Turner is a former Social Worker and currently a Lecturer in the School of Education and Social Work at the University of Sussex. Her teaching and research interests include auto-ethnography; methodological innovation and the psychosocial. She has been a contributor to both conferences and publications in the field of social work and social networking and is interested in how social work, with its traditional ethical boundaries negotiates the 'brave new world' created by digital platforms. Within her current teaching Denise has worked experientially with students to create video clips and social media conversations which explore the challenges of digital spaces in social work, whilst also embracing the opportunities.

Santanu Vasant
City University London, santanu@santanuvasant.com, @santanuvasant

Santanu is an Educational Technologist at City University London. He has over 10 years' experience in education having previously worked at Brunel University London and Imperial College London and as a secondary school teacher of ICT. His current work involves investigating the impact of classroom technologies and mobile technologies to learning and teaching and learning spaces design, which he greatly enjoys exploring with staff to bring about a better student experience. He is also a school governor at the Northwood School in North West London.

Ros Walker
University of Sheffield, ros.walker@sheffield.ac.uk, @roswalker

Ros is Faculty Learning Technologist for Social Sciences at the University of Sheffield. She trained originally as a teacher of languages (EFL / MFL) and specialised in computer assisted language-learning. This expanded to cross-curricular work and led to posts as an adviser in the schools sector for 15 years, undertaking research projects and managing professional development programmes for teachers in the UK and overseas. Her Masters dissertation (2013) focussed on how pupils aged 14-16 were using their smart phones for learning and led to a particular interest in the area of mobile learning. She moved into higher education in 2014.

Simon Warwick
*Sheffield Hallam University, s.warwick@shu.ac.uk, @Simon_W_*

Simon is the Technology Enhanced Learning Adviser for Sheffield Business School. Over the last 7 years, he has worked in partnership with academic colleagues to create innovative approaches to teaching and learning and, more recently, using multifunctional mobile devices to enhance and enrich the student learning experience.

Helen Webster
Newcastle University, helen.webster@ncl.ac.uk, @scholastic_rat

Helen is a learning developer and Head of the Writing Development Centre at Newcastle University. She has over a decade's experience in teaching and learning in Higher Education, working with students, researchers and staff to develop their academic and digital literacies. Having begun her career with a PhD on the role of the manuscript in medieval lay women's education, she is now interested in how more modern technologies shape literacy and learning for C21st students.

Natalie Wilmot
Sheffield Hallam University, n.wilmot@shu.ac.uk, @NatalieWilmot

Natalie is a lecturer in the International Business and Business Economics subject group. Prior to joining Sheffield Hallam University, her professional background is in export sales and global supply chain management, and she has worked extensively with organisations in Spain and South America, and is fluent in Spanish and French. She obtained both her BA (Hons) in Business and Management and her MSc in Leadership and Management at Sheffield Hallam University, and is currently studying for a PhD examining foreign language diversity in international supply chain relationships. She teaches on a range of undergraduate and postgraduate modules, dealing with many different aspects of international business, and her research interests relate to cross cultural management, the role that language plays in the management of multinational enterprises, and international business pedagogy. She is an Associate Member of the Institute of Export, and a Fellow of the Higher Education Academy.

Juliette Wilson
University of Salford, J.V.Wilson@edu.salford.ac.uk, @JuliettePhD

Juliette is a Social Sciences Graduate Teaching Assistant at the University of Salford which means that teaching responsibilities are part of her role as a funded PhD student. Juliette's PhD is a qualitative study of social exclusion and the third sector through a case study of a community group called a time bank. Juliette worked to become a fellow of the Higher Education Academy early in her career because she is led by a passion for teaching and the desire to help students achieve their potential.

Neil Withnell
University of Salford, n.withnell@salford.ac.uk, @neilwithnell

Neil is Associate Head Academic Enhancement at the University of Salford. Neil is a qualified Mental Health Nurse who started working in Higher Education 12 years ago. He enjoys the challenge of developing (and supporting others in) creative technologies in teaching and learning. Neil is a Fellow of the Higher Education Academy.

Bianca Wright
Coventry University, ab6597@coventry.ac.uk, @bmtwright

As a freelance journalist since 1996, Bianca Wright has been published in a variety of magazines and online publications in the UK, the US and South Africa, including Global Telecoms Business, Office.com, SA Computer Magazine, M-Business, Discovery.com, Business Start-ups, Cosmopolitan and ComputorEdge. She has also ghost-written two books on the health community in South Africa for ISDS, a European Union initiative and has contributed to the 2001 Black ICT Achievers' Awards Handbook, published by BMI-TechKnowledge. Bianca was first runner-up in the print business magazine category at the 2002 Telkom ICT Journalist of the Year Awards. She also won second place in the 2002 AISI Media Awards' special category IDRC Award for Reporting on Research and Innovation. In 2012, she was selected as one of the Top 40 Under 40 business achievers by the Nelson Mandela Bay Business Chamber. She holds an MPhil degree in Journalism from the University of Stellenbosch and a DPhil in Media Studies from Nelson Mandela Metropolitan University.

CPSIA information can be obtained
at www.ICGtesting.com
Printed in the USA
LVHW031724140519
617804LV00013B/915/P

9 781843 873839